Oxford Living Grammar
pre-intermediate

Mark Harrison

OXFORD
UNIVERSITY PRESS

Great Clarendon Street, Oxford OX2 6DP

Oxford University Press is a department of the University of Oxford.
It furthers the University's objective of excellence in research, scholarship,
and education by publishing worldwide in

Oxford New York

Auckland Cape Town Dar es Salaam Hong Kong Karachi
Kuala Lumpur Madrid Melbourne Mexico City Nairobi
New Delhi Shanghai Taipei Toronto

With offices in

Argentina Austria Brazil Chile Czech Republic France Greece
Guatemala Hungary Italy Japan Poland Portugal Singapore
South Korea Switzerland Thailand Turkey Ukraine Vietnam

OXFORD and OXFORD ENGLISH are registered trade marks of
Oxford University Press in the UK and in certain other countries

© Oxford University Press 2009

The moral rights of the author have been asserted

Database right Oxford University Press (maker)

First published 2009
2013 2012 2011
10 9 8 7 6 5 4

No unauthorized photocopying

All rights reserved. No part of this publication may be reproduced,
stored in a retrieval system, or transmitted, in any form or by any means,
without the prior permission in writing of Oxford University Press,
or as expressly permitted by law, or under terms agreed with the appropriate
reprographics rights organization. Enquiries concerning reproduction
outside the scope of the above should be sent to the ELT Rights Department,
Oxford University Press, at the address above

You must not circulate this book in any other binding or cover
and you must impose this same condition on any acquirer

Any websites referred to in this publication are in the public domain and
their addresses are provided by Oxford University Press for information only.
Oxford University Press disclaims any responsibility for the content

ISBN: 978 0 19 455705 4   Student's Book
ISBN: 978 0 19 455706 1   Student's CD-ROM Pack

Printed in China

This book is printed on paper from certified and well-managed sources.

ACKNOWLEDGEMENTS

Illustrations by: Tim Bradford pp 2, 4, 6 (on the bus), 6 (man and woman), 8 (eating a meal), 8 (in the kitchen), 10, 12, 14, 16, 18, 20, 22, 24, 26, 28, 30, 32, 34, 36 (offering a lift), 36 (video game), 38, 40 (calendar), 42, 44, 46 (backpackers), 46 (bus stop), 48, 50, 52, 54, 56, 58, 60, 62, 64, 64, 66, 68, 70, 72, 76, 78 (man ironing), 80, 82, 84, 88, 90, 92, 94, 96, 98, 100, 102, 104, 106, 108, 110, 112, 114, 118, 120; Lisa Hunt pp 11, 19, 21, 27, 29, 35, 36 (waiter and customer), 46 (going to London), 47, 49, 61, 69, 75, 77, 83, 85, 91, 93, 99, 101, 107, 109, 115, 117; Julian Mosedale pp 3, 6 (cricket batsman), 8 (reporter), 17, 23, 31, 33, 39, 40 (weather forecaster), 55, 63, 65, 78 (some facts about my job), 81, 89, 95, 97, 103, 105, 111, 121

We would also like to thank the following for permission to reproduce the following photographs: Alamy p 43 (Chris Howes/Wild Places Photography); Getty Images pp 51 (Kyle Newton), 71 (MIXA); Punchstock p 45 (Image Source); Royalty-free pp 5 (Photodisc), 15 (Tetra Images), 31 (Stockbyte), 32 (skyscraper/Photodisc), 32 (call centre/Stockbyte), 58 (Polka Dot Images), 67 (Image Source), 113 (A J James/Digital Vision), 119 (Photodisc)

Images sourced by: SuzanneWilliams/Pictureresearch.co.uk

Introduction

What is Oxford Living Grammar?

Oxford Living Grammar is a series of three books which explain and practise grammar in **everyday contexts**. They show how grammar is used in **real-life situations** that learners themselves will experience. The books can be used for self-study, for homework, and in class.

Elementary: CEF level A1+ (towards KET level)
Pre-intermediate: CEF level A2 (KET and towards PET level)
Intermediate: CEF level B1 (PET and towards FCE level)

How are the books organized?

The books are divided into four-page units, each of which deals with an important grammar topic. Units are divided into two two-page parts. Each unit begins with an explanation of the grammar point, and includes a unique **Grammar in action** section which shows how the grammar is used in typical everyday situations. It explains **when** to use the grammar point. This is followed by a number of **contextualized exercises** for learners to practise the grammar they have read about. The second part of each unit introduces additional explanation of the topic, more Grammar in action, and more contextualized exercises. The last exercise in every unit provides practice of a variety of the points and contexts introduced across the four pages.

The intention is that the fully contextualized explanations and exercises will show real English in real situations, which learners can recognize and apply to their own experience.

Word focus boxes highlight unfamiliar words or expressions and enable learners to widen their vocabulary.

The **Over to you** section at the back of the book provides a **comprehensive bank of review exercises**. Learners are encouraged to do more creative tasks about themselves and their own experience, using what they have learned. Sample answers are provided for these tasks.

There is an *Oxford Living Grammar* **Context-Plus CD-ROM** at each level with further grammar practice and Word focus exercises. Learners can also build longer texts, and build and take part in dialogues; learners can record and listen to their own voice to improve pronunciation. There are six grammar tests at each level so learners can see if there are any areas they would like to study again.

What grammar is included?

At Pre-intermediate level, you will study all the grammar necessary for Cambridge KET and much of the grammar required for PET. The choice of contexts in the exercises has been informed by the Common European Framework of Reference and the framework of the Association of Language Testers in Europe at A2.

How can students use Oxford Living Grammar on their own?

You can work through the book from beginning to end. All the units will present and practise the grammar in typical everyday situations. When you have finished the exercises, you can go to the Over to you tasks for that topic at the back of the book for extra practice, and then check your answers.

Or, when you have a particular grammar problem, you might want to study that topic first. You can look up the topic you need in the Contents at the front of the book, or in the Index at the back.

How can teachers use the material in the classroom?

Oxford Living Grammar enables your students to learn and practise English grammar in context. The contexts themselves are typical everyday situations that your students will experience, such as talking about their own experiences, having conversations with people they have met, talking about other people, and discussing common topics.

The syllabus is divided into 30 four-page units, which we hope will make the book ideal for study over an academic year. Units can be studied in any order, or you and your students can work through the book from beginning to end. The Over to you tasks provide freer practice and more creative review tasks.

Contents

Introduction *page iii*

Verbs and tenses

01 Present continuous   2
Talking about the present
Talking about the future

02 Present simple   6
Forms, uses, and contexts
Present simple or present continuous?

03 Past simple and past continuous   10
Past simple
Past continuous; past simple or continuous?

04 Present perfect   14
Forms, uses, and contexts
Present perfect with *just, yet, already, never, ever*

05 Past simple and present perfect   18
Comparison of uses
Comparison with *for, since, ago, ever, never*

06 The future   22
Going to
Will and *shall*

Questions

07 Question words   26
When, where, why, how, which, whose, who, what
How long, how many, etc.

08 Subject and object questions   30
Questions with *who*
Questions with *what, which*, and *whose*

Modal verbs

09 *Can, could*, and *would*   34
Ability
Requests and permission

10 *May, might, could*, and *should*   *page 38*
May and *might* for possibility
Could and *should*: possibility and probability

11 *Must* and *have to*   42
Positive forms, their uses, and their contexts
Negative forms, their uses, and their contexts

12 *Should*   46
Uses and contexts
Should compared with other modals

Verb forms and structures

13 The infinitive   50
The *to* infinitive
The infinitive without *to*

14 The *-ing* form   54
Form, uses, and contexts
Infinitive or *-ing* form?

15 The passive   58
Forms, uses, and contexts
Active and passive compared

16 Conditionals   62
First conditional
Second conditional

17 Connecting future sentences   66
Conditional clauses
Time clauses

Nouns, pronouns, determiners

18 Articles   70
A/an and *the*
A/an, the, and no article

19 Pronouns and possessives   74
Subject and object pronouns; possessive adjectives and pronouns
Reflexive pronouns; *each other*

20 Quantifiers *page 78*
   All, most, some, a lot of, any, a few, a little
   Much, many, none, no

21 Pronouns and determiners 82
   One, ones; another, other, others
   Something, everybody, nowhere, anyone, etc

22 *There, it, this, that,* etc. 86
   There and *it*
   This, that, these, and *those*

Adjectives and adverbs

23 Comparison of adjectives 90
   Comparative adjectives
   As … as; superlative adjectives

24 Adverbs 94
   Adverbs of manner; comparison of adverbs
   Adverbs of degree

Prepositions

25 Prepositions (1) 98
   Prepositions of place
   Prepositions of movement

26 Prepositions (2) 102
   In, with, by, without
   Prepositional phrases

Building sentences

27 Reported speech 106
   Say and *tell*
   Tell and *ask*

28 Relative clauses 110
   Who, which, that
   Which, that, who, where, when, whose

29 Conversational English 114
   Short answers and short questions;
      question tags
   Short responses: *so, too, neither/nor, either*

30 Clause and sentence building *page 118*
   Still, only, also
   Because, so, so that; instead; apart from, except; although/though

Over to you 122

Form tables 129

Verb tenses 133

Answer key 134

Answer key Over to you 149

Index 153

01 Present continuous
Talking about the present

1 Some examples of the **present continuous** (be + -ing):
   I'm reading a good book at the moment.
   She isn't working at this office today.
   What *are* you *doing* now?

2 Forms of the **present continuous**:

   POSITIVE
   I **am/'m** starting
   you/we/they **are/'re** starting
   he/she/it **is/'s** starting

   NEGATIVE
   I **am not / 'm not** starting
   you/we/they **are not / 're not / aren't** starting
   he/she/it **is not / 's not / isn't** starting

   QUESTIONS
   am I starting
   are you/we/they starting
   is he/she/it starting

3 The **-ing** form:

   For most verbs, add **-ing**:
   work → work**ing**   play → play**ing**

   For verbs ending **-e**, take away **-e** and add **-ing**:
   tak**e** → tak**ing**   writ**e** → writ**ing**

For many verbs ending with one vowel and one consonant, double the last letter and add **-ing**:
   ru**n** → run**ning**   si**t** → sit**ting**

(For more information on the **-ing** form, see p. 130.)

Grammar in action

1 We use the **present continuous** to talk about actions and describe situations at the present moment:
   What are you doing at the moment? ~ I'm sitting on the sofa. It's raining outside.

2 We use the **present continuous** for actions and situations in the present period of time, but not at this exact moment:
   What's Jack doing these days? ~ He's travelling around the world. He's visiting lots of countries.

3 We use the **present continuous** for present situations that are temporary or different from usual. This example decribes a change in someone's usual routine:
   Kathy has an office but she's working at home today.

A What I'm doing now

Alice is on a train. Complete what she says using the present continuous and the words in brackets. Use short forms if possible.

0 *I'm sitting* on a train. (I/sit)
1 .... a cup of coffee. (I/drink)
2 .... the station now. (We/leave)
3 .... to Manchester. (The train/go)
4 .... to a meeting. (I/travel)
5 What .... at the moment? (you/do)
6 Me? .... a phone call to you! (I/make)

B The big match

Complete the descriptions of the football match using the words in brackets and the present continuous forms of the correct verbs from the box.

leave   run   blow   ~~talk~~   wear   look   shine   celebrate   play

0 Good afternoon. _I'm talking_ to you from the National Stadium. (I)
1 It's a lovely day at the stadium. .... and it's warm. (The sun)
2 .... out onto the field. (The teams)
3 .... white shirts and Wales are in red. (The England players)
4 .... well and it's a good game. (Both teams)
5 .... happy. It's 1–0 to England. (The England fans)
6 It's half-time. .... the field. (The players)
7 Another goal for England and .... (the players)
8 .... his whistle and it's the end of the game. (The referee)

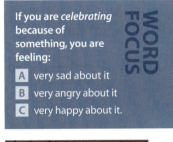

WORD FOCUS

If you are *celebrating* because of something, you are feeling:
A very sad about it
B very angry about it
C very happy about it.

C News of friends

Tom and Rose are talking about people they know. Complete their conversation using the present continuous and the words in brackets. Use short forms.

TOM   How's Michael?
ROSE He's fine. _He's working_ ⁰ (He/work) in Italy at the moment.
TOM   Really? .... ¹ (What/he/do) there?
ROSE .... ² (He/spend) a year at his company's office in Rome.
      .... ³ (He/learn) Italian and .... ⁴ (he/have) fun.
TOM   And what about Olivia?
ROSE .... ⁵ (She/live) in a different flat now. And .... ⁶
      (she/not go out) with Frank any more. In fact, ... ⁷ (they/not talk)
      to each other now.
TOM   Oh dear. Poor Frank.
ROSE He's fine. .... ⁸ (He/enjoy) himself. .... ⁹ (He/not sit)
      at home alone. .... ¹⁰ (He/take) lots of girls to bars and night clubs.
TOM   Oh, I see. Lucky Frank!

D Changes in my town

Complete this report about changes in a town using the present continuous and the correct verbs from the box.

not use   talk   go   tell   not do   ~~change~~   cause   move   not listen
not travel   get

My town _is changing_ ⁰ a lot. The population .... ¹ bigger because
people .... ² from the countryside to the town. This .... ³
traffic problems. People .... ⁴ public transport very much and they
.... ⁵ on bikes. Too many cars .... ⁶ into the town centre.
The authorities .... ⁷ people to stop using their cars so much, but
people .... ⁸. People .... ⁹ about the problem but they
.... ¹⁰ anything to solve it.

Verbs and tenses | 3

01 Present continuous
Talking about the future

4 We also use the **present continuous** to talk about the **future**:
I'm meeting some friends tonight.
Jane is starting a new job next week.
What are you doing next weekend?

(For more information on future verb forms, see unit 6 on p. 22 and unit 17 on p. 66.)

Grammar in action

4 We use the **present continuous** for fixed, arranged, and organized actions. These actions are certain to happen in the future.
I'm going on holiday tomorrow.
I'm catching the 8.30 flight.

E My plans next week

Look at Zena's schedule for next week and complete her description of her plans, using the present continuous. Use short forms.

Monday	start new course 9 a.m., go to Main Hall Principal gives talk attend lectures rest of day	**Friday**	write essay in library have meeting with tutor
Tuesday	we take test we go on trip to History Museum (leave 2 p.m., arrive back 5 p.m.)	**Saturday**	morning, go shopping with Alex afternoon, play tennis with Pam go to concert, Morris Hall
Wednesday	play for college basketball team no college work to do	**Sunday**	do nothing! stay at home, take it easy
Thursday	evening, cook meal for Sam and Olga (eat 8.30 p.m.) watch film at home	April	1 2 3 4 5 6 7 8 9 10 11 12 13 14 15 16 17 18 19 20 21 22 23 24 25 26 27 28 29 30

On Monday morning, ...*I'm starting*...⁰ a new course. At 9 a.m., ...¹ to the Main Hall and ....² a talk about this course. After that, ...³ lectures for the rest of the day.
On Tuesday morning, ...⁴ a test. In the afternoon, ...⁵ on a trip to the History Museum. ....⁶ the college at 2 p.m. and ....⁷ back at the college at 5 p.m.
On Wednesday, ...⁸ for the college basketball team. ....⁹ any college work that day.
On Thursday evening, ...¹⁰ a meal for Sam and Olga. ....¹¹ at 8.30 p.m. and then ....¹² a film at home.
On Friday, ...¹³ an essay in the library and then ....¹⁴ a meeting with my tutor.
On Saturday morning, ...¹⁵ shopping with Alex. In the afternoon, ...¹⁶ tennis with Pam and in the evening ....¹⁷ to a concert at the Morris Hall.
On Sunday, ...¹⁸ anything. ....¹⁹ at home and ....²⁰ it easy all day.

4 | Verbs and tenses

F The college party

Tara and Leon and talking on the phone. Complete their conversation using the present continuous and the words in brackets.

TARA Are you busy at the moment?
LEON Yes, *I'm trying* ⁰ (I/try) to finish some work. _____¹ (I/do) an assignment and _____² (I/find) it very difficult. What _____³ (you/do)?
TARA _____⁴ (I/get) ready for the party tonight. _____⁵ (I/leave) in about twenty minutes. _____⁶ (The taxi/come) for me at 7.30 p.m.
LEON Well, _____⁷ (I/not go), unfortunately. I've got too much work to do. _____⁸ (Who/go) to this party?
TARA Everyone. _____⁹ (We/celebrate) the end of the exams. _____¹⁰ (A band/play) and about 120 _____¹¹ (people/come).
LEON Well, _____¹² (I/stay) here and _____¹³ (I/work) all evening. And then _____¹⁴ (I/go) to bed.

G My life in London

Complete this email from Carmen to her friend, using the present continuous and the correct verbs from the box. Use short forms.

> go   not miss   study   learn   take   have   visit   practise   ~~stay~~
> happen   treat   do   look   not study   make

Hi

As you know, I *'m staying* ⁰ in London with a family. I _____¹ at a local college and I _____² a really good time. Everyone _____³ me very well and I _____⁴ lots of new friends. I _____⁵ home at all because I _____⁶ so many fantastic things.

At college, I _____⁷ a lot of English and of course I _____⁸ my English with the family. When I _____⁹, I _____¹⁰ all sorts of places with the family. For example, on Saturday they _____¹¹ me to a theme park and next week we _____¹² to a very famous old castle, somewhere outside London. I _____¹³ forward to that.

Let me know what _____¹⁴ with you.

Carmen

OVER TO YOU   Now go to page 122.

02 Present simple
Forms, uses, and contexts

1 Some examples of the **present simple**:
   I **read** a newspaper every day.
   She **doesn't like** this kind of music.
   When **does** the party **start** tomorrow?

2 Forms of the **present simple**:

   POSITIVE
   I/you/we/they **know**
   he/she/it **knows**

   NEGATIVE
   I/you/we/they **do not know / don't know**
   he/she/it **does not know / doesn't know**

   QUESTIONS
   do I/you/we/they **know**
   does he/she/it **know**

3 The **he/she/it** form:

   For most verbs, add **-s**:
   work → works   like → likes   buy → buys

   For verbs ending **-ch, -o, -sh, -x** and **-ss**, add **-es**:
   catch → catches   go → goes
   wash → washes   fix → fixes
   pass → passes

   For verbs ending with a consonant and **-y**,
   take away **-y** and add **-ies**:
   study → studies   cry → cries   fly → flies

For **have**:
   have → has

(For more information on the **he/she/it** form, see p. 129.)

Grammar in action

1 We use the **present simple** for facts and things that are always true:
   Some doctors work in hospitals.

2 We use the **present simple** for habits and repeated actions:
   She takes the bus to work.

3 We use the **present simple** to talk about thoughts or feelings, for example to say what we *like, want, think,* or *know*:
   He loves her very much.

4 We use the **present simple** for the **future**, to talk about events on a timetable. Here, someone is looking at a TV schedule:
   The film tomorrow starts at 8.30 and finishes at 11.

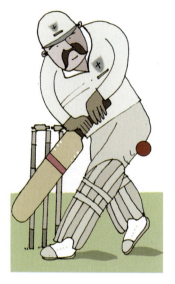

A Some facts about cricket

These are some facts about the sport of cricket. If the verb form is correct, put a tick (✓). If the verb form is incorrect, write the correct verb form.

0 A cricket team have ...has... 11 players and they usually wear ...✓... white.
1 Cricket has .... a lot of rules and lots of people aren't understand .... it.
2 In a game of cricket, the bowler throws .... the ball and the batsman tries .... to hit it.
3 The fielders stand .... around the field and they stop .... the ball.
4 If a fielder catchs .... the ball, the batsman is 'out', and he leaves .... the field.
5 If the batsman doesn't hits .... the ball and the ball hits .... the wicket, he is also out.
6 You win .... a game if you score .... more 'runs' than the other team.
7 Some cricket matches lasts .... for five days and nobody wins .... !
8 Some people doesn't like .... cricket but millions watch .... it on TV.

B A typical day at work

Complete this magazine article by a businesswoman, using the present simple forms of the verbs in brackets. Use short forms for negatives.

Business as usual

I usually _arrive_ ⁰ (arrive) at the office very early. My assistant Cheryl ....¹ (bring) me the mail and ....² (tell) me what is in my diary for the day. She ....³ (do) a lot of very important work for me – she ....⁴ (organize) my day and ....⁵ (deal) with a lot of people for me. Then I ....⁶ (have) a meeting with my team of managers – we ....⁷ (discuss) plans and problems. Sometimes they ....⁸ (not agree) with me but the meetings usually ....⁹ (not last) for very long.

I ....¹⁰ (not eat) much at lunchtime – the others ....¹¹ (go) to the canteen but I ....¹² (stay) in my office and someone ....¹³ (get) me a sandwich. My day usually ....¹⁴ (finish) at about 6 p.m.

I ....¹⁵ (not go) to the office every day. I ....¹⁶ (work) at home some days and I sometimes ....¹⁷ (travel) to meetings or conferences.

WORD FOCUS

Which of these words in exercise B is not used only in connection with work?
- A office
- B diary
- C canteen
- D conferences

C Using the library

Complete the questions and answers in a survey of people using a library, using the present simple and the words in brackets.

INTERVIEWER	_Do you live_ ⁰ in the local area? (you/live)
WOMAN	Yes, _I live_ ⁰ close to here. (I/live)
INTERVIEWER	..........¹ this library very often? (you/visit)
WOMAN	No, ...² here very often. (I/not come)
INTERVIEWER	What ....³ in the library? (you/do)
WOMAN	..........⁴ the newspapers and ....⁵ books. (I/read) (I/borrow)
INTERVIEWER	What kind of books ....⁶? (you/borrow)
WOMAN	Fiction. ....⁷ a good fiction section. (The library/have)
INTERVIEWER	..........⁸ the library? (other members of your family/use)
WOMAN	Yes, ...⁹ some of her college work here. (my daughter/do)

D Timetable for tomorrow's school trip

Complete this notice about a school trip in the future, using the present simple and the correct verbs from the list.

> go   start   ~~meet~~   show   leave   return   finish   get   attend   arrive   have

Here are the details for tomorrow's trip. We _meet_ ⁰ outside the school at 8. The coach ....¹ at 8.30 so don't be late! We ....² at the museum at 10. A guide ....³ us round the museum from 10 to 12. We ....⁴ to the museum restaurant for lunch at 12 and we ....⁵ lunch from 12 to 1. In the afternoon, we ....⁶ a lecture in one of the lecture rooms. It ....⁷ at 1 and ....⁸ at 2.30. We ....⁹ back on the coach at 3 and we ....¹⁰ to the school at 4.30.

02 Present simple
Present simple or present continuous?

4 Compare the **present simple** and the **present continuous**:
He **sits** at a desk every day.
He's **sitting** at his desk at the moment.

Grammar in action

5 We use the **present simple** to talk about facts that are always true. We use the **present continuous** to talk about things that are only true at the moment or in the present period of time:

You cook wonderful meals.
(= always or usually)

He's cooking a meal in the kitchen.
(= right now)

6 We use the **present simple** for permanent situations. We use the **present continuous** for temporary situations:
My husband works for a computer company, but he's working at home today.

7 We use the **present simple** for things we do regularly (e.g. in our daily routine). We can use it with words and phrases describing how often something happens (*always, sometimes, often, never, usually, every day*, etc.):
I go to bed at ten and get up at six every day.

We do not use the present continuous with this meaning:
I sometimes wear a hat.
(NOT *I'm sometimes wearing a hat.*)

8 We often use the **present continuous** with 'now' and phrases meaning 'now', for example *at the moment, right now, this week, this month*. We do not use the present simple with these words and phrases:
I'm sitting in a traffic jam at the moment. (NOT *I sit* …)

9 We use the **present simple** with verbs that describe what we feel and think. These verbs are connected with what is in our minds, not with actions. They describe what we like (for example *like, dislike, hate, love*), what we want (*want, need*), what we know (*know, understand, realize, remember*) and what we believe (*believe, think*). We do not use the present continuous with these verbs:
I don't understand this letter.
(NOT *I'm not understanding this letter.*)

E Over to our reporter

Complete what the television reporter says by choosing the present simple or present continuous form.

Hello, ….I'm standing…. ⁰ outside a very famous person's house. …………… ¹ in films and …………… ² millions of dollars for every film. …………… ³ on the front cover of magazines and people all over the world …………… ⁴ her and …………… ⁵ her. And people …………… ⁶ about her at the moment because the media …………… ⁷ stories about her private life. She …………… ⁸ her private life but right now everyone …………… ⁹ to know about it. Can you guess who it is?
Dozens of photographers are here too and …………… ¹⁰ for her to come out. Ah, the front door …………… ¹¹ now and someone …………… ¹² out.

0 I stand / I'm standing
1 She stars / She's starring
2 she earns / she's earning
3 She appears / She's appearing
4 know / are knowing
5 love / are loving
6 talk / are talking

7 tell / are telling
8 doesn't usually discuss / isn't usually discussing
9 wants / is wanting
10 we wait / we're waiting
11 opens / is opening
12 comes / is coming

F Someone to write to

Complete this letter in an international magazine for teenagers, using the present simple or present continuous form of the verbs in brackets. Use short forms.

Letter of the month

I **'m looking** ⁰ (look) for someone to write to in another country. I .... ¹ (speak) quite good English but I .... ² (want) to get better at it. And I .... ³ (think) it's good to have friends in different parts of the world.
I .... ⁴ (go) to a local school and this term we .... ⁵ (study) for our exams. I .... ⁶ (work) very hard at school now because I .... ⁷ (need) to get good results. In my spare time, I .... ⁸ (like) classical music but I .... ⁹ (not like) much modern pop music. I .... ¹⁰ (not play) video games and I .... ¹¹ (not watch) TV much – I .... ¹² (read) a lot of books and at the moment I .... ¹³ (try) to read fiction in English. I .... ¹⁴ (take) an interest in sports but I .... ¹⁵ (not play) any sports regularly.
My family? My father .... ¹⁶ (work) for an international company and he .... ¹⁷ (travel) a lot - right now he .... ¹⁸ (travel) in South-East Asia. He always .... ¹⁹ (buy) me something interesting from these trips and at the moment I .... ²⁰ (use) a computer that he bought me. I hope that I .... ²¹ (not make) too many mistakes!

G Adverts

Complete the extracts from adverts, using the present simple or present continuous and the words in brackets.

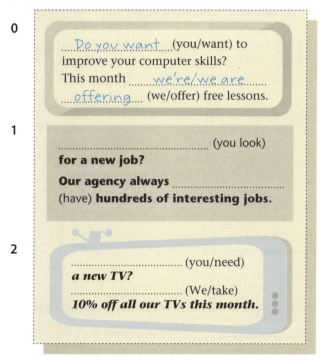

0 **Do you want** (you/want) to improve your computer skills? This month **we're/we are offering** (we/offer) free lessons.

1 .... (you look) for a new job? Our agency always .... (have) hundreds of interesting jobs.

2 .... (you/need) a new TV? .... (We/take) 10% off all our TVs this month.

3 People .... (love) this area and .... (it/become) very popular with tourists.

4 .... (We/serve) thousands of customers every week and many of them .... (come) back to us again.

5 Our company .... (grow) and .... (we/look) for more staff.

6 The box office .... (open) at 8 a.m. every day, but hurry, tickets .... (sell) fast.

OVER TO YOU Now go to page 122.

03 Past simple and past continuous
Past simple

1 Some examples of the **past simple**:
   I **walked** to college yesterday.
   She **didn't phone** me last week.
   When **did** you **arrive** in this country?

2 Forms of the **past simple**:

POSITIVE
I/you/he/she/it/we/they **finished**
NEGATIVE (did not / didn't + verb)
I/you/he/she/it/we/they **did not / didn't finish**
NOT ~~didn't finished~~
QUESTIONS (did + subject + verb)
did I/you/he/she/it/we/they **finish**
NOT ~~did it finished~~

3 **Regular verbs** (positive forms):

   We form the **past simple** by adding **-ed** to the verb:

walk → walk**ed**	visit → visit**ed**

   For verbs ending with **-e**, we add **-d**:

live → live**d**	love → love**d**

   For verbs ending with a consonant and **-y**, we take away **-y** and add **-ied**:

carry → carr**ied**	try → tr**ied**

   For many verbs ending with one vowel and one consonant, we double the last letter and add **-ed**.

stop → sto**pped**	plan → pla**nned**

   (For more regular past simple forms, see p. 130.)

4 **Irregular verbs**:

   Many very common verbs are irregular:

go → went	come → came	do → did
speak → spoke	run → ran	have → had
take → took	see → saw	buy → bought
think → thought	leave → left	make → made

   (For more irregular past simple forms, see p. 131.)

5 The **past simple** forms of **be**:
   I/he/she/it **was/was not/wasn't**
   you/we/they **were/were not/weren't**
   was I/he/she/it
   were you/we/they

Grammar in action

1 We use the **past simple** to talk about actions completed in the past, for example when we describe a sequence of events:
   He came out of the door, locked it, got into his car and drove away.

2 We use the **past simple** to talk about past situations (situations that are not true now). For example, we can use it to describe earlier times in our lives:
   I was a waiter when I lived in Spain.

3 With the **past simple**, we often say when something happened. Sometimes we don't say when something happened because we understand what point in time in the past we are talking about:
   What did you do last night? ~ I listened to some music, I read a book and then I went to bed.
   (= last night)

A Family history

Complete this description using the past simple forms of the verbs in brackets.

My name is Gurnam and my family originally ___came___ [0] (come) from India. My grandparents _____ [1] (move) to Britain in 1975 and they went to live in the city of Leicester. My grandfather _____ [2] (open) a restaurant there and he _____ [3] (become) very successful. He _____ [4] (not speak) much English when he _____ [5] (arrive) in Britain but he _____ [6] (learn) very

quickly. Lots of people .... ⁷ (eat) at his restaurant. He .... ⁸ (work) very hard for many years and he .... ⁹ (make) plenty of money.
My father .... ¹⁰ (be) born in Leicester and he .... ¹¹ (go) to school there. He .... ¹² (do) very well at school and .... ¹³ (pass) all his exams. Then he .... ¹⁴ (study) at university for three years and .... ¹⁵ (get) a Business degree. After that, he .... ¹⁶ (set) up his own business. At first he .... ¹⁷ (sell) clothes in a shop near the city centre, and after a few years he .... ¹⁸ (own) five shops all over the city. When I was a small child, we .... ¹⁹ (live) in a small house but my father .... ²⁰ (buy) a bigger one two years ago.

B An unpleasant journey

Complete this story about a journey, using the past simple and the correct verbs from the box. Use short forms for negatives.

> get not stay drive be (x2) shout not speak come not go make
> not start not say arrive start ~~go~~ not arrive want

Yesterday I ..*went*..⁰ on a day trip. My friend Liam .... ¹ with me. The day .... ² well because Liam .... ³ at my house late. He .... ⁴ why he .... ⁵ late and I .... ⁶ at him. Then we .... ⁷ our journey. I .... ⁸ the car. A bit later, we .... ⁹ lost. We .... ¹⁰ to go to the seaside but we .... ¹¹ a bad mistake and we .... ¹² in the right direction. We .... ¹³ at the beach until very late in the day, so we .... ¹⁴ for a long time. On the way home, we .... ¹⁵ to each other at all. We .... ¹⁶ both very angry.

C The road to fame

Complete this interview with a famous singer, using the past simple and the correct words from the box.

> offer play you feel happen appear be not earn
> you become help it happen see leave enjoy buy want make
> ~~you start~~ take ask know have

INTERVIEWER   When ..*did you start*..⁰ singing in the band?
MIA   Well, I .... ¹ 19 years old. The original singer .... ² the band and the others .... ³ me to replace him.
INTERVIEWER   .... ⁴ successful very quickly?
MIA   No, it .... ⁵ a long time. We .... ⁶ in small clubs for many years and we .... ⁷ much money.
INTERVIEWER   .... ⁸ unhappy then?
MIA   No, we .... ⁹ ourselves. We .... ¹⁰ a great time. But we .... ¹¹ to succeed.
INTERVIEWER   How .... ¹²?
MIA   Well, a manager .... ¹³ us playing in a small club and he .... ¹⁴ to be our manager. He .... ¹⁵ a lot about the music business and he .... ¹⁶ us a lot. Because of him, we .... ¹⁷ on a TV show. Then we .... ¹⁸ a record and lots of people .... ¹⁹ it. Everything .... ²⁰ very quickly then.

Verbs and tenses | 11

03 Past simple and past continuous
Past continuous; past simple or continuous?

6 Some examples of the **past continuous**:
*In 2003, I **was studying** at college.
Please repeat that, I **wasn't listening**.
What **were** you **doing** at 6 o'clock yesterday evening?*

7 Forms of the **past continuous**:

POSITIVE (was/were + -ing)
I/he/she/it **was walking**.
you/we/they **were walking**.
NEGATIVE (was not / wasn't / were not / weren't + -ing)
I/he/she/it **was not** / **wasn't walking**.
you/we/they **were not** / **weren't walking**.
QUESTIONS (was/were ... + -ing ...?)
was I/you/he/she/it **walking**
were you/we/they **walking**

(For rules on the *-ing* form, see p. 130.)

Grammar in action

4 We use the **past continuous** for actions and situations that were in progress at a particular time in the past (e.g. *in 1981, at 6 a.m. yesterday morning*):
At 7.30 p.m. last night, I was playing a video game, my sister was doing her homework and my parents were reading.

5 We often use the past continuous in sentences with the past simple to talk about two actions. We use the **past simple** for a completed action and the **past continuous** to describe something in progress when the second action happened:
*I was walking down the street when I met an old friend.
While/When I was walking down the street, I met an old friend.*

> **TIP**
> We use **when** before the past simple and **while/when** before the past continuous:
> *When the doorbell rang, I was lying in bed.
> While/When I was lying in bed, the doorbell rang.*

D What was happening five years ago

Complete this description of situations five years ago, using the past continuous and the verbs in brackets. Use short forms for negatives.

Five years ago, I ....was living.... ⁰(live) in a different city. I .... ¹ (study) for my final school exams and I .... ² (try) to decide what to do after school. I .... ³ (do) homework every evening and I .... ⁴ (not go) out much. My friends .... ⁵ (have) more fun than me. They .... ⁶ (go) to clubs and they .... ⁷ (enjoy) themselves while I .... ⁸ (sit) at home. But I'm glad now that I .... ⁹ (not do) that, because I passed my exams and now I've got a good job.

Five years ago, my father .... ¹⁰ (work) very hard. He .... ¹¹ (get) up early every morning and he .... ¹² (come) home quite late at night. He .... ¹³ (feel) under pressure and he .... ¹⁴ (not enjoy) life. He is retired now and he is much happier because he has a lot more free time.

Five years ago, my sister .... ¹⁵ (go) out with a local boy. They .... ¹⁶ (save) money to get married and they .... ¹⁷ (plan) their wedding. She .... ¹⁸ (serve) in a shop and he .... ¹⁹ (live) with his parents. Now they're married and they've got three children.

E A day at the office

Complete these sentences about someone's day at work, using the past simple or the past continuous forms of the verbs in brackets.

0   While I _was travelling_ (travel) to work, I _got_ (get) stuck in traffic jam.
1   When I _____ (arrive) at work, my boss _____ (speak) to someone on the phone.
2   At 11 a.m., I _____ (do) some work when the boss _____ (ask) to see me.
3   While I _____ (talk) to my boss, his phone _____ (ring) several times.
4   When I _____ (come) out of the boss's office, people _____ (not work), they _____ (look) at me.
5   At 1 o'clock, I _____ (stop) work and I _____ (go) for lunch.
6   While I _____ (eat) my lunch, a colleague _____ (come) to my table.
7   While we _____ (sit) together, he _____ (ask) me a question.
8   He asked me: 'What _____ (the boss/talk) about while you _____ (sit) in his office?'
9   I said: 'When I _____ (go) into his office, I _____ (feel) nervous, but he _____ (smile).
10 While we _____ (talk), he _____ (offer) me a much better job.'

WORD FOCUS

In exercises B, D and E, there are three phrases with *get*. Complete each phrase. The meaning of each one is in brackets:

A get _____ (be unable to find your way to a place)

B get _____ (marry someone)

C get _____ (be unable to move or progress)

F Travel writers

Complete this story, using the past simple or the past continuous form of the correct verbs from the box. You will need to use some of the verbs more than once.

plan   ask   have   decide   meet   travel   come   sit   write   give
discover   become   start   make   do   chat   continue   not like   ~~live~~

Joan _was living_ ⁰ in Paris when she _____ ¹ Paul. She _____ ² in a café when he _____ ³ to her table and _____ ⁴ if he could sit there. They _____ ⁵ talking and while they _____ ⁶, they _____ ⁷ that they _____ ⁸ a lot in common. Both of them _____ ⁹ novels and both of them _____ ¹⁰ jobs that they _____ ¹¹. They _____ ¹² very good friends.

One day, while they _____ ¹³ lunch in the same café, they _____ ¹⁴ an idea. They _____ ¹⁵ to travel around the world together. While they _____ ¹⁶ their trip, they _____ ¹⁷ working. Then they _____ ¹⁸ up their jobs and they _____ ¹⁹ their journey. While they _____ ²⁰, they _____ ²¹ all sorts of adventures, and they _____ ²² all sorts of interesting people. They _____ ²³ lots of notes while they _____ ²⁴ these experiences. When they _____ ²⁵ home again, both of them _____ ²⁶ books about their journey.

OVER TO YOU   Now go to page 122.

04 Present perfect
Forms, uses, and contexts

1 Some examples of the **present perfect** (**have/has** + **past participle**):
   I've posted the letters.
   She hasn't replied to my email.
   Have you seen this programme before?

2 Forms of the **present perfect**:

POSITIVE
I/you/we/they **have/'ve worked**
he/she/it **has/'s worked**
NEGATIVE
I/you/we/they **have not / haven't worked**
he/she/it **has not / hasn't worked**
QUESTIONS
have I/you/we/they **worked**
has he/she/it **worked**

3 For regular verbs, the **past participle** is the same as the past simple form:

   add **-ed**: finish → finish**ed**   start → start**ed**
   add **-d**: live → live**d**   save → save**d**
   take away **-y** and add **-ied**: reply → repl**ied**
   try → tr**ied**
   double the last letter and add **-ed**:
   stop → sto**pped**   plan → plan**ned**

4 The **past participle** of some irregular verbs is different from the past simple form:

   write → written   be → been   do → done

   The **past participle** of some irregular verbs is the same as the past simple form:

   buy → bought   think → thought   leave → left

The **past participle** of some irregular verbs is the same as the infinitive form:

   read → read   come → come   put → put

(For more information on forming past participles, see p. 130 and p. 131.)

Grammar in action

1 We use the **positive present perfect** for past actions and situations. We do not say the time in the past, and we often use the present perfect with the meaning 'in my life' or 'in the life of the person we are talking about':
   She's travelled to many countries.

2 When we use the **present perfect**, the point in the past when something happened is not important, or we do not know or cannot remember exactly when it happened:
   I've read that book and it's great. (The fact of reading the book is important, not when you read it.)

3 We use the **present perfect** when something that happened in the past has a result now. The result is more important than when the action or event happened:
   I've lost my keys. (= I can't find them now.)

4 We use the **negative present perfect** with the meaning 'at any time before now':
   I've met his brother but I haven't met his sister.
   (= in all of the past before now)

5 We also use the **negative present perfect** with the meaning 'in the period of time before now':
   You haven't eaten much.

A My life until now

It is Olivia's 40th birthday and she is thinking about her life until now. Complete her sentences, using the present perfect and the verbs in brackets. Use short forms.

0 *I've met* (meet) lots of people and *I've done* (do) lots of exciting things.
1 _____ (work) hard but _____ (not become) rich.
2 _____ (live) in different cities but _____ (not live) in another country.
3 _____ (study) on several courses and _____ (learn) a lot.
4 _____ (buy) lots of books but _____ (not read) all of them.
5 _____ (try) lots of sports but _____ (not find) one I enjoy.

B Surprising news

Complete this conversation between two friends about a friend of theirs, using the present perfect, the correct verbs from the box and *he*. Use short forms if possible.

> find   give   not say   buy   ~~hear~~   not tell   decide   sell   not contact
> plan   do

JACK Have you heard⁰ about Marlon?
TOM No, ...¹ me recently. What ....²?
JACK ....³ to leave the country. ....⁴ a job in Australia.
TOM I'm very surprised about that. ....⁵ anything to me.
JACK No, it's a secret. ....⁶ his family, so they don't know.
TOM Wow. ....⁷ everything in secret?
JACK Yes, ...⁸ up his job, ...⁹ his car and ....¹⁰ his plane ticket.
TOM I don't know what to say. I'm amazed.

WORD FOCUS

At the end of the conversation, Tom says 'I'm amazed'. Find a two-word phrase earlier in the conversation that means *amazed*:
amazed
....

C Things said in a classroom one day

Anna is a college student and her teacher is Mr Cross. Complete what Anna says one day at college, using the present perfect and the correct verbs from the box. You will need to use negative forms in some sentences. Use short forms if possible.

> be   join   come   have   do   ~~lose~~   eat

0 I need to borrow a pen because I 've lost mine.
1 Sharon is unhappy because she .... an argument with her boyfriend.
2 The class is bigger today because two new students .... it.
3 Mr Cross is angry with me because I .... my homework.
4 Jane .... to school today because she's ill.
5 I .... lunch because I .... too busy.

D News from home

Complete this email from Georgia to her friend Paul, who now lives in another country. Use the present perfect and the words in brackets. Use short forms if possible.

Hi Paul, I'm sorry I haven't replied ⁰ (I/not reply) to your email before now, but finally here's some news. ....¹ (Helen/leave) college now and ....²(she/start) her first job. ....³ (She/buy) lots of new clothes to wear at work because she needs to look smart. ....⁴ (Things/get) better for Harry. ....⁵ (He/find) a new girlfriend and ....⁶ (he/become) a lot happier. She's called Martha and ....⁷ (I/not meet) her, but ....⁸ (people/tell) me that she's really nice. ....⁹ (The weather/be) terrible. ....¹⁰ (The rain/not stop) for ages. ....¹¹ (You/make) a good decision – I'm sure it's lovely where you are!

Verbs and tenses | 15

04 Present perfect
Present perfect with *just, yet, already, never, ever*

5 We use **just**, **already**, and **never** with the **positive** present perfect in the pattern:

> subject + have/has + just/already/never + past participle

I've just arrived at the airport.
I've already given you this information.
I've never heard this singer before.

6 We use **yet** with the **negative** present perfect in the pattern:

> subject + haven't/hasn't + past participle + yet

We haven't bought any tickets *yet*.

We use **yet** in **questions** with the present perfect in the pattern:

> have/has + subject + past participle + yet

Have you *bought* any tickets *yet*?

7 We use **ever** in **questions** with the present perfect in the pattern:

> have/has + subject + ever + past participle

Have you *ever written* a song?

Grammar in action

6 We use **just** with the present perfect with the meaning 'a short time ago' or 'a very short time before now':
I've just arrived at the station.

7 We use **already** with the present perfect with the meaning 'before now'. We use **already** to emphasize that something happened before now or to express surprise that something happened before now:
The bus has already left. ~ But we're not late.

8 We use **yet** with the present perfect to say that something has not happened but we think it will happen. Here the speaker expected something to happen before now, and is waiting for it to happen:
He hasn't fixed the car yet.

9 We use **never** with the present perfect with the meaning 'at no time in the past':
He has never scored a goal for the team.

10 We use **ever** in questions with the present perfect with the meaning 'at any time in the past':
Have you ever met a famous person?

E In the shopping centre

Decide whether these sentences and questions said by people in a shopping centre are correct or not. If a sentence or question is correct, put a tick (✓). If it is not correct, write it correctly.

0 I spent already all my money. *I've already spent all my money.*
1 The book hasn't arrived in the shops yet.
2 I've just seen something I really want.
3 We didn't go to that shop yet.
4 I've bought already lots of things.
5 Did you yet buy anything?
6 We've been already here for three hours.
7 I didn't look yet in all the shops.
8 The shop over there has opened just.
9 The shop has already sold out of the DVD.
10 Have you found any bargains yet?

F Fans

Complete this conversation between two fans of a singer. Use the words given for each gap, and put *just*, *yet* and *already* in the correct places. Use short forms if possible.

KATE *Have you bought his new CD yet* ⁰?
         ¹.
JIM   Yes, ².
      but ³.
      ⁴?
KATE Yes, ⁵ several times and it's great. ⁶?
JIM   No, ⁷ and ⁸. But ⁹ several times so I don't mind.
KATE Well, ¹⁰ and I really want to. ¹¹ and asked him if he's got a spare ticket.
JIM   And has he got one?
KATE I don't know. ¹².

0	you/buy/his new CD	yet	7	I/phone the box office	just
1	I/get/my copy	already	8	they/sell out	already
2	I/buy it	just	9	I/see him	already
3	I/not listen to it	yet	10	I/not see him	yet
4	you/hear it	yet	11	I/phone a friend	just
5	I/play it	already	12	He/not phone back	yet
6	you/buy tickets for his concert	yet			

G Are you sporty?

Complete the questions and answers in this conversation, using the words in brackets and *ever* or *never* and the present perfect. Use short forms if possible.

MICK *Have you ever done* ⁰ (you/do) any dangerous sports?
PETE No, ¹ (I/do) anything like that. ² (I/jump) out of an aeroplane, ³ (I/climb) a mountain and ⁴ (I/dive) deep under the sea.
MICK ⁵ (you/want) to do any of those things?
PETE No, ⁶ (I/be) interested in them and ⁷ (I/understand) why people do them.
MICK Well, ⁸ (you/play) any sports?
PETE Yes, but ⁹ (I/be) any good at them. ¹⁰ (I/win) a race and ¹¹ (I/score) a goal in a football match.
MICK ¹² (you/try) to do those things?
PETE Yes, but ¹³ (I/succeed). ¹⁴ (Sport/be) one of my strong points.
MICK ¹⁵ (you/feel) bad about that?
PETE No, ¹⁶ (it/worry) me. I'm good at other things.

OVER TO YOU Now go to page 122.

05 Past simple and present perfect
Comparison of uses

1 Compare the **past simple** and the **present perfect**:
He **left** school last year.
He **has left** school and he has a job now.

Grammar in action

1 We use the **past simple** to talk about things happening at a particular time in the past. We use the **present perfect** to talk about things happening in the past when we don't say or are not interested in exactly when they happened:
I watched this programme last week.
I've watched this programme many times.

2 We use the **past simple** to talk and ask about particular times in the past. We use the **present perfect** to talk and ask about the past in general. These examples are about experiences in the past:
When did he visit France? ~ He visited France in 2006.
Has he ever visited France? ~ Yes, he's visited France and many other countries in his life.

3 We use the **past simple** to talk about the past only. We use the **present perfect** to talk about things that happened in the past but have an important result now:

I finished my work and then I went home.

I've finished my work. ~ OK, you can go home now.

4 We use the **past simple** if we understand exactly when something happened, but don't say when. We use the **present perfect** if we don't know when something happened in the past:
What did she do last weekend? ~ She did some shopping and she went to a party. (= last weekend)
She's given up smoking. (= at an unknown time in the past)

A Kitchen conversation

Complete the conversation using the past simple or the present perfect and the words in brackets. Use short forms if possible.

JULIA   I hope _you haven't eaten_ ⁰ (you/not eat). _____¹ (I/cook) a very big meal.
CAROL   No, I'm hungry. This looks interesting. _____² (you/cook) this dish before?
JULIA   Yes, _____³ (I/cook) it many times.
CAROL   Oh, _____⁴ (I/not see) it before. When _____⁵ (you/learn) how to cook it?
JULIA   _____⁶ (Someone/teach) me when _____⁷ (I/be) in Sweden.
CAROL   Oh. When _____⁸ (you/live) in Sweden?
JULIA   _____⁹ (I/live) there from 2003 to 2006. _____¹⁰ (I/have) a job there.
CAROL   Oh, that's interesting. _____¹¹ (you/live) in any other countries?
JULIA   Yes, _____¹² (I/have) jobs in various parts of the world.
CAROL   For example?
JULIA   Well, _____¹³ (I/work) in Brazil last year.
CAROL   _____¹⁴ (you/enjoy) that?
JULIA   Yes, _____¹⁵ (I/have) a great time. _____¹⁶ (I/make) lots of friends and _____¹⁷ (I/enjoy) my time there. Anyway, _____¹⁸ (I/finish) the cooking now. Let's eat.

B No tickets

Complete this conversation between two people arriving at the theatre, by choosing the past simple or the present perfect form.

DANIEL Oh no! _I've made_ ⁰ a terrible mistake.
TOBY What _____¹?
DANIEL _____² the tickets. _____³ them at home.
TOBY What?
DANIEL Yes, _____⁴ them in my bag this morning but then _____⁵ to use a different bag. _____⁶ the tickets out of the first bag this evening and so _____⁷ them with me.
TOBY When _____⁸ the tickets?
DANIEL Last week. I _____⁹ it by phone and then _____¹⁰ me the tickets in the post.
TOBY How _____¹¹?
DANIEL _____¹² by credit card.
TOBY _____¹³ a receipt?
DANIEL Yes. Oh, just a minute. Look, _____¹⁴ the receipt. It's in my wallet.
TOBY Great. Let's go to the box office. I'm sure _____¹⁵ a record of the seat numbers and we can solve the problem.

0 I made / I've made
1 did you do / have you done
2 I forgot / I've forgotten
3 I left / I've left
4 I put / I've put
5 I decided / I've decided
6 I didn't take / I haven't taken
7 I didn't bring / I haven't brought
8 did you book / have you booked
9 I did / I've done
10 they sent / they've sent
11 did you pay / have you paid
12 I paid / I've paid
13 Did they send / Have they sent
14 I found / I've found
15 they kept / they've kept

C My guest tonight …

The host of a chat show is introducing his special guest. Complete what he says, using the past simple or the present perfect and the correct verbs from the box.

> want play be leave see change ~~become~~ get choose go
> win work vote not be have

My guest tonight _has become_ ⁰ a household name in this country. He _____¹ the lead role in many successful TV dramas and he _____² several awards. Last year viewers _____³ him the Most Popular Actor on TV.
But it _____⁴ easy for him to get where he is today. Ten years ago, he _____⁵ school without any qualifications. He _____⁶ a job in a restaurant and he _____⁷ as a waiter. But he _____⁸ desperate to be an actor and he _____⁹ to drama school at weekends. Then he _____¹⁰ a big piece of luck. The writer Sheila Grace _____¹¹ him acting in a small theatre and she _____¹² him to be the main character in her new police series. At that moment his life _____¹³ , and he is now one of the most well-known people on TV. I _____¹⁴ to meet him for a long time. Please welcome Terry McCann!

WORD FOCUS

What is the correct definition of *household name*?

A a name someone gives to their house, often on a sign on the door

B a person who is very famous and known by the majority of people

05 Past simple and present perfect
Comparison with *for*, *since*, *ago*, *ever*, *never*

2 Compare these sentences:
   I **worked** in Rome **for a year**.
   I **have worked** in Rome **for years** and I love it here.

3 We use the pattern **past simple + for + period of time** to talk about something that continued and ended in the past:
   She **lived** in Paris **for two years**. (= She does not live in Paris now.)

   We use the pattern **present perfect + for + period of time** to talk about something that began in the past and continued until now (it may also continue after now):
   She's **lived** in Paris **for a year**. (= She lives in Paris now.)

4 We use the pattern **past simple + period of time + ago** to talk about how long in the past something happened:
   He **started** this job **two months ago**.

   We use the pattern **present perfect + since + point in time** to talk about something that began in the past and continued until now (it may also continue after now):
   He's **worked** in this job **since March**.

   Remember that we use **for** with a **period of time** and **since** with a **point in time**.

Grammar in action

5 We use **for** and **since** with the **negative present perfect** to talk about the period of time between when something happened and now. We often use this pattern to talk about the last time something regular happened:
   He hasn't phoned me for four days. / He hasn't phoned me since Tuesday. (= The last time he phoned me was four days ago/Tuesday.)

6 We use the **present perfect**, not the past simple, with **never** and **ever** to talk and ask about the past in general:
   'Have you ever cooked this dish before?' (NOT *Did you ever cook?*)
   'No, I've never cooked it before. It's my first time.' (NOT *I never cooked ...*)

> **TIP**
> The verb **go** has two present perfect forms. We use **have/has been** to talk about going to a place but <u>not being in that place now</u>:
>   I've been to Poland six times.
>
> We use **have/has gone** to talk about going to a place and <u>not being here now</u>:
>   Matt's gone to Poland. He'll be back next week.

D Football reports

Complete the rewritten sentences about various football clubs, using *for*, *since*, or *ago*.

0 The club last won a trophy 20 years ago.
   The club hasn't won a trophy *for 20 years* .

1 The club has been successful for 5 years.
   The club started to be successful _____.

2 The team last won a home game in April.
   The team hasn't won a home game _____.

3 He hasn't scored a goal for 3 months.
   He last scored a goal _____.

4 The club started to play at this stadium in 1996.
   The club has played at this stadium _____.

5 He became the team captain 6 months ago.
   He has been the team captain _____.

6 He last played for the team 2 months ago.
   He hasn't played for the team _____.

7 He got injured 3 weeks ago.
   He has been injured _____.

E My friend Steve

Write the sentences about a friend, using the present perfect and *for* or *since*.

0 Steve/be/a friend of mine/many years.
   Steve has been a friend of mine for many years.

1 I/know/him/2002.

2 Steve/work/for the same company/five years.

3 I/not see/Steve/a couple of months.

4 Steve/not phone/me/March.

5 We/not play/tennis together/a long time.

6 Steve/be/very busy/several months.

7 Steve/not have/ a holiday/last year.

F Where are they?

Complete this conversation at a party, using the past simple or the present perfect and *ever*, *never*, *went*, *go*, *been*, or *gone*. Use short forms if possible.

BRIAN   I haven't seen Nick or Karen. Where are they?
VALERIE Nick? *He's gone to Canada.* ⁰
BRIAN   Really? When _____ ¹?
VALERIE _____ ² about three weeks ago. He's got relatives there.
BRIAN   It's a really good country. _____ ³?
VALERIE No, _____ ⁴, but I'd like to go one day. What about you?
BRIAN   Yes, _____ ⁵ several times. Anyway, where's Karen?
VALERIE _____ ⁶. She's not feeling very well. _____ ⁷.
BRIAN   Oh dear. But it's a good party, isn't it?
VALERIE Yes, _____ ⁸ before but I think it's a very good place.
BRIAN   Yes, it is. Where's Trudy? It's her party and I'd like to speak to her. I saw her a few minutes ago but I can't see her now. Where _____ ⁹?
VALERIE I don't know. Maybe _____ ¹⁰.
BRIAN   Well, I'll try to find her later. See you.

0 He / to Canada
1 he / there?
2 He
3 you / there?
4 I / there
5 I / there
6 She / home
7 She / to bed
8 I / here
9 she
10 she / outside

OVER TO YOU   Now go to page 122.

06 The future
Going to

1 Some examples of **going to** (**be going to** + verb):
   We**'re going to have** a party next week.
   It **isn't going to rain** today.
   Are you **going to watch** the match on TV tonight?

2 Forms of **going to**:

POSITIVE
I **am**/**'m going to** eat
you/we/they **are**/**'re going to** eat
he/she/it **is**/**'s going to** eat
NEGATIVE
I **am not** / **'m not going to** eat
you/we/they **are not** / **'re not** / **aren't going to** eat
he/she/it **is not** / **isn't** / **'s not going to** eat
QUESTIONS
am I **going to** eat
are you/we/they **going to** eat
is he/she/it **going to** eat

Grammar in action

1 We use **going to** for actions that we have decided to do in the future. First we think and decide, then we say what we have decided about the future, using **going to**:
   I'm going to catch the 8.30 train.

2 Sometimes we say when the action will happen and sometimes we understand when the action will happen and do not say it:
   I'm going to wear my new dress tonight.
   I'm going to a party tonight. ~ What are you going to wear? (= tonight) ~ *I'm going to wear my new dress.* (= tonight)

3 We use **going to** for actions in the future that we have planned and organized. We can also use the present continuous for these actions (see p. 4).
   Here, someone is talking about travel plans:
   I'm going to fly/I'm flying to Milan on Friday.

4 We use **going to** for things that we believe or predict about the future, often because the present situation or a past event gives us a good reason for our prediction:
   You're going to fall.

A In future, I'm going to …

Suzanne has decided to change her life. Complete her decisions for the future, using *going to* and the correct verbs from the list. Use short forms.

prepare   enjoy   do   learn   not watch   not spend   get
not sit   join   not worry   ~~study~~   save   go   be   read
lose   not shout   ~~pass~~   not eat   run

0 *I'm going to study* hard at college and *I'm going to pass* my exams.
1 _____ more exercise and _____ fit.
2 _____ a running club and _____ a marathon.
3 _____ on the sofa so much and _____ for walks.
4 _____ so much money and _____ more money.
5 _____ so much TV and _____ more books.
6 _____ some weight and _____ so much chocolate.
7 _____ nicer to my brother and _____ at him.
8 _____ how to cook and _____ healthy meals.
9 _____ about small problems and _____ life more.

B Plans for tonight's event

Luke is the organizer of a college event. He is talking to the students who are helping him. Complete the questions and answers, using *going to* and the words in brackets.

LUKE OK, _the show is going to start_.⁰ at 8 p.m. (the show/start)
AMY When ....¹ here? (you/get)
LUKE ....² here at 6 p.m. (I/get)
................................³ at the same time. (The rest of you/come)
KATE When ....⁴ ? (the refreshments/arrive)
LUKE ....⁵ at 6.30 p.m. (They/arrive)
................................⁶ them in the kitchen immediately. (We/put)
Then ....⁷ the chairs for the audience. (we/arrange)
PAUL When ....⁸ arriving? (people/start)
LUKE ....⁹ arriving for the event at 7.30 p.m. (People/start)
................................¹⁰ the parking outside. (Robin and Thelma/organize)
................................¹¹ the tickets at the door. (Pamela/collect)
................................¹² her. (Alan/help)
SALLY What ....¹³ ? (the timetable for the show/be)
LUKE ....¹⁴ at 9 p.m. (The first part of the show/finish)
................................¹⁵ the food and drinks in the interval. (Elaine and Frank/serve)
................................¹⁶ for 20 minutes. (The interval/last)
................................¹⁷ at 9.20 p.m. (The second part of the show/begin)
................................¹⁸ at 11 p.m. (The show/finish)
PAUL ....¹⁹ afterwards? (we/stay)
LUKE Yes, ...²⁰ the hall after the show. (we/tidy)

WORD FOCUS

Find words in the conversation with these meanings. The words are all connected with public events:

A people watching/listening

B food and drink

C pause between parts

D performance

C Predictions at home

Bob and Louise are doing various things at home. Complete their predictions, using *going to* and the correct verbs from the box.

> be drop not work taste ~~finish~~ ruin fall not look

0 We _'re going to finish_ this wall soon.
1 This meal .... great.
2 Be careful. That shelf .... on you.
3 This letter .... a bill.
4 You .... those books.
5 That picture .... good there.
6 The computer .... There's something wrong with it.
7 You .... that shirt.

06 The future
Will and shall

3 Some examples of **will** (**will** + verb):
  I**'ll speak** to you later.
  It **won't cost** a lot.
  Will you **help** me?

4 The forms of **will** are the same for all persons:

POSITIVE
I/you/he/she/it/we/they **will**/**'ll help**
NEGATIVE
I/you/he/she/it/we/they **will not** / **won't help**
QUESTIONS
will I/you/he/she/it/we/they **help**

5 We use **shall** in questions with **I** and **we**:
  Shall I go with you?
  Shall we have something to eat?

Grammar in action

5 We use **will** for actions in the future that we decide to do at the moment of speaking. We think first and speak using **will** at the same time that we decide. In this example, someone is looking at a menu in a restaurant:
  I'm not sure what to order … OK, I'll have the Chef's Special dish.

6 We use **will** for offering to do something. Here, the speaker offers help after a meal:
  Sit down! I'll do the washing-up.

7 We use **will** for promises:
  Don't worry. I won't tell anyone your secret.

8 We use **will** to give opinions about the future. We often use phrases like *I'm sure*, *I think*, and *I don't think* before **will** to give opinions about the future:
  I'm sure you'll feel better soon.

9 We use **will** for facts about the future:
  My daughter will be 5 years old next year.

10 We use **shall** in questions for offering to do something for another person. Here, the speaker offers help to someone who has a problem:
  Shall I carry that heavy case for you?

11 We use **shall** in questions for suggesting possible actions and asking if an idea is good:
  Shall we stop now?

D Tomorrow's an important day

Complete this conversation, using *will* or *shall* and the words in the box. You will need to use negative verbs in some gaps. Use short forms if possible.

| I/cook   I/bring   I/be   you/do   I/have   I/keep   I/tell   you/be   I/leave |
| you/get   ~~I/watch~~   you/wake   I/go   I/forget |

JANE   I don't think ......**I'll watch**...... ⁰ the rest of this programme. I think .... ¹ to bed now, I'm very tired.

SUE   OK. I think .... ² watching. .... ³ you what happens at the end tomorrow.

JANE   .... ⁴ me up in the morning? Please remember. It's important.

SUE   Don't worry, ... ⁵. And .... ⁶ you a cup of tea in bed. .... ⁷ you some breakfast, too?

JANE   No, ... ⁸ time to eat breakfast.

SUE   Of course .... ⁹ able to have breakfast!

JANE   OK, maybe some toast. And then .... ¹⁰ for the interview. .... ¹¹ very nervous about it.

SUE   Don't be nervous. I'm sure .... ¹² well and I think .... ¹³ the job.

JANE   Oh, I hope so.

E The visit next week

Michael is going to stay at Andrew's house next weekend. Complete their phone conversation about his visit, using *will* or *shall* and the words in brackets. You will need to use negative verbs in some gaps. Use short forms if possible.

MICHAEL I'll see ⁰ you next Friday. (I/see)
ANDREW Shall I meet ¹ you at the bus station? (I/meet)
MICHAEL No, it's OK. I'll walk ² from there to your house. (I/walk)
ANDREW Will you find ³ my house? (you/find)
MICHAEL Yes, it'll be ⁴ easy. (it/be) I won't get ⁵ lost. (I/get)
ANDREW Shall I send ⁶ you a map? (I/send)
MICHAEL No, I won't need ⁷ one. (I/need) Shall I bring ⁸ a sleeping bag with me? (I/bring)
ANDREW No, that won't be ⁹ necessary. (that/be) I'll put ¹⁰ you in the spare room. (I/put) You'll be ¹¹ very comfortable there. (You/be)
MICHAEL That's great. Shall I call ¹² you when I get to the bus station? (I/call)
ANDREW Yes, and then I'll wait ¹³ for you to arrive. (I/wait)
MICHAEL Fine. I'm sure we'll have ¹⁴ a great weekend. (we/have)
ANDREW Me too.

F A new life

Sam's friend Eddie is going to live in another country. Complete Sam's email to Eddie, using *will* or *shall* and the correct verbs from the box. You will need to form negatives and questions in some gaps and you will need to use one of the verbs three times. Use short forms if possible.

> tell   come   meet   talk   be   learn   ~~have~~   write   send
> fix   wonder   contact   forget   miss   keep

I'm sure you 'll have ⁰ a great time in your new country. You 'll meet ¹ lots of new people and you 'll learn ² all about a different culture. And you 'll be ³ so busy when you get there that you won't miss ⁴ your friends or this country too much.
Of course things won't be ⁵ the same here without you. I'm sure we'll wonder ⁶ about you and we'll talk ⁷ about what you're doing. We certainly 'll miss ⁸ you. Shall I write ⁹ to you first or will you write ¹⁰ me first? I'll keep ¹¹ you up to date with all the news from here. Will you tell ¹² me all about what happens when you get there? And will you send ¹³ me some photographs of your new home?
I'm sure it won't be ¹⁴ long before we see each other again. Perhaps I'll come ¹⁵ and visit you some time next year. We'll fix ¹⁶ a date for that soon.

OVER TO YOU   Now go to page 122.

07 Question words
When, where, why, how, which, whose, who, what

1 Some examples of questions with these words:
   Where are you going?
   Which film are you going to see?
   What did you do last weekend?

2 To form questions with **when**, **where**, **why** and **how**, we use these patterns:

   > question word + auxiliary (do, have, etc.) + subject + verb

   When does the film *start*?

   > question word + be + subject

   When was the exam?

3 To form questions with **which** and **whose**, we use this pattern:

   > which/whose + noun + auxiliary/be

   Which course is he taking?
   Whose coat is this?

   We can also use a noun with **what**, with the same meaning as **which**:
   What/Which sports do you play?

4 To form questions with **who**, **what**, **which** and **whose**, we can use both of the patterns in **2**:
   Who do you *live* with?
   What is your address?
   Which restaurant do you *prefer*?
   Whose books are these?

   (For more information on questions with **who**, **what**, **which** and **whose**, see unit 8 on p. 30.)

Grammar in action

1 We use **when** to ask about time and **where** to ask about places:
   When did you arrive here?
   Where are my keys?

2 We use **why** to ask for a reason:
   Why are you wearing a coat?

3 We use **how** to ask about a process or a series of actions or events that produce a certain result. In this example, someone is asking what you do to make a certain meal:
   How do you cook this dish?

4 We use **which** or **what** with a **plural noun** to ask someone to specify when there are a number of possibilities:
   Which countries in Europe have you been to? ~ Italy, Spain, Germany, …

   We usually use **which** with a **singular noun** when we are asking someone to specify one thing from more than one possibility:
   Which country in Europe have you been to the most? ~ Italy.

5 We use **whose** to ask who owns something:
   Whose hat is this?

6 We use **what** to ask about things or actions and **who** to ask about people:
   What do you want to eat?
   Who is that man over there?

A The concert ticket

Complete the questions in this conversation by putting in the correct question words.

0 *What'* s in this envelope? ~ A ticket.
1 _____ ticket is it? ~ It's my ticket.
2 _____ did you get a ticket for the concert? ~ I queued at the box office.
3 _____ is the concert? ~ Next Friday.
4 _____ are your seats? ~ At the back of the hall.
5 _____ did you choose those seats? ~ Because it's going to be very loud.
6 _____ are you going to the concert with? ~ Two of my friends.
7 _____ friends are you going with? ~ Pete and Dave.

26 | Questions

B The new dress

Write the questions in this conversation, using the words in brackets and the correct question words and verb tenses.

0 *What are you wearing?* (you/wear) ~ I'm wearing a new dress.
1 .... (you/buy a new dress) ~ I bought a new dress because I'm going to a party tomorrow.
2 .... (you/buy/it) ~ I bought it in a new shop in town.
3 .... (the shop/called) ~ It's called 'Beautiful People'.
4 .... (street/the shop/be/in) ~ It's in Taylor Street.
5 .... (party/it/be) ~ It's Stella's party.
6 .... (be/Stella) ~ She's a new friend of mine.

C London Quiz

Write or complete the questions for a quiz about London, using the words in brackets and the verb tenses in italics.

0 *What do people call* the financial district of London? (people/call) *present simple*
1 ....? (London Marathon/end) *present simple*
2 .... in Trafalgar Square? (statue/be) *present simple*
3 .... in Portobello Road? (people/buy) *present simple*
4 ....? (Heathrow Airport/open) *past simple*
5 ....? (street/the Prime Minister/live in) *present simple*
6 .... to the Tate Modern? (people/go) *present simple*

ANSWERS 0. The City 1. On Westminster Bridge 2. Lord Nelson's 3. Antiques 4. In 1946 5. Downing Street 6. Because it's a famous art gallery

D Police investigation

Write the questions asked by a police officer while investigating various crim[es]. short answers to each question are underlined.

0 *Where were you at 3 o'clock yesterday afternoon?*
   I was <u>at home</u> at 3 o'clock yesterday afternoon.
1 ....
   I ran away <u>because I was scared</u>.
2 ....
   I last saw the missing person <u>three weeks ago</u>.
3 ....
   The burglars got into my house <u>by breaking a window</u>.
4 ....
   They broke <u>the kitchen window</u>.
5 ....
   The burglars took <u>my laptop and some jewellery</u>.

07 Question words
How long, how many, etc.

5 Some examples of questions with **how**:
How often do you check your emails?
How many people did you invite?

6 We use **how long**, **how far** and **how often** in the pattern:

> How long/far/often + auxiliary + subject + verb?

How long does the film last?

7 We also use **how far** in these patterns:

> How far + be + it + from A to B?

How far is it from your home to your office?

> How far + be + A from B?

How far is your home from your office?

8 We use **how much** in these patterns:

> How much + auxiliary + subject + verb?

How much did you pay?

> How much + be + subject?

How much was the ticket?

> How much + uncountable noun + auxiliary + subject + verb?

How much money have you spent?
(Uncountable nouns have no plural form. See p. 72.)

9 We use **how many** in these patterns:

> How many + plural noun + auxiliary + subject + verb?

How many tickets did you buy?

> How many + plural noun + verb?

How many people live in your house?

10 We can form questions with the pattern **how + adjective + be + subject**:
How old is he?
How expensive was it?

Grammar in action

7 We use **how long** to ask about a period of time:
How long is this film?

8 We use **how far** to ask about a distance:
How far is it from London to Paris?

9 We use **how often** to ask about the number of times something happens:
How often do the trains go to London?

10 We use **how much** to ask about the cost or amount of something:
How much is that guitar?
How much milk would you like?

11 We use **how many** to ask about a number of things or people:
How many potatoes would you like?

12 We use **how** with **an adjective** to ask for personal details:
How old are you?
How tall are you?

We also use **how** with **an adjective** to ask questions which can be answered 'very' or 'not very', etc.:
How angry are you?

E Travel survey

Complete this survey about public transport by putting in the question words.

0	*How long*	have you lived in this area?	*For about 2 years.*
1	....	do you spend on travel per week?	*About £30.*
2	....	does it take you to travel to work?	*About 20 minutes.*
3	....	is it from your home to the nearest bus stop?	*About 500 metres.*
4	....	journeys do you make by bus?	*About 3 a week.*
5	....	do you buy a travel card?	*Every month.*
6	....	do you think the transport service is?	*I think it's very good.*

F Museum questions

Write the questions in this conversation between a tourist and a tour guide about a museum. Begin each question with *How* and use the words in brackets.

0 How far is it from the bus stop to the museum? (it/be/the bus stop/the museum)
   The bus station is quite close to the museum.
1 .... (be/the building)
   It's over 500 years old.
2 .... (it/be/a museum)
   It's been a museum for about 30 years.
3 .... (it/be/popular)
   It's extremely popular.
4 .... (tourists/visit/it/every year)
   About a million tourists visit it every year.
5 .... (there/be/special exhibitions)
   There are special exhibitions three times a year.
6 .... (season ticket for the museum/cost)
   A season ticket for the museum costs £60.

G Brian is leaving

Complete this conversation between work colleagues by completing or writing the questions. The short answers to each question are underlined.

CLIVE   Who were you talking to ⁰ just now?
KATE   I was talking to <u>Brian</u>. He's an assistant here.
CLIVE   .... ¹ ?
KATE   He's <u>Fiona's</u> assistant.
CLIVE   .... ² you?
KATE   He told me <u>that he was leaving the company</u>.
CLIVE   Really? .... ³ ?
KATE   He's leaving <u>because he doesn't like working here any more</u>.
CLIVE   .... ⁴ ?
KATE   He's going to leave <u>next month</u>.
CLIVE   .... ⁵ ?
KATE   He's going to work <u>in Birmingham</u>.
CLIVE   .... ⁶ ?
KATE   He's going to work for <u>a company called Gregory Systems</u>.
CLIVE   .... ⁷ ?
KATE   That company is <u>not very big</u>.
CLIVE   .... ⁸ that job?
KATE   He got that job <u>by answering an advert</u>.
CLIVE   .... ⁹ ?
KATE   He's going to earn <u>over £100,000 a year</u>.

WORD FOCUS

Before you do exercise G, answer this question: If two people are *colleagues*, they:
A live in the same place.
B work in the same place.
C are close friends.
D travel together.

OVER TO YOU Now go to page 122.

08 Subject and object questions
Questions with *who*

1 Some examples of **subject questions** with **who**:
   Who knows the answer to this question?
   Who's that girl with George?

2 In a **subject question** with **who**, the pattern is:

   who + singular verb

   Who wants something to eat?
   Who's/Who is going to help me?

   In these questions, **Who?** is the subject. The order of words in the question is the same as in a statement:
   Who won the game? = *Somebody won the game. Who?*

3 The answer to a **subject question** with **who** is the subject of the verb:
   Who went to the concert with you? ~ *Irene.* (Irene went to the concert with me. 'Irene' is the subject of 'went'.)

4 Some examples of **object questions** with **who**:
   Who did you meet last night?
   Who have you told about this?

5 In an **object question**, the pattern is:

   who + auxiliary (are, do, did, etc.) + subject + verb

   Who do you live with?
   Who did you phone?

   In these questions, **Who?** is the object of the verb. The order of words in the question is the same as in any other question:
   Who did you phone? = *You phoned somebody. Who?*

6 The answer to an **object question** with **who** is the object of the verb:
   Who do you live with? ~ **My parents**. (= I live with my parents. 'I' is the subject of 'live' and 'my parents' is the object.)

Grammar in action

1 We use a **subject question** with **who** when we want to know which person does the action mentioned in the verb:
   Who broke this window?

> **TIP**
> We use the third person (*he/she/it*) form of the verb in a subject question. The answer may be more than one person but the verb after **who** is singular. Here, a teacher is speaking to a class:
> *Who knows the answer to this question?*

2 We use an **object question** with **who** when we are asking which person is the object of the verb. A different person is the subject of the verb and that person is not the answer to the question:
   Who did Lucy marry?

A Classroom questions

Write the subject questions asked by a teacher in a classroom, using the same verb tenses as the student's answers.

0 *Who's/Who has done the homework?* ~ We've all done the homework.
1 .... ~ I know the answer.
2 .... ~ I'm going to hand out the books.
3 .... ~ Nobody got every answer right.
4 .... ~ We're all listening carefully.
5 .... ~ I left a pen here yesterday.
6 .... ~ I've finished the exercise.

B Class gossip

One student is asking another student about the people in their class.
Write the object questions using the same verb tenses as the answers.

0 Who did you go to the café with? ~ I went to the café with Anna.
1 .... ~ Elaine is going out with Phil.
2 .... ~ Mark sat next to Irene on the bus.
3 .... ~ I like Jack the most in the class.
4 .... ~ I'm going to be Ruth's partner next week.
5 .... ~ Eric has invited most of the class to his party.
6 .... ~ Tom was phoning his brother in the break.

C Soap opera stories

Read the summary of what has been happening in a television series and then write the correct subject and object questions about it.

TV CHOICE

CITY PEOPLE *An Update*

In last week's episodes of this popular series, a lot happened. Harry and Chris had a big argument and Harry killed Chris. Olivia saw what happened and she ran away. Now Harry is trying to find her because he wants to kill her too.

Sharon has left her husband and she is now living with her parents again. She's given up her job and she's going to start a new life in Australia. But Geoff is in love with her and he wants her to live with him.

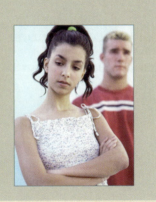

WORD FOCUS

On television, an *episode* is:

A something that happens during a programme.
B one programme in a series that shows a continuing story.
C one of the main characters in a series.

0	Who / a big argument?	Who had a big argument?	Harry and Chris
0	Who / Harry?	Who did Harry kill?	Chris
1	Who / Chris?	....	Harry
2	Who / what happened?	....	Olivia
3	Who / Harry / to find?	....	Olivia
4	Who / to find Olivia?	....	Harry
5	Who / to kill?	....	Olivia
6	Who / her husband?	....	Sharon
7	Who / now?	....	Her parents
8	Who / a new life in Australia?	....	Sharon
9	Who / Sharon?	....	Geoff
10	Who / Geoff?	....	Sharon

08 Subject and object questions
Questions with *what*, *which*, and *whose*

7 A **subject question** has the same form as a statement:
Who invited you to the party? ~ Jake invited me to the party.

An **object question** has an auxiliary in the same way as any other question:
Who did you invite to the party? ~ I invited 10 people from college and about 20 other people.

8 We can also ask both **subject** and **object questions** with *what*, *which*, and *whose*:
What's on TV tonight? (= Something is on TV tonight. What?)
What did you watch on TV last night? (= You watched something on TV last night. What?)
Which newspapers are the most popular? (subject)
Which newspapers do you read? (object)
Whose house is this? (subject)
Whose house did you stay in? (object)

Grammar in action

3 We use a **subject question** to ask about the subject of the verb in the question. We use an **object question** to ask about the object of the verb in the question:
Who invented the worldwide web?
The answer is the subject of 'invented': *An Englishman called Tim Berners-Lee (invented the worldwide web).*

What did an Englishman called Tim Berners-Lee invent?
The answer is the object of 'invented':
(He invented) the worldwide web.

4 We often use **subject questions** with **what** + **be** to ask for information and facts:
What's the capital of Venezuela?

5 We often use **subject questions** with **what** + **happen** to ask about situations and events:
What's happening in this programme? I can't follow it.

D Workplace questions

Write the questions about the place where someone works, beginning with *Who* or *What*.

0 *Who started the company?* ~ A man called Evans started the company.
0 *What does the company make?* ~ The company makes computer parts.
1 .... ~ My job title is 'Sales Executive'.
2 .... ~ Karen sits next to me in the office.
3 .... ~ I have lunch with Anna most days.
4 .... ~ Ian Butler runs the department.
5 .... ~ Something strange happened at work today.
6 .... ~ I'm working on a new product at the moment.
7 .... ~ I worked with Jane on that project.
8 .... ~ The project involved a lot of meetings.
9 .... ~ Ron and Zena applied to be the new boss.
10 .... ~ They appointed Ron as the new boss.

E Quiz questions

Write the questions for a general knowledge quiz.

0   Something happened on 20 July 1969. What?
    What happened on 20 July 1969?

1   Edward Jenner discovered something. What?
    ....

2   The author JK Rowling created a very famous character. Which?
    ....

3   John Wilkes Booth shot someone in Washington in 1865. Who?
    ....

4   Something caused the Great Fire of London in 1666. What?
    ....

5   Someone won the award for Best Actor at last year's Oscars. Who?
    ....

6   One king of England had six wives. Which?
    ....

7   Someone has had more Number 1 hits in Britain than any other singer. Who?
    ....

F The painting competition

Complete the questions about a painting competition at a school. The short answers to each question are underlined.

0   What *took place last week?*
    A painting competition (took place last week).
1   Who ....
    Daniel (won the painting competition).
2   Whose ....
    Daniel's (painting won the painting competition).
3   What ....
    (Daniel painted) a forest.
4   Which ....
    (The teacher chose) Daniel's painting.
5   Who ....
    (The teacher gave the first prize to) Daniel.
6   Which ....
    Sarah's painting (came second in the competition).
7   What ....
    (The title of my painting was) 'Summer Fields'.
8   Whose ....
    (I liked) mine (the most, of course!).

OVER TO YOU Now go to page 123.

09 Can, could, and would
Ability

1 Some examples of **can** and **could**:
She **can play** the guitar and the piano.
She **couldn't go** to work yesterday.

2 Forms of **can**:

POSITIVE
can + verb
I **can swim** quite well.
NEGATIVE
cannot/can't + verb
We **can't afford** a new car.
QUESTIONS
can + subject + verb
Can you **speak** any other languages?

3 We use **can** and **can't** for the present and the future:
I **can't talk** to you now.
I **can do** it tomorrow.

4 We use **could** and **couldn't** for the past:
He **could drive** at the age of 17.
It was so hot that I **couldn't breathe**.

He can't play football very well.

He can't play football this month.

2 We use **can/can't** or **will/won't be able to** to say that something will/won't be possible in the future. Here someone is discussing a future arrangement:
I **can see** you on Friday but I **can't see** you on Saturday.
I'll **be able to see** you on Friday but I **won't be able to see** you on Saturday.

3 We use **could** and **couldn't** to talk about past abilities in general:
She **could play** the piano when she was young but she **couldn't play** the guitar.

We usually use **was/were able to** or **managed to** (NOT could) to talk about being able to do something successfully at a particular time in the past. This might be to describe something that was difficult to do:
After several days, the climbers **were able to get / managed to get** to the top of the mountain.

Grammar in action

1 We use **can** and **can't** to talk or ask about the ability to do something, in general or at a particular moment in time:

4 We use **couldn't** to say that something was impossible for someone in the past:
He was listening to music on headphones and he **couldn't hear** me.

A The lost key

Complete this phone conversation using can, can't **or** couldn't **and the words in brackets.**

JUDY Hi, Frank, _can you hear_ ⁰ (you/hear) me?
FRANK Well, ...¹ (I/hear) you very well, there's something wrong with your phone. Where are you?
JUDY I'm outside the house. ....² (I/get) in because ....³ (I/find) the key.
FRANK ....⁴ (you/speak up)? ....⁵ (I/hear) what you said.
JUDY ....⁶ (I/open) the door!!!
FRANK ....⁷ (you/remember) when you last had the key?
JUDY ....⁸ (I/remember) putting it in my pocket this morning. But when I got home a few minutes ago, ...⁹ (I/find) it.
FRANK How did you lose it?
JUDY I don't know. ....¹⁰ (I/explain) it.
FRANK OK. ....¹¹ (you/wait) there? ....¹² (I/drive) over there now and ....¹³ (I/open) the door for you.

B Language ability

Complete this description of a personal experience using *can*, *can't*, *could* or *couldn't* and the verbs in brackets.

I <u>can remember</u> ⁰ (remember) my first year of living in this country very clearly. When I first arrived here, I _____ ¹ (speak) the language very well. I _____ ² (understand) a few words and phrases and I _____ ³ (go) shopping but I _____ ⁴ (have) real conversations with people. Then I took a course and now I _____ ⁵ (speak) the language quite well. I _____ ⁶ (make) friends and I _____ ⁷ (do) most things I want to do. Sometimes I _____ ⁸ (remember) certain words but usually I _____ ⁹ (think of) the right word and people _____ ¹⁰ (understand) what I'm saying.

C Possibilities for the game tomorrow

Complete this conversation using *can/can't* or *will/won't be able to* and the words in brackets. Put two answers into a gap if this is possible.

JAMES   <u>Can you go / Will you be able to go</u> ⁰ (you/go) to the game tomorrow?
PAUL   Yes, _____ ¹ (I/go) and I'm looking forward to it.
JAMES   _____ ² (we/discuss) our plans for going to the game now?
PAUL   Yes, of course. I'm sure _____ ³ (we/arrange) everything now.
JAMES   OK. _____ ⁴ (we/go) in your car tomorrow night? _____ ⁵ (We/use) my car because it isn't working.
PAUL   Oh. _____ ⁶ (you/borrow) your father's car?
JAMES   No, _____ ⁷ (he/lend) it to me because he needs it then.
PAUL   _____ ⁸ (we/get) there on public transport?
JAMES   Well, _____ ⁹ (we/take) a train that goes all the way but _____ ¹⁰ (we/get) one that stops near the stadium. _____ ¹¹ (I/look up) the train details on the internet now.
PAUL   Oh, _____ ¹² (you/do) that now? That's great.
JAMES   Yeah, and _____ ¹³ (I/phone) you back later and _____ ¹⁴ (I/tell) you the best plan then.

D Problems on the trip

Complete this description of a trip using *were able to*, *managed to* or *couldn't* and the verbs in brackets.

We had some bad problems on our trip. First of all, we <u>couldn't get</u> ⁰ (get) a taxi to the airport because they were all busy. We rang lots of numbers and eventually we _____ ¹ (get) one and we _____ ² (arrive) at the airport just in time. When we arrived at the other end, we _____ ³ (find) a trolley for all our bags but we _____ ⁴ (carry) them to the bus. We _____ ⁵ (find) our hotel without any problems so that was good. The next day, we _____ ⁶ (book) a tour of the city and we _____ ⁷ (see) all the famous sights. Unfortunately, we _____ ⁸ (take) any photos because the camera wasn't working. The next day, I _____ ⁹ (get) any money because I _____ ¹⁰ (use) my card in any of the cash machines. After several hours, we _____ ¹¹ (find) a bank which accepted my card, which was lucky. At the end of the trip, we _____ ¹² (come) home without any problems, I'm pleased to say!

09 Can, could, and would
Requests and permission

5 We use **can**, **could**, **may**, and **would** in questions:
Can I help you?
Could I borrow your pen, please?
May I ask a question?
Could you phone back later?
Would you wait for a moment, please?

6 We use **can/can't** and **be allowed to** with the same meaning:
You can park here. / You're allowed to park here.
I can't use my father's computer. / I'm not allowed to use my father's computer.

Grammar in action

5 We use **Can I…?** (NOT ~~Could I~~…? or ~~May I~~…?) to offer to do something for someone:
Can I give you a lift?

6 We use **Can I/we?**, **Could I/we?** and **May I/?** to ask for something or for permission to do something.
Can I have a go now?

Can I? is not as polite as **Could I?** **May I?** is very polite and is used in formal situations. Here, someone is talking to an interviewer in a job interview:
Could/May I ask a question?

7 We use **Can you?**, **Could you?** and **Would you?** to ask someone to do something. **Can you?** is not as polite as **Could you?** and **Would you?** Here, someone is talking to a friend:
Can you be quiet?
Here, someone is talking to a person they don't know:
Could/Would you be quiet, please?

8 We use **can** and **can't** to give or refuse permission to someone:
Yes, you can use my phone.
You can't sit there, it's my friend's seat.

9 We use **can/can't** and **be allowed to** to talk about what is permitted or not permitted by rules and laws:
You can go to this club if you're over 18. /
You're not allowed to go to this club if you're under 18.

E In a restaurant

Complete the questions asked in a restaurant, using the words in brackets. There is more than one way of completing each question.

0	WAITER	*Can/Could/May I take* your coat, sir? (I/take)
0	CUSTOMER	*Could/Can we sit* at a table by the window? (we/sit)
1	CUSTOMER	.... me the menu please? (you/show)
2	CUSTOMER	.... me what this dish is, please? (you/tell)
3	WAITER	.... the chef's special, madam? (I/recommend)
4	CUSTOMER	.... now, please? (I/order)
5	WAITER	.... your order now? (I/take)
6	CUSTOMER	.... to another table, please? (we/move)
7	CUSTOMER	.... my order please? (I/change)
8	CUSTOMER	.... me another knife, please? (you/bring)
9	CUSTOMER	.... some more bread, please? (we/have)
10	CUSTOMER	.... me the bill, please? (you/get)

F Home rules

Complete this interview with a child in a children's magazine about what he is permitted to do at home. Change 'can/can't' to 'be allowed to' and 'be allowed to' to 'can/can't'.

(Can you eat) _Are you allowed to eat_ ⁰ meals in front of the TV?
(We aren't allowed to do) _We can't do_ ⁰ that usually but (we're allowed to do) ....¹ it if there's a special programme on TV.
(Are you allowed to watch) ....² films on your own?
(I can't watch) ....³ violent films. One of my friends, Ben, (is allowed to watch) ....⁴ anything he wants, but

(I can't do) ....⁵ that. (I can watch) ....⁶ films for my age but (I'm not allowed to watch) ....⁷ (films for teenagers or adults.
(Can you play) ....⁸ computer games on school days?
(I'm allowed to play) ....⁹ computer games when I get home but (I'm not allowed to play) ....¹⁰ them for more than half an hour on school days.

G Booking a hotel room

Complete this phone conversation using the phrases in the box. You need to form questions and positive and negative verbs.

could/wait   may/have   can/park   could/tell   could/give   could/book
can/go   can/smoke   would/spell   can/leave   can/use   would/send
~~can/help~~   could/stay   could/make

RECEPTIONIST   _Can I help_ ⁰ you?
MR LEACH   Yes, ...¹ a room for next week?
RECEPTIONIST   Sure. ....² a moment, please? … OK, ...³ your surname?
MR LEACH   Yes, it's Leach.
RECEPTIONIST   ....⁴ that for me?
MR LEACH   Yes it's L-E-A-C-H.
RECEPTIONIST   OK, Mr Leach. ....⁵ me when you want to stay here?
MR LEACH   Yes, ...⁶ a reservation for next weekend?
RECEPTIONIST   A single or a double room?
MR LEACH   ....⁷ in a luxury single, please?
RECEPTIONIST   Sure. I must just tell you that ....⁸ in the room.
MR LEACH   That's OK. Now, I have a question. ....⁹ at the hotel?
RECEPTIONIST   Yes, ...¹⁰ your car in the private car park for guests.
MR LEACH   And ....¹¹ the hotel gym?
RECEPTIONIST   Yes, ...¹² to the gym free of charge at any time.
MR LEACH   OK, I'll book the room.
RECEPTIONIST   Fine. ....¹³ me your credit card details, please?
MR LEACH   Yes, and ....¹⁴ me confirmation of the booking by email?
RECEPTIONIST   Yes, of course.

WORD FOCUS

In exercises B, C and F, there are three phrasal verbs with *up*. Complete each phrasal verb. The meaning of each one is in brackets:

A .... up (talk louder)

B .... up (find information in a book, on a website, etc.)

C .... up (not go to bed until a later time)

OVER TO YOU Now go to page 123.

10 May, might, could, and should
May and might for possibility

1 Some examples of **may** and **might**:
*Take an umbrella because it **might rain** later.
We **may not have** enough money.*

2 Forms of **may/might**:

POSITIVE
may/might + verb
*I **might buy** a new guitar next week.*
NEGATIVE
may not/might not + verb
*The traffic **may not be** bad today.*

We do not usually form questions with **may** or **might**.

We usually use the full forms (**may not / might not**) for negatives.

We can use the negative short form **mightn't** but we do not use a short form of **may not**:
*She **mightn't be** angry with you.*

3 We use **may** and **might** for the present and the future:
*I **might not have** enough money with me now.
I **may not have** enough money next month.*

Grammar in action

1 We use **may** and **might** to say that something is possible, but not certain, in the future:
Runner number 7 may/might win the race. (= It's possible that number 7 will win.)

2 We use **may** and **might** to say that it is possible, but not certain, that something is true in the present:
This shirt may/might fit me.

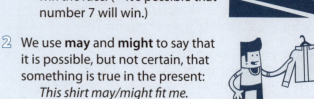

> **May** is often less certain than **might**. We often use **may** to make it clear that something is possible but that we do not think it will happen. We often use **might** to make it clear that it really is possible that something will happen. Here, someone is talking about the possibility of getting tickets for a concert by a very popular band:
> *We **may** get tickets but I don't think we will.
> We **might** get tickets if we phone today.*

A The cinema tonight

Complete this conversation, using *might* or *might not* and the verbs in brackets.

LUKE   I _might go_ ⁰ (go) the cinema tonight. I think I _____¹ (see) that new film, *Wild Thing*.

STANLEY   Oh, I _____² (come) with you. I think it _____³ (be) good.

LUKE   Well, you _____⁴ (not enjoy) it. I think you _____⁵ (find) it boring.

STANLEY   Why?

LUKE   Well, it's a comedy, but you _____⁶ (not think) that it's very funny.

STANLEY   You _____⁷ (not be) right about that. It _____⁸ (make) me laugh a lot. The reviews say that it's very funny.

LUKE   Yes, that's true. But we _____⁹ (have) a problem. We _____¹⁰ (not get in) because the cinema _____¹¹ (be) full.

STANLEY   Oh, yes. Lots of people _____¹² (want) to see it. There _____¹³ (be) a big queue. We _____¹⁴ (have to) get there very early.

LUKE   Just a minute! We _____¹⁵ (be able to) book tickets on the phone.

STANLEY   Ah, good idea! I'll find the number and phone it.

38 | Modal verbs

B What are you going to do next summer?

Complete these sentences written by a group of students about their plans for the summer, using *might* or *might not* and the correct verbs from the box. Use each verb in the box only once.

| visit | do | come | get | read | rain | take |
| spend | want | ~~find~~ | travel | have | ~~work~~ | be |

0 I **might work** in a shop but I **might not find** a job easily.
1 I .... a summer job, but it .... easy to find one.
2 I .... Spain, but I .... enough money to do that.
3 I .... around Europe and my friend .... with me.
4 I .... some books for school, but I .... to do that.
5 It .... at all and I .... every day outdoors.
6 I .... anything, I .... it easy all the time.

C Possible but unlikely

Complete this voicemail message, using *may* or *may not* and the verbs in the box.

| get | be able to | have | leave | ~~be~~ | have to | last | arrive | get back |

Hi Kate, it's Charles here. I'm just calling to tell you that I **may be** ⁰ a bit late tonight. I don't think it's going to happen but I .... ¹ at the restaurant at exactly 8 o'clock. The problem is that I .... ² work late today. There's a meeting here at 4 and it .... ³ until 6, so I .... ⁴ the building until about 6.30. At that time, I .... ⁵ stuck in traffic and I .... ⁶ home until about 7.30. Then I have to get changed and I .... ⁷ a shower, so I .... ⁸ get to the restaurant for 8. Sorry about that. See you this evening, anyway.

D The visitor

Complete this email about a visit, using the phrases in the box. For some gaps you will need to form negatives.

may/organize	may/say	might/get on	might/want
may/do	might/speak	might/forget	may/book	may/go
~~might/have~~	might/offer	might/be	might/be able to

A French girl is coming to stay with me and my family next month and I'm not quite sure what to do with her when she's here. I think we **might have** ⁰ some language problems because she .... ¹ very good English, but I .... ² right about that. She .... ³ to spend her time going to museums and art galleries. I .... ⁴ a guided tour of one of them but I'm not sure about that. Another thing that I .... ⁵ with her is that I .... ⁶ a party for her. Some of my friends .... ⁷ very well with her and they .... ⁸ to go places with her. But I .... ⁹ organize a party so I .... ¹⁰ about that idea. I'm a bit worried that her visit .... ¹¹ well and that she .... ¹² that she's had a good time when she gets home. But I'm hoping that everything will be fine.

10 May, might, could, and should
Could and should: possibility and probability

4 We can use the positive form **could** to say that we believe that something is possible in the present or future. (In this way, **could** has the same meaning as **may** and **might**.)
   It **might rain** tomorrow or it **could be** sunny.

5 We cannot use **couldn't** to talk about a future or present possibility. We only use the negative form **couldn't** to talk about possibility in the past. (See unit 9 on p. 34.)

> **TIP**
> We often use phrases like **I think, I should think, I suppose, I guess, I reckon**, etc., before **may**, **might** and **could** to give our opinion that something is possible:
>   *I think my dad might phone tonight.*
>   *I guess that shop may have what you want.*
>   *I reckon I could finish this work today.*

Grammar in action

3 We use **could** to say that something is possible because the subject is able to do it or has the opportunity to do it:
   I could see you at 12 o'clock on Wednesday.

4 We can use **should** and **shouldn't** for the present and future to say that we think that something good in the future probably will or probably won't happen. (We are more certain when we use **should** than when we use **may** or **might**.) Here, someone is talking about a journey:
   I should arrive at 7 p.m. but I'll be later if there's a lot of traffic.
   I might be late because the traffic might be bad.

E The weather forecast

Complete this weather forecast, using *might* and *could* and the verbs in brackets. If both *might* and *could* are correct, use both of them.

Tomorrow will be a wet day in many parts of Britain. The rain _might/could be_ ⁰ (be) very heavy in the North but it _might not be_ ⁰ (be) so heavy in the South. In the north, thunderstorms _____ ¹ (arrive) early in the morning and the weather conditions _____ ² (make) driving difficult. However, it _____ ³ (be) as cold as it was today and temperatures _____ ⁴ (rise) to 12°C. In the Midlands, fog _____ ⁵ (appear) on high ground early in the morning but this will clear away by lunchtime. There will be rain in the afternoon, but this _____ ⁶ (last) for very long and there _____ ⁷ (be) only light showers. Temperatures will be around 10°C but it _____ ⁸ (feel) as warm as that because of the cold winds. The weather will be better in the South and people there _____ ⁹ (enjoy) some sunny periods. There will be some rain, but it _____ ¹⁰ (rain) at all in some parts of the South.

F Plans for the weekend

Complete these plans for the weekend, using *might* or *could* and the verbs in brackets. Use *could* if it is more appropriate than *might*.

0 I *might buy* (buy) a new coat because I need one.
0 I *could meet* (meet) you tomorrow night because I'm not doing anything then.
1 I .... (invite) some friends for dinner but I haven't decided yet.
2 I .... (get) my hair cut because it's very long at the moment.
3 I .... (do) some training at the gym because I want to get fit.
4 I .... (go) to the match tomorrow because there are plenty of tickets.
5 I .... (do) some cleaning because my flat is very dirty.
6 I .... (give) you a lift to the party because my brother is lending me his car.
7 I .... (stay) at home all weekend because I'm quite tired.
8 I .... (have) a great time because I can do anything I want.

WORD FOCUS

Before you do exercise F, answer this question. If someone offers you a *lift*, that person is offering to:
A take you to a place you want to go to.
B give you some useful information.
C buy something for you.
D tell you how to get to a place.

G A possible arrangement

Complete this conversation between students at the end of a day at college, using *might* or *should* and the phrases below the text. Use *should* if it is more appropriate than *might*.

LILY   What did you think of that test?
GLENN I don't know. *I might not pass*⁰ because I didn't know some of the answers.
LILY   Oh, *you should get* ⁰ a good mark. You always do well in the tests.
GLENN Well, ... ¹ this time. .... ² this one.
LILY   No, ... ³ that badly. It wasn't that difficult. Anyway, where are you going now?
GLENN A friend's house.
LILY   Is it a long way from here?
GLENN No, ... ⁴ long to get there, it's not very far. In fact, ... ⁵ there in about half an hour.
LILY   What are you going to do there?
GLENN I don't know. I guess .... ⁶ some computer games and I reckon .... ⁷ a film.
LILY   So you're not going out tonight?
GLENN Well, ... ⁸ at his house the whole evening. I suppose .... ⁹ to go out.
LILY   Ah. Well, I'm going to that new club, The Workhouse. I think .... ¹⁰ good fun. I've heard about it from other people and they say it's great.

0 I/pass	3 you/do	7 we/watch
0 you/get	4 it/take	8 we/stay
1 it/happen	5 I/get	9 we/decide
2 I/fail	6 we/play	10 it/be

OVER TO YOU   Now go to page 123.

11 Must and have to
Positive forms, their uses, and their contexts

1. Some examples of **must** and **have to**:
   You **must obey** the rules.
   I **have to make** a phone call.

2. The positive form of **must** is:

   > must + verb

   You **must listen** to the instructions.
   NOT ~~You must to listen ...~~

   The form of **must** is the same for all subjects:
   I/You/He/She/It/We/You/They **must work**.

   The form of **must** is the same for the present and the future:
   You **must do** this now/tomorrow.
   NOT ~~You will must do ...~~

3. The positive form of **have to** is:

   > have to + verb

   I **have to go** home now.

   The form of **have to** changes in the same way as *have*:
   I/You/We/They **have to work**. He/She/It **has to work**.

   We can use the present simple form of **have to** for the present and the future:
   You **have to do** this now/tomorrow.

   For the future, we can also use **will have to** + verb:
   You**'ll have to do** this tomorrow.

   The past form is **had to** + verb:
   I **had to get up** early yesterday.

Grammar in action

1. We use **must** in a formal way for rules, particularly written rules. Here is an example of a company rule:
   All staff must wear smart clothes.

2. We use **have to** in an informal way for talking about rules:
   Sanjay has to wear a smart suit for work.

3. We use **must** and **have to** for giving orders and instructions to someone:
   You must wear your helmet! /
   You have to wear your helmet!

4. We use **must** and **have to** for actions that we believe are necessary or very important:
   We must get a new car. /
   We'll have to get a new car.

5. We use **have to** for actions that are necessary because there is no choice in the circumstances:
   I had to stand because there were no empty seats.

6. We use **must** and **have to** (often after *really*) for strongly recommending or offering something:
   You (really) must / have to try this cake, it's delicious!

A **College course rules and instructions**

(i) Complete the rules from a college brochure, using *must* and the correct verb.

> tell   get   ~~enrol~~   arrive   pay   complete

0 Students *must enrol* for the course by 10 July.
1 Students .... the fee before the start of the course.
2 Students .... a student identity card.
3 Students .... on time for classes.
4 Students .... their assignments on time.
5 Students .... the college if they change address.

(ii) Complete the sentences about the rules written by one of the students, using *have to*.

0 We *have to enrol* for the course by 10 July.
1 I .... the fee before the start of the course.
2 I .... a student identity card.
3 We .... on time for classes.
4 We .... our assignments on time.
5 You .... the college if you change address.

B   The Problem Friend

Tom and Rose are talking at the end of a class. Complete their conversation using *must* and *have to* and the words in brackets. If both *must* and *have to* are possible, write both of them. Sometimes only a form of *have to* is possible.

TOM   Would you like to go for a cup of coffee?
ROSE   No, I can't. I _must leave / have to leave_ ⁰ (leave) now. ....¹ (I/meet) a friend of mine. She says that ....² (she/speak) to me because she's got a problem that ....³ (she/discuss) with me. So ....⁴ (I/hurry) now because I don't want to be late.
TOM   Oh, OK. I hope it isn't a serious problem.
ROSE   Probably not. Last week, ...⁵ (she/borrow) some money from me and before that ....⁶ (I/give) her some advice about a boyfriend.
TOM   So she has lots of problems?
ROSE   Yes, and she always contacts me about them. ....⁷ (I/tell) her to talk to someone else sometimes!

C   No choice

Complete this description of a family's situation using the correct forms of *have to* and the correct verbs from the box.

> walk   find   catch   get   ~~travel~~   drive   leave   have

I live with my family in a small village a long way from the nearest town. I _have to travel_ ⁰ a long way to my school. I ....¹ up very early in the morning and I ....² my house at 7.30 a.m. Then I ....³ a bus. Last month, I ....⁴ to school because it snowed and there were no buses. My brother ....⁵ to work because the buses don't go there. So he ....⁶ a car. He doesn't like the journey every day. He thinks that in the future he ....⁷ an apartment in the town and live there.

D   Recommendations

Complete this email from one friend to another using *must* and the correct verbs from the box.

> spend   bring   see   meet   go   take   ~~do~~   eat   look

0   Here are some things that you really _must do_ when you come here:
1   You .... to the Transport Museum – it's fascinating.
2   You .... my friends Rob and Jerry – they're really funny.
3   We .... at Sparks Restaurant – it's new and I've never been there.
4   You .... the fireworks display on 1 May – it's spectacular.
5   We .... some time walking in the countryside – it's beautiful.
6   You .... round the old part of the city – it's very historic.
7   You .... a trip to the next town – it's got some great buildings.
8   You .... warm clothes with you – it can get very cold here!

Modal verbs | 43

11 Must and have to
Negative forms, their uses, and their contexts

4 The negative form of **must** is:

> **must not/mustn't + verb**

You **mustn't forget** to take your passport.
NOT ~~You mustn't to forget …~~
NOT ~~You don't must forget …~~

The form of **must not/mustn't** is the same for all subjects:
I/You/He/She/It/We/You/They **mustn't leave**.

The form of **must not/mustn't** is the same for the present and the future:
It **mustn't happen** today and it **mustn't happen** tomorrow.

5 The present negative form of **have to** is:

> **don't/doesn't have to + verb**

You **don't have to book** tickets in advance.
She **doesn't have to work** hard in her job.

We can use the present negative form of **have to** for the present and the future:
You **don't have to do** this now/tomorrow.

For the future, we can also use **won't have to + verb**:
You **won't have to do** this tomorrow.

The past form is **didn't have to + verb**:
I **didn't have to get up** early yesterday.

6 The question forms of **have to** are:

> Do   I/you/we/they   have to + verb?
> Does he/she/it   have to + verb?

Do I **have to fill** in a form?

We do not usually use **must** in a question form.

Grammar in action

7 We use **must not/mustn't** for rules, to say that something is forbidden or not allowed. Here is an example of a company rule:
Staff must not eat at their desks.

8 We use **must not/mustn't** for orders and instructions, to say that an action is bad or wrong:
You mustn't forget your helmet.

9 We use **must not/mustn't** to say that it is necessary or very important <u>not</u> to do something:
We mustn't use this car again, it's dangerous.

10 We use **don't have to** to say that an action is not necessary:
I didn't have to stand because there was one empty seat.

> **TIP**
> Compare **mustn't** and **don't have to**.
> *You mustn't shout, you're making too much noise.* (= Don't shout, it's bad/not allowed.)
> *You don't have to shout, I can hear you easily.* (= It is not necessary to shout.)

E Sports rules

Complete these rules for various sports, using *have to* or *mustn't* and the correct verbs.

> jump   kick   touch   cross   ~~run~~   win   get   start

0 In a 1500m race, you _have to run_ round the track four times. (✓)
1 In football, the players _____ the ball with their hands. (✗)
2 In golf, you _____ the ball into the hole. (✓)
3 In tennis, you _____ a certain number of points in each game. (✓)
4 In a hurdles race, a runner _____ over hurdles. (✓)
5 In a grand prix race, the drivers _____ before the green light goes on. (✗)
6 In a rowing race, you _____ the line before the other boats. (✓)
7 In most sports, you _____ your opponent, even if you are very angry! (✗)

F   **Activity Centre Information**

Complete this speech made by a course leader to people arriving at an activity centre, using *mustn't* or *don't have to*.

OK, welcome to the Bridges Activity Centre. Let me tell you some things about your stay here. First of all, for safety reasons you ....*mustn't*....⁰ use any of the equipment without one of the teachers. When you're doing the activities, you ....¹ take any unnecessary risks. I'm sure I ....² tell you that – I'm sure you're all sensible people. And thirdly, you ....³ make a lot of noise at night – other people want to sleep. You ....⁴ be completely silent, but you ....⁵ disturb other people.

Now, the activities. Of course, you ....⁶ do anything that you don't want to do. You can choose which activities to do and you ....⁷ choose anything you don't fancy. All the activities are included in the price and you ....⁸ pay extra for any of them.

Finally, remember that you ....⁹ leave the centre without telling someone where you're going – that's one of our rules. You ....¹⁰ stay here every minute of the day, but we need to know where you are.

So, enjoy your time here. Any questions?

WORD FOCUS

Find words in exercise F that have these meanings (fill each space with one word only):

A not doing stupid things
....

B dangerous actions that can have bad results
....

C want to do
....

D wake up someone who wants to sleep
....

G   **The Secret Job**

Complete this conversation, in which Jane asks Nick about his job, using *mustn't* or the correct form of *have to* and the words in brackets.

JANE   What ...*do you have to do*...⁰ (you/do) in your job exactly?
NICK   ....¹ (I/tell) you too much about it. A lot of my work is secret.
JANE   Really? Well, ...² (you/tell) me anything if you don't want to.
NICK   Well, I can tell you that I do research work for various companies about games products.
JANE   ....³ (you play) a lot of games?
NICK   I can, but ....⁴ (I/do) that.
JANE   ....⁵ (you/go) to other countries to do your research?
NICK   Sometimes. I've just been on a trip but ....⁶ (I/go) abroad again until next year.
JANE   ....⁷ (you/get) any particular qualifications before you got that job?
NICK   No, ...⁸ (I/do) a course – experience was more important.
JANE   So, are there any exciting new games coming out soon?
NICK   Yes, there is one that's going to be really popular. ....⁹ (You/repeat) this to anyone, but it's called 'Weird'. ....¹⁰ (I/say) any more. Only a few people know about this game.
JANE   Don't worry. I won't say a word.

OVER TO YOU Now go to page 123.

Modal verbs | 45

12 Should
Uses and contexts

1 Some examples of **should**:
*I **should** go to bed now – it's late.
You **shouldn't** work so hard.
What **should** I say?*

2 Forms of **should**:

POSITIVE
should + verb
You **should do** more exercise.
NEGATIVE
shouldn't + verb
You **shouldn't watch** so much TV.
QUESTIONS
should + subject + verb
Should I **phone** them again?

3 We use **should** for the present and the future:
*You **should speak** to him now.
You **should speak** to him tomorrow.*

Grammar in action

1 We use **should** to say that we believe that something is a good idea or the right thing to do, and **shouldn't** to say that we believe that something is a bad idea or the wrong thing to do:
*We **shouldn't** keep walking. We **should** find a place to eat now.*

2 We use **should** and **shouldn't** to give or ask for advice:
*You **should** go home – you're ill.
You **shouldn't** spend so much money.
What **should** I wear for the party?*

> **TIP**
> We often use **I think, I don't think**, and **Do you think?** with **should** to give or ask for advice and to give opinions:
> *I think we **should** look for a better hotel.
> I don't think we **should** stay at this hotel.
> Do you think we **should** look for another hotel?*

3 We use **should** to talk about things that we expect to be true now but in fact are not true:
*The bus **should** be here now.*

A Going to London

Complete this conversation, using *should* or *shouldn't* and the phrases below the text.

SAM I'm going to London next month. You've been to London, haven't you?
      ...What should I do...⁰ while I'm there?
LUCY Well, of course, ...¹ some sightseeing. ....² to the famous places but ....³ only the places the tourists always go to. ....⁴ in the parks and ....⁵ interesting things to buy in the markets. ....⁶ all your time doing the things that every tourist does. ....⁷ the real city.
SAM ....⁸ a car?
LUCY No, ...⁹ that. ....¹⁰ public transport.
SAM ....¹¹ a travel card?
LUCY Yes, but ....¹² too far every day. ....¹³ that London is a very big city and ....¹⁴ to do too much every day.

0	What/I/do	5	you/look for	10	You/use
1	you/do	6	You/spend	11	I/get
2	You/go	7	You/experience	12	you/travel
3	you/visit	8	you/think/I/hire	13	You/remember
4	I/think/you/walk	9	I/think/you/do	14	you/try

46 | Modal verbs

B Helping the environment

Complete this blog about the environment, using *should* or *shouldn't* and the verbs in brackets.

In my opinion, people ___should do___ ⁰ (do) a lot more to help the environment and they ___shouldn't continue___ ⁰ (continue) to damage it. We _____ ¹ (use) our cars so much because cars produce pollution. We _____ ² (walk) more and we _____ ³ (cycle) more. Some people say that we _____ ⁴ (fly) so much because aeroplanes are very bad for the environment.

We _____ ⁵ (buy) products that are bad for the environment and we _____ ⁶ (throw away) so many things. People _____ ⁷ (recycle) more and governments _____ ⁸ (organize) more ways of recycling things. Companies _____ ⁹ (produce) more products that aren't bad for the environment. And we _____ ¹⁰ (destroy) the land by cutting down trees and building on it. Also, we _____ ¹¹ (look for) other ways of getting the fuel we need, for example by using solar energy. We _____ ¹² (use up) all the world's natural resources. We _____ ¹³ (wait) – we _____ ¹⁴ (take care) of the planet now.

> **WORD FOCUS**
>
> Before you do exercise B, complete phrasal verbs with these meanings by putting in the correct prepositions:
>
> **A** use .... (use all of something)
> **B** look .... (try to find)
> **C** throw .... (put into dustbin)

C The new computer

Alan has bought a new computer and his girlfriend Sarah is helping him to get it ready for use. Look at the pictures and complete Alan's statements, using *should* or *shouldn't* and the verbs in brackets.

0 The instruction manual ___should tell___ (tell) us everything.

1 The screen _____ (come on) now.

2 It _____ (make) that noise when you switch it on.

3 The time _____ (be) in that corner.

4 That message _____ (appear) on the screen. Something's wrong.

5 I'm sure the screen _____ (look) like that.

Modal verbs | 47

12 Should
Should compared with other modals

4 Compare:
- **could**, **should** and **would**
- **should** and **must / have to**
- **should** and **might**

Grammar in action

4 We can use **could** (but not *couldn't*) to give advice and to suggest that we think that something is a good idea. With this meaning, **could** is not as strong as **should**:
We could try to repair it.

We often use **I suppose** or **I guess** before **could** with this meaning:
I suppose we could try to repair it.

We can also use **I'd** (= **I would**) and **I wouldn't** to give advice to someone and to tell someone that we think that something is a good or a bad idea. We often say 'if I were you' when we give advice in this way:
I wouldn't argue with him (if I were you).

5 We use **should** to talk about actions that we believe are right or correct, and **shouldn't** to talk about actions that we believe are wrong or bad. We use **must/mustn't** for official rules and laws:
People shouldn't drop litter in the street. (= it's wrong)
People mustn't drop litter here. (= it's against the law)

Should is not as strong as **must** or **have to** – we use **should** for giving advice and **must/have to** for giving orders.
(See also unit 11 on p. 42.)

6 **Should** is stronger than **might**. We use **might** to say that something is possible, and **should** to say that something is likely or probable:
They should win the game. There are only five minutes left.
They might win the game. There are five minutes left.

(See also unit 10 on p. 38.)

D Advice on personal problems

Change the advice given in a teenage magazine, using the word in brackets. You will need to use some negative forms.

0 Perhaps you should discuss the problem with him. (could)
I guess *you could discuss* the problem with him.

0 You should tell him how you feel. (would)
If I were you, *I'd/I would tell* him how you feel.

1 Maybe you should start doing a different sport. (could)
I suppose .... doing a new sport.

2 I think you should speak to your teacher about the problem. (would)
.... to your teacher about the problem, if I were you.

3 You shouldn't get upset about the problem. (would)
If I were you, ... upset about the problem.

4 Maybe you should apologize to her. (could)
I suppose .... to her.

5 I don't think you should listen to those people. (would)
.... listen to those people, if I were you.

6 You should forget about him and get a new boyfriend. (would)
If I were you, ... about him and get a new boyfriend.

48 | Modal verbs

7   You should eat healthier food. (would)
    .... healthier food, if I were you.
8   I don't think you should feel bad about what happened. (would)
    .... bad about what happened, if I were you.

E The school trip

Complete what a teacher says to a class before a school trip by putting the correct word from the choices in brackets in each gap.

OK, tomorrow's trip to the museum. Everyone ....*must*........ ⁰ (might/must) meet at the school entrance by 8.30 a.m. This is very important – you ....¹ (mustn't/might not) be late because we ....² (might/must) get to the museum in time for our guided tour.

You ....³ (must/should) enjoy the museum because it's a very interesting place. We ....⁴ (might not/shouldn't) have time to see all of the interesting exhibitions but we ....⁵ (should/must) be able to see most of them. The museum ....⁶ (mustn't/shouldn't) be too crowded.

The journey back ....⁷ (mustn't/shouldn't) take more than an hour and we ....⁸ (might/should) arrive back here at 6 p.m. However, we ....⁹ (shouldn't/might not) get back for 6 p.m. because there ....¹⁰ (must/might) be a lot of traffic on the way. So you ....¹¹ (might/should) tell your parents to get here by 6 p.m. but they ....¹² (might/should) have to wait for you.

F When you come to this country

Complete this email, using one of the modal forms from the box. Use each of the choices only once.

> ~~should~~   shouldn't   could   would   wouldn't   must   mustn't   might   might not

Hi Martha,

When you come to this country, I think you ....*should*........ ⁰ see as much of the country as possible. I ....¹ stay in the city all the time if I were you – you ....² spend the whole trip in such a busy and crowded place. I ....³ see some of the countryside if I were you, it's very varied and very beautiful. I don't know if you want to drive while you're here, but I guess you ....⁴ hire a car and take a little tour. But don't forget that you ....⁵ have a proper licence to do that and that you ....⁶ drive on the right in this country; they drive on the left here.

Unfortunately, I ....⁷ see you while you're here because I ....⁸ have to go away during that period. I'm not sure about that but I'll let you know later.

Eleanor

OVER TO YOU   Now go to page 123.

13 The infinitive
The *to* infinitive

1. Some examples of the *to* infinitive:
   *I want **to go** home now.*
   *He promised **not to do** it again.*

2. We use the pattern **verb + *to* infinitive** with various common verbs:
   *I've **arranged to meet** some friends tonight.*
   *She's **hoping to get** a better job.*

3. The negative form is **not + *to* infinitive**:
   *We **decided not to buy** the cheapest one.*

4. We use the pattern **verb + object + *to* infinitive** with some common verbs:
   *I **don't want her to come** with me.*

   See also *tell* and *ask* on p. 108.

Grammar in action

1. We use the *to* infinitive after various verbs connected with saying that we will or will not do something: **agree, refuse, offer, promise**
   *She **refused to go** to bed.*

2. We use the *to* infinitive after various verbs connected with wanting or planning to do something: **hope, intend, plan, want**.
   Here, someone is talking to a waiter:
   *I **want to order** my meal now.*

3. We use the *to* infinitive after various verbs connected with thinking: **decide, forget, remember**
   *I've **forgotten to bring** my money.*

4. We use the *to* infinitive after various verbs connected with doing something in order to produce a certain result: **try, manage, arrange, fail**
   *He **tried not to drop** the plates.*

5. We use **want + object + *to* infinitive** to give an order or request. Here, a teacher is giving instructions to a class:
   *I **want you to write** a story called 'The Long Journey'.*

A Postcard from Paris

Complete this postcard from one friend to another, using the *to* infinitive form of the correct verbs in the box.

> see ~~understand~~ pay take go arrive bring spend get in improve

Hi Nick,
I'm having a good time in Paris. My French isn't very good but I'm managing *to understand* ⁰ what people say to me, and fortunately I remembered _____¹ my phrase book. I'm hoping _____² my French while I'm here. And I'm planning _____³ a lot of my time sightseeing. I want _____⁴ a riverboat trip on the Seine, I intend _____⁵ to the top of the Eiffel Tower and I've also decided _____⁶ for a guided tour of The Louvre. Yesterday, I tried _____⁷ some of the famous paintings at another museum but I failed _____⁸ at the place early enough. There were long queues but I managed _____⁹ after about an hour and the paintings were great. I'll write to you again in a few days.
William

Nick Smith
9 Park Street
Oxford
ENGLAND

B The school team's next match

Some people had a meeting to discuss the school team's next match at another school. Complete what some of the boys and their parents said, using *agreed*, *offered*, *promised* or *refused* and the *to* infinitive.

'Will you wear the number 4 shirt, Andy,' said the coach. 'No,' said Andy'.

'I'm not going to play in the match. I don't want to,' said Eric.

'I'll take Eric's place,' said Simon.

'Will you bring some snacks and drinks, Mrs Davies?' 'OK,' said Mrs Davies.

'Don't be late, Don,' said the coach. 'No, I'll be there on time.'

0 Andy _refused to wear_ the number 4 shirt.
1 Eric _____ in the match.
2 Simon _____ Eric's place.
3 Mrs Davies _____ some snacks and drinks.
4 Don _____ there on time.

C The new motorbike

Complete this conversation between Joe and Neil about Joe's new motorbike. Use the verbs in brackets in the same verb tenses as the questions before them, and use the negative *to* infinitive form of the correct verbs in the box.

| do   get   scare   ~~spend~~   discuss   go |

NEIL Did you buy a motorbike last week?
JOE   Yes, and I _managed not to spend_ ⁰ (manage) too much. I found a cheap one.
NEIL What have your parents said about it?
JOE   We _____ ¹ (agree) the subject any more. They're not pleased.
NEIL Did you get the one you told me about?
JOE   No, I _____ ² (decide) that one. I got a different one.
NEIL Can I come for a ride on it with you? Will I be safe?
JOE   Yes, I _____ ³ (try) anything risky if you're with me. And I _____ ⁴ (remember) too fast.
NEIL Do you promise? I don't want to get frightened.
JOE   Yes, I _____ ⁵ (promise) you. You'll love it.

D Janet's party

Complete each pair of sentences about Janet's birthday party, using the phrases in the box. Use the past simple form of *want* in each first sentence and the present simple form of *want* in each second sentence.

| not want/her old boyfriend/go   want/people/have   ~~want/people/remember~~
~~want/everyone/enjoy~~   want/everyone dance   not want/people/sit
not want/him/be   not want/food/run out |

0 She _wanted everyone to enjoy_ ⁰ the party.
   She said 'I _want people to remember_ ⁰ it for a long time.'
1 She _____ to the party.
   She said 'I _____ there. I hate him!'
2 She _____ plenty to eat.
   She said 'I _____ quickly.'
3 She _____ down all evening.
   She said 'I _____ to the music.'

WORD FOCUS

Which of these sentences means the same as 'The food ran out'?

A There was no more food.
B The food was excellent.
C There was a lot of food.
D The food was poor.

13 The infinitive
The infinitive without *to*

5 Some examples of the use of the **infinitive without *to***:
I'll see you tomorrow.
The teacher made him do the work again.

6 We use the **infinitive without *to*** after modal verbs (*will, can, may, might, should, could, would, must*):
Can you hear me?
You might not like this.

7 We use the **infinitive without *to*** after **make** and **let** in this pattern:

make/let + object + infinitive without *to*

His story made us laugh.
The boss let them go home early.

Grammar in action

7 We use the **infinitive without *to*** to make statements and ask questions using modal verbs:
I can't see anything.

8 We use **make** with an object and the infinitive without *to* to talk about the cause of an action or feeling:
It was a sad film and it made me cry.

9 We use **make** with an object and the infinitive without *to* to say that someone forces another person to do something that the person does not want to do:
His mother made him tidy his room.

10 We use **let** with an object and the infinitive without *to* with the meaning 'allow' or 'give permission':
They let their children do anything they want.

We usually use the patterns in 9 and 10 to talk about the actions of people in authority, e.g. parents, teachers, bosses at work.

> **TIP**
> To form negatives with **let**, we often use **won't** for the present and **wouldn't** for the past:
> *His parents won't let him stay up late at night.* (in the present and in general)
> *He wanted to watch the programme but his parents wouldn't let him watch it.*

E Travel card information

Complete this conversation in a tourist information office using the phrases in the box and the appropriate modals. More than one modal may be correct in some gaps.

| I/get   you/find   they/be   I/use   ~~you/give~~   it/be |

TOURIST ......Could/Would you give......⁰ me some information on travel cards?
ASSISTANT Yes, of course. What do you want to know?
TOURIST ....¹ the card on trains and buses?
ASSISTANT Yes, it's for trains and buses.
TOURIST I'm staying here for three weeks. ....² weekly cards or a monthly card?
ASSISTANT Well, that's up to you. If you travel a lot, ...³ a good idea to get a monthly card, but I'm not sure.
TOURIST Are children free?
ASSISTANT ....⁴ under the age of 12 for free travel.
TOURIST How much are the cards?
ASSISTANT Here's a leaflet with all the details. ....⁵ everything you need to know there.
TOURIST Oh, OK thanks.

F My teacher

Complete this description of a teacher using the correct forms of *make* or *let*, the words in brackets and the correct verbs in the box.

> go   bring   concentrate   enjoy   behave   read   do   ~~stay~~   give

Mr Gregory is a good teacher and I like him but he's very strict. Sometimes *he makes all of us stay* ⁰ (all of us) at school after lessons if only one person has done something wrong. Last week, he ....¹ (us) home because he was angry with us, and he ....² (us) a lot of extra work. He certainly never ....³ (people) badly.

He ....⁴ (everyone) on their work, but he sometimes ....⁵ (us) ourselves when we've finished a particular piece of work. One thing he's very strict about is doing our homework on time – he ....⁶ (students) it to him late. Last Thursday was an unusual day in our class, because he ....⁷ (us) books to school that we wanted to read. That was great, but he also ....⁸ (me) from my book to the rest of the class.

G Email from California

Bill is visiting the US. Complete his email to his friend Ellie, using the *to* infinitive or the infinitive without *to* and the correct verbs or phrases in the box.

> visit   bring   stay   pay   not laugh   me/miss   describe   go   everyone/sing
> not look   be   take   me/meet   do   ~~tell~~   rent   say   have   not get

Hi Ellie,

I'm staying with some friends of my parents here in California and I'm having a good time. I've done lots of things and I won't *tell* ⁰ you about all of them now but I can ....¹ one or two of my experiences. Last week, the family offered ....² me to Hollywood because I wanted ....³ on a tour of a film studio. It was great – you must ....⁴ the place one day. And yesterday they wanted ....⁵ some of their friends and so they arranged ....⁶ a picnic in some beautiful woods. At the end, they made ....⁷ a song. At first I refused ....⁸ it, but they wouldn't let ....⁹ my turn, so I had to sing. I tried ....¹⁰ embarrassed and they promised ....¹¹ if I sang badly. I did OK, I think, and I managed ....¹² too stupid.
Next week, I'm planning ....¹³ a visit to San Francisco on my own. The family I'm staying with are really good to me, and perhaps I shouldn't ....¹⁴ this, but it'll ....¹⁵ good to spend some time exploring on my own. I might ....¹⁶ in a hotel there for a couple of days, I'm not sure. And I've also decided ....¹⁷ a car and drive to some other places before I come home – I remembered ....¹⁸ my international licence with me. That's all for now,

Bill

OVER TO YOU   Now go to page 124.

14 The -ing form
Form, uses, and contexts

1 Some examples of the **-ing** form:
   *I enjoy **listening** to music.*
   *Would you mind **waiting**?*

2 We use the **-ing** form of a verb after various common verbs:
   *He **hates getting up** early in the morning.*
   *My computer **keeps breaking down**.*
   *She **loves travelling**.*
   *Please **stop making** so much noise.*

3 We use **go + -ing** in various common phrases:
   *Let's **go swimming**.*

4 We can use the **-ing** form of a verb as the subject of a sentence. When the **-ing** form is the subject, we can also use an object after it:
   ***Swimming is** a good form of exercise.*
   ***Travelling long distances** every day is very tiring.*

Grammar in action

1 We use the **-ing** form after various verbs connected with liking or not liking something: **like**, **love**, **enjoy**, **hate**
   I like walking in the countryside.

2 We use the **-ing** form after **mind** in negative statements to say that we are not angry or unhappy about doing something:
   I don't mind lending you some money.

We use **Do/Would you mind** with the **-ing** form in questions to ask someone politely to do something. Here, a shop assistant is talking to a customer in a busy shop:
   Would you mind waiting, please?

3 We use the **-ing** form after **keep** to say that something happens regularly or too often:
   My team keeps losing matches.

4 We use the **-ing** form after **stop** to say that something does not continue:
   The phone stopped ringing before I could answer it.

We use the **-ing** form after **finish** to talk about completing an action or process that continues for a period of time:
   She hasn't finished painting the picture.

5 We use **go + -ing** to talk about various activities and hobbies that we go out of our homes to do:
   He goes fishing in the river near where I go swimming.

6 We use the **-ing** form as the subject of a sentence when the subject is an action or situation, not a person or thing:
   Playing the violin is very difficult.

A Going to rock festivals

Complete the blog about rock festivals, using a positive, negative or *to* infinitive form of the verb in brackets and the -ing form of the correct verb from the list.

| be   work   sit   listen   do   ~~go~~   travel   spend   wait   join   get |

Next month I'm going to a rock festival that's taking place quite a long way from where I live. I really ___like going___ ⁰ (like) to these festivals and I've been to a few before. My friend Jake usually comes with me, but he's decided _____ ¹ (stop) me. He says that he _____ ² (like) down in muddy fields, he _____ ³ (hate) in long queues for food and he _____ ⁴ (enjoy) long distances to get there and back. But I'm going _____ ⁵ (keep) it because I really _____ ⁶ (love) to the music, I _____ ⁷ (enjoy) in a big crowd of people and I _____ ⁸ (mind) wet when it rains. So, when I _____ ⁹ (finish) in the shop this week, I'm going to set off on my journey to the festival. I really _____ ¹⁰ (like) my free time out in the countryside listening to music with thousands of people.

54 | Verb forms and structures

B Busy people

Lucy and her friends do a lot of activities. Look at the pictures and complete the sentences using the correct tense of *go* and the *-ing* form of the correct verb.

0 I sometimes ......*go cycling*...... with a friend at weekends.
1 We .... in the mountains two months ago.
2 I sometimes .... with my friend Hannah.
3 I .... with some friends last night.
4 We often .... in the local pool.
5 I .... in the winter but I wasn't very good at it.

C Living in a new city

Suzanne has gone to live in a big city in her own country. Here, she talks about her experience. Complete what she says, using the *-ing* form of the correct verbs from the box.

| cross be understand meet drive leave ~~find~~ shop go park travel |

I came to live in this city about a year ago. At first, it wasn't easy. ......*Finding*...... ⁰ somewhere to live was difficult. .... ¹ people was another problem, because they speak with a strong accent in this part of the country. But things are better now. I'm living in an apartment in the centre of the city. .... ² is easy and I can get anything I want. .... ³ is a bit tiring because I have to go on crowded trains to the place where I work. I have a car but .... ⁴ is a problem in this area. And .... ⁵ here is risky because there's so much traffic – .... ⁶ the road can be dangerous, too. But .... ⁷ in the centre of the city is great. .... ⁸ out is great fun and .... ⁹ people is easy. I'm really glad I came here. .... ¹⁰ my home town wasn't an easy thing to do but I don't regret it.

D A special offer

Complete the conversation between two friends, using the correct phrases from the box and the *-ing* form of the verbs.

| try hate/do love/shop stop/complain mind/come not enjoy/be ~~like/wear~~ not like/buy go/shop keep/talk not mind/help not like/spend not finish/tell mind/listen |

OLIVIA   ......*Do you like wearing*...... ⁰ nice clothes?
CLAUDIA Yes, you know I do. But I .... ¹ them.
OLIVIA   Are you busy this afternoon? .... ² to the shops with me?
CLAUDIA Look, I .... ³ you with most things but I don't want to .... ⁴. You know I .... ⁵ that. It's so boring. I .... ⁶ my time in shopping centres and I .... ⁷ in crowds. .... ⁸ on clothes is horrible, too.
OLIVIA   .... ⁹! I .... ¹⁰ you why I want you to come. .... ¹¹ to me?
CLAUDIA OK, sorry, ... ¹².
OLIVIA   Well, it's your birthday soon. I thought I'd buy something special for you.
CLAUDIA Ah, why didn't you say that before? I .... ¹³! When can we go?

WORD FOCUS

Find words in exercise D that mean the opposite of these words:

A unpleasant, horrible
   ....
B ordinary, usual, typical
   ....
C interesting, exciting
   ....
D free, doing nothing
   ....

Verb forms and structures | 55

14 The -ing form
Infinitive or -ing form

5 Some examples of the **to** infinitive and the **-ing** form:
I **promised to help** her.
I **didn't mind helping** her.
I **like learning** English.
I**'d like to learn** Spanish.

6 We use the **to** infinitive after some verbs and the **-ing** form after other verbs:
I **want to have** something to eat.
I **enjoy eating** good food.

(For more examples of verbs followed by the **to** infinitive see p. 50, and for more examples of verbs followed by the **-ing** form see p. 54.)

7 We can use the **-ing** form with **like** but we always use the **to** infinitive with **would like**:

| like + -ing |

I **like living** in Paris.

| would like + to + infinitive |

I **would like to live** in Paris.

> **TIP**
> We usually use the short form of **would like**:
> I**'d like to live** in Paris.

8 We can use the **to** infinitive (not the **-ing** form) to link two parts of a sentence:
I went to the library **to borrow** a book.
We can use the **-ing** form as the subject of a sentence:
Borrowing books from the library is easy.

Grammar in action

7 We use the **-ing** form after **like** to talk about actions that we actually do and situations that actually exist. We use **like** + **-ing** to say that we enjoy these actions and situations in general and they make us feel good:
I **like spending** time with my friends.

8 We use the **to** infinitive after **would like** to say that we want to do something that we are not doing, or to say that we want a situation that is not happening. **Would like** is more polite than **want**:
I**'d like to spend** time with my friends.

9 We use the **to** infinitive to talk about the reason for or purpose of an action – when we explain why someone does something, for example:
He went to a gym **to get** fit
We can put the **to** infinitive clause at the beginning of the sentence, with the same meaning:
To get fit, he went to a gym.

E The picnic

Julie and Ruth are having a picnic together. Complete their conversation using positive or negative forms of *like* or *would like* and the correct verbs in the box. Use short forms if possible.

| earn spend give up ~~sit~~ be come happen talk work have go |

JULIE   _I like sitting here_ ⁰, it's very pleasant.
RUTH   Me too. And _____ ¹ time with good friends. _____ ²
        on picnics more often but it isn't always possible. _____ ³ to
        places like this and _____ ⁴ to friends like you when we're able to
        do it.
JULIE   I agree. _____ ⁵ less. What _____ ⁶ to you in the
        future?
RUTH   Me? _____ ⁷ a lot of money and _____ ⁸ work
        completely! _____ ⁹ under pressure and I'm under pressure at work
        a lot.
JULIE   I know what you mean. _____ ¹⁰ more free time.

F Plans with John

Charlie has a friend called John. Complete what he says about a situation with John, by putting in the *to* infinitive or *-ing* form of the correct verbs in the box.

| stop plan phone ~~discuss~~ help do get make speak leave fix |

I rang John ___to discuss___ ⁰ something important with him. _____¹ in touch with John isn't always easy because he's a very busy man. _____² him at a time when he can talk is often difficult. When I phoned _____³ to him, he was out. Then I phoned _____⁴ him a message. Eventually, he called me back. I said that I wanted to speak to him _____⁵ the arrangements for his visit to me. _____⁶ isn't something that John is good at and _____⁷ decisions sometimes takes him a long time. _____⁸ me plan for his visit, I made him agree on a definite weekend. _____⁹ that took a long time but I managed to do it in the end. And _____¹⁰ him forgetting all about it, I sent him a message with the dates in it.

G Plans for a tour of Europe

Complete this text about travel plans, using the *to* infinitive or *-ing* forms of the verbs in brackets.

I like ___travelling___ ⁰ (travel) and I've done quite a lot of it. Last year, I decided _____¹ (take) a big trip around Europe. _____² (save) money for the trip, I stopped _____³ (go) to night clubs. I like _____⁴ (have) fun in those places and I enjoy _____⁵ (spend) time with my friends there, but I wanted _____⁶ (keep) my money for the trip. So I didn't go _____⁷ (dance) at all and in fact I didn't go out much. And I managed _____⁸ (save) enough money for the trip.

_____⁹ (choose) which countries I would visit wasn't easy. I wanted _____¹⁰ (experience) lots of places because I love _____¹¹ (see) new places, and I think that _____¹² (find out) about different cultures is fantastic. _____¹³ (choose) the countries I would visit, I borrowed some books from the library and tried _____¹⁴ (learn) as much as I could about different places. Then I made a list of the countries I planned _____¹⁵ (visit). I don't mind _____¹⁶ (stay) in cheap hotels so _____¹⁷ (find) places to stay didn't worry me. I wanted the places _____¹⁸ (be) interesting.

I finished _____¹⁹ (do) my research and then I booked my flight from here. _____²⁰ (get) a cheap flight, I did a lot of research online. In fact, _____²¹ (book) a cheap flight wasn't at all difficult because there were lots available. _____²² (organize) my timetable was great fun, and I looked in lots of guidebooks _____²³ (help) me decide what do to in the different places I visited.

And then I went on my trip and it was great. I'd like _____²⁴ (travel) all the time and I'm hoping _____²⁵ (be) able to go on a trip to Africa next year.

OVER TO YOU Now go to page 124.

15 The passive
Forms, uses, and contexts

1. Some examples of **passive** sentences:
   *English **is spoken** all over the world.*
   *This product **was invented** in Sweden.*

2. We use this pattern to form the **passive**:

   > subject + be + past participle

   (For details on forming past participles, see p. 14.)

3. The form of **be** is different for different verb tenses:

   PRESENT SIMPLE PASSIVE
   subject + am/is/are + past participle
   I'm employed by a big company.

   PRESENT CONTINUOUS PASSIVE
   subject + am/is/are + being + past participle
   The road is being repaired.

   PAST SIMPLE PASSIVE
   subject + was/were + past participle
   It was made in China.

   PAST CONTINUOUS PASSIVE
   subject + was/were + being + past participle
   People were being interviewed.

   PRESENT PERFECT PASSIVE
   subject + has/have + been + past participle
   He has been given a new job.

   MODAL PASSIVE
   subject + modal + be + past participle
   Applications must be received before 12 May.

   GOING TO PASSIVE
   subject + am/is/are going to + be + past participle
   I'm not going to be chosen for the team.

Grammar in action

1. We use the **passive** when the person who 'does' the verb is not important or we don't know who 'does' the verb. The object of the verb is more important, so it becomes the subject of the sentence and we use a passive verb:
   The college was built in 1947.
   (= Some people built the college in 1947.)

   Here, *the college* is the subject of the sentence because the man is talking about the college. He is not talking about who built the college, and he may not know who built it. He uses a passive verb because *the college* is not the subject of the verb (the college did not build anything).

2. We often use the **passive** in formal contexts, such as public information (rules, signs, brochures, etc.) and media reports:
   Cycling is not permitted in this area. (*Cycling* is the subject of the rule, not who does not allow it.)
   Bookings can be made online. (*Bookings* is the subject of the sentence, not the people making them).

A A bad journey

Complete this story about a journey, using the past simple passive or past continuous passive form of the verbs in brackets. You will need to use one past continuous passive form and one negative form.

The journey to Italy was terrible. First of all, I got to the airport quite late. I ......*was driven*......⁰ (drive) there in a taxi, but my taxi got stuck in traffic because the road ....¹ (repair). When I got to the airport, I ....² (tell) that there was a problem and the flight ....³ (delay). Then I ....⁴ (put) in a seat on the plane next to some very loud children. During the flight, we ....⁵ (give) a really horrible meal. When we landed, my bags ....⁶ (search) and this took a long time. Everything ....⁷ (take out) of them. When I came out of the airport, I was too late for the bus to my hotel. I had to get a taxi and I ....⁸ (charge) a lot of money for the journey. When I finally got to the hotel, all the staff were busy. I ....⁹ (show) to my room and I had to find it myself. It was a terrible way to start the trip.

B Tonight's news

Complete these news stories, using the passive form of the correct verbs in the box. In each paragraph, use the same verb tense as the example.

leave   create   ~~announce~~   complete
~~build~~   choose   show   name

New bridge planned for north

A new bridge _is going to be built_ ⁰ in the north of the country next year. The plan .... ¹ to the public in June and the work .... ² within three years. Thousands of new jobs .... ³ in that part of the country.

World Cup shock

The national team for the World Cup _has been announced_ ⁰ and it contains some surprises. Several new players .... ⁴ for the squad for the first time, a new captain .... ⁵ and a number of established players .... ⁶ out.

C Ordering online

Complete the information and instructions from a company's website, using the verbs in brackets and the passive forms given after each sentence.

0 All our products _can be ordered_ (order) online. (can)
1 Orders .... (make) 24 hours a day. (can)
2 All major credit cards .... (accept). (present simple)
3 Orders .... (deliver) within 14 days. (will)
4 A delivery address .... (provide). (must)
5 Please wait. Your order .... (process). (present continuous)
6 Your order .... (send). (present perfect)

D Harry's party

Complete this conversation between two friends, using the words below it and the correct passive forms.

ADAM _Where was this photograph taken_ ⁰ ? And .... ¹?
IAN   At Harry's party last week.
ADAM Oh. .... ² to that.
IAN   No, I know. .... ³ far in advance and .... ⁴ about it.
ADAM Was it a good party? .... ⁵?
IAN   Only about 20 people came. But it was good fun.
ADAM What exactly is happening in this photograph?
IAN   .... ⁶ in water and his friends are laughing.
ADAM Well, ... ⁷ if someone did that to me. But Harry deserves it!

0 Where/this photograph/take
1 when/it/take
2 I/not/invite
3 The party/not/plan
4 lots of people/not/tell
5 How many people/invite
6 Harry/cover
7 I/not/would/amuse

15 The passive
Active and passive compared

4 Here is a comparison between **active** and **passive** forms:

PRESENT SIMPLE
ACTIVE	The price **includes** meals.
PASSIVE	Meals **are included** in the price.

PRESENT CONTINUOUS
ACTIVE	Police **are interviewing** a man.
PASSIVE	A man **is being interviewed** by police.

PAST SIMPLE
ACTIVE	He **caused** the problem.
PASSIVE	The problem **was caused** by him.

PAST CONTINUOUS
ACTIVE	People **were repairing** the road.
PASSIVE	The road **was being repaired**.

PRESENT PERFECT
ACTIVE	They **have sold** all the tickets.
PASSIVE	All the tickets **have been sold**.

MODAL
ACTIVE	You **can buy** this book in most bookshops.
PASSIVE	This book **can be bought** in most bookshops.

GOING TO
ACTIVE	The manager **is going to choose** the team tomorrow.
PASSIVE	The team **is going to be chosen** tomorrow.

5 We often use **by** after a **passive** verb form to say who or what is the subject of the verb. We use **by** before the 'agent' (the person or thing that 'does' the action):
> The programme **is watched by millions of people**.
> (= Millions of people watch the programme.)
> Children **must be accompanied by an adult**.
> (= An adult must accompany children.)

Grammar in action

3 We use the **active** or the **passive** depending on what is the main topic we are talking about or what we are most interested in. We use the **active** if the subject of the verb is the main topic, and the **passive** if the subject of the sentence is not the subject of the verb because the subject of the verb is not important or not known:
> Lions live in parts of Africa and southern Asia. They belong to the cat family. Lions are hunted and killed in some places. They can be seen in many zoos.

Here, the topic is 'lions'. 'Lions' is the subject of 'live' and 'belong', and so those verbs are active. 'Lions' is not the subject of 'hunted', 'killed' or 'seen' – other people hunt, kill and see lions – and so those verbs are passive.

4 We use **by + agent** after a passive verb when it is important to say who 'does' the verb because the sentence would have no real meaning without this information:
> The painting 'Sunflowers' was painted by Vincent Van Gogh. It is a very famous painting.

In the example, the main topic is the painting – it is the subject of the next sentence. But the artist's name is important information. We use **by + agent** because the sentence is about both the painting and the artist, and the artist (the agent) is not the subject of the verb.

E College information

Complete the information from a college brochure by changing the active sentences into passive sentences.

0 We offer excellent tuition at the college.
1 You can find details of all our courses on our website.
2 We do not give lessons on public holidays.
3 You must pay all course fees in advance.
4 We are introducing new courses at the college.
5 Students take tests at the end of every course.

Excellent tuition is offered at the college.
.... on our website.
.... on public holidays.
.... in advance.
.... at the college.
.... at the end of every course.

F Short story competition

This is an announcement on a children's TV programme about a competition. Rewrite the announcement, changing the active forms into passive forms with *by*.

As you know, this programme runs a short story competition every year, and every year, children from all over the country send in stories for the competition. And I know that many of you are creating fantastic stories right now. Last year a story called 'Creeps' won the competition and Ellie Stone, aged 12, wrote that story. The teenage magazine YLP published it and many thousands of people all over the country read it. This year the film director Marvin White is going to judge the competition. And this year, a film studio in London is offering the top prize – Marvin will make the winning story into a short film after the competition. This channel will show that film later in the year.

As you know, *a short story competition is run by this programme* ⁰ every year, and every year _____¹ from all over the country for the competition. And I know that _____² right now. Last year _____³ called 'Creeps' and _____⁴, aged 12. _____⁵ YLP and _____⁶ all over the country. This year, _____⁷ Marvin White. And this year, _____⁸ in London – _____⁹ after the competition. _____¹⁰ later in the year.

G Crime report

Complete this conversation in a police station by putting in the correct active and passive verbs in the box.

> will be seen   ran   will be found   will help   appeared   was grabbed
> will throw   will be written   took   has happened   contained
> was being served   will be asked   might remember   wasn't seen
> ~~has been stolen~~   am being robbed   will be returned

WOMAN   Can you help me? My bag *has been stolen* ⁰. Someone _____¹ it while I was in a shop. I _____² by an assistant and suddenly it _____³ by someone. I shouted 'I _____⁴' but it was too late.

OFFICER   OK. Can you wait here? In a few minutes you _____⁵ by one of my colleagues. You _____⁶ to give a description of this person and a report _____⁷.

WOMAN   I don't know what he looked like and the incident _____⁸ by anyone else. The thief simply _____⁹ and then he _____¹⁰ away.

OFFICER   OK. My colleague _____¹¹ you and you _____¹² more than you think.

WOMAN   I hope so. It's very important. My bag _____¹³ my passport but no money. Perhaps the thief _____¹⁴ it away and it _____¹⁵ by somebody.

OFFICER   Yes, it's possible that it _____¹⁶ to you by a member of the public. That kind of thing _____¹⁷ before.

WORD FOCUS

Which of these words from exercise G describes a person, which one describes an action and which one describes an event? Write *person*, *action* or *event*.

A incident _____

B grab _____

C thief _____

OVER TO YOU   Now go to page 124.

16 Conditionals
First conditional

1 Some examples of **first conditional** sentences:
   I'll phone you later if I have time.
   If you leave now, you won't be late.

2 The **first conditional** pattern is:

   if + subject + present simple + subject + will

   If I pass my exams, I'll go to university.

   We use a comma (,) after the 'if' part of the sentence in this pattern.

   The *if* clause can come second:
   I'll go to university if I pass my exams.

   We can use negative verbs in the same patterns:
   If I don't pass my exams, I won't go to university.
   I won't go to university if I fail my exams.

   We can form questions with all these patterns:
   What will you do if you don't pass your exams?

   > **TIP**
   > Remember to use the present simple (NOT *will/won't*) after *if* in a first conditional sentence:
   > *If I pass …* (NOT ~~if I will pass~~)
   > *If I don't pass …* (NOT ~~if I won't pass~~)

Grammar in action

1 We use the **first conditional** to talk about possible actions and situations in the future, and the results of those actions and situations. The 'if' part of the sentence contains a possible action or situation, and the 'will/won't' part of the sentence contains the result:
   If you run, you'll catch the bus.

2 We use the **first conditional** when we are talking about possibilities immediately after the present moment:
   You'll be late for work if you don't get up now.

   We also use the **first conditional** when we are imagining and talking about possibilities a long time in the future. Here, a child imagines life as an adult:
   If I make a lot of money, I'll live in a big house.

3 We can use **may/might** for the result, to say that the result is only possible, not certain:
   If I post this letter today, it might get there tomorrow.

   We can use **should** for the result, to say that the result is probable but not certain:
   If I post this letter today, they should get it before the end of the week.

   We can use an **imperative** for the result, to give an instruction or advice:
   Here's my card – if you need any help, give me a ring.

A Possibilities in my future

Complete this email from one friend to another by putting in the correct positive or negative forms of the verbs in brackets. Use the present simple or *will/won't*. Use short forms.

Thanks for your message, it was great to hear your news. I'm very busy at the moment because my exams start next week. If I ……*get*……⁰ (get) the right grades, I`ll start……⁰ (start) my university course in September. But if I ………………¹ (do) well enough in them, I ………………² (be able to) go to that university. So I'm working very hard.

Thanks for inviting me to come and stay with you during the summer. I ………………³ (do) it if the flights ………………⁴ (be) too expensive. I'm planning to get a job for a few weeks and I ………………⁵ (save) enough money to come if I ………………⁶ (find) one. It ………………⁷ (be) a pity if we ………………⁸ (see) each other, so I'll do my best.

Other news? Well, the weather's terrible here at the moment. If it ………………⁹ (improve), I think I ………………¹⁰ (go) mad! I hope you're OK. If you ………………¹¹ (write) to me again soon, I ………………¹² (reply) as quickly as I can.

B What might happen tonight

Judy and Brian are getting ready to go out for the evening. Complete their conversation, using the words below it and the present simple or will/won't.

JUDY If you don't hurry⁰, ...¹ to the restaurant on time.
BRIAN Well, ...² if ....³ a bit late. Don't worry about it.
JUDY I am worried. What ....⁴ if ....⁵ there?
BRIAN I'm sure ....⁶ if ....⁷ wait for us for a few minutes.
JUDY But it's a very important evening. It's Frank's birthday and ....⁸ angry with us if ....⁹ on time.
BRIAN Look, I'm nearly ready. If ....¹⁰ calm, ...¹¹ fine.
JUDY Do you think that Frank is going to make a speech?
BRIAN If ....¹² a speech, ...¹³ embarrassed, I'm sure.
JUDY Why? If ....¹⁴ to make a speech on his special day, ...¹⁵. If ....¹⁶ his funny stories, ...¹⁷.
BRIAN You might laugh. But if ....¹⁸ about things that happened when he and I were small children, ...¹⁹ leave the room!

0 you/not hurry	7 they/have to	14 he/want
1 we/not get	8 people/be	15 nobody/mind
2 it/not matter	9 we/not turn up	16 he/tell
3 we/be	10 you/keep	17 we/laugh
4 the others/do	11 everything/be	18 he/talk
5 we/not be	12 he/make	19 I/have to
6 they/not panic	13 everyone/be	

WORD FOCUS

Find verbs in the words below exercise B that have these meanings:

A arrive (phrasal verb)
....

B do something quickly
....

C become extremely worried or frightened
....

D be annoyed, disapprove
....

E be important
....

C If you visit this city …

Match the second halves of the tips from a travel guide (a–i) giving advice to tourists visiting a city with the beginning of each sentence (1–8). Write the letters of the correct sentence endings in the spaces.

0 If you book accommodation early, ...i...
1 If you get lost in the city, ...
2 If you visit the Central Museum, ...
3 If you want to go to the opera, ...
4 If you go to the market, ...
5 If you want to avoid the crowds, ...
6 If you buy a tourist pass, ...
7 If you feel energetic one day, ...
8 If you come here in the winter, ...

a you might like to climb to the top of the cathedral tower.
b you should be able to get tickets easily.
c some of the tourist attractions might not be open.
d don't panic.
e you shouldn't have to queue at museums and art galleries.
f you might find some good souvenirs.
g go straight to the third floor.
h don't come at the height of the tourist season.
i you shouldn't have difficulty getting a good hotel.

Verb forms and structures | 63

16 Conditionals
Second conditional

3 Some examples of **second conditional** sentences:
If I lived by the sea, *I'd go* swimming every day.
If I could find a better job, *I wouldn't stay* here.

4 The **second conditional** pattern is:

> if + subject + past simple + subject + would

If I had enough money, *I would/I'd buy* that car.

We use a comma (,) after the 'if' part of the sentence in this pattern.

The *if* clause can come second:
I would/I'd buy that car *if I had* enough money.

We can use negative verbs in the same patterns:
If I didn't have friends, *I wouldn't be* happy.
I wouldn't be happy *if my friends left* the country.

5 We also use **could/couldn't** in the *if* clause:
If I could find a better job, *I would/I'd leave* this company.

6 We can form questions with all these patterns:
If you had lots of money, which car *would you buy*?
How *would you get* to work *if you couldn't drive*?

Grammar in action

4 We use the **second conditional** to talk about the present, and to imagine that a present fact or situation is different from what it really is. We use the second conditional to imagine the present or future result of a different present situation:

If I lived by the sea, I'd go swimming every day. (But I don't go swimming every day because I don't live by the sea.)

5 We also use the **second conditional** to talk about actions and events in the future that we think probably will not happen, and to imagine the results of those actions and events. For example, we can use it to talk about our dreams:

If I won $1 million, I would travel the world.
(But I probably won't win $1 million so I probably won't travel the world.)

6 We use **could** in second conditional sentences to talk about abilities and possibilities that do not exist in the present or probably won't exist in the future:
If I could swim, I'd go in the water. (But I won't go in the water because I can't swim.)

7 **Compare the first and second conditionals.** We use the **first conditional** to talk about things that really are possible in the future. Here, someone is talking on a TV gameshow:
If I win the prize, I'll be very happy.

We use the **second conditional** to talk about things that probably won't happen in the future. Here, someone is watching other people on a TV gameshow:
If I won the prize, I'd be very happy.

D A different world

A teenage magazine asked readers to imagine a world that is different from the world they live in. Complete what they wrote, using the verbs in the box and the second conditional. Use short forms. You will need to use one of the choices more than once.

> not eat   not suffer   help   not be   use   ~~not start~~   do   not like   ~~be~~

0 If people _didn't start_ wars, the world _would be_ a better place.
1 If everyone _____ their cars less, there _____ so much pollution.
2 If people _____ more recycling, they _____ the environment a lot.
3 People _____ so unhealthy if they _____ junk food.
4 People _____ from stress if life _____ so fast.
5 Celebrities _____ popular if people _____ reading about them.

E It probably won't happen, but …

Complete this extract from a magazine interview with an actor called Paul, using the words in brackets and the second conditional. Use short forms if possible.

INTERVIEWER If _you could have_ ⁰ (you/can have) another job, what ……………… ¹ (it/be)?

PAUL Well, if ……………… ² (I/can be) a musician, ……………… ³ (I/be) really happy. If ……………… ⁴ (I/be) a good singer or if ……………… ⁵ (I/can play) an instrument really well, ……………… ⁶ (it/be) great.

INTERVIEWER What instrument ……………… ⁷ (you/play) if ……………… ⁸ (you/can choose) one?

PAUL ……………… ⁹ (I/love) to be a lead guitarist. ……………… ¹⁰ (I/join) a band and ……………… ¹¹ (I/play) really loud. ……………… ¹² (I/stand) on the stage and ……………… ¹³ (I/enjoy) being a rock star. But of course, it's not going to happen.

INTERVIEWER No, and you have a very successful career as an actor.

PAUL I know, and I love it, but if ……………… ¹⁴ (I/stop) enjoying it, ……………… ¹⁵ (I/give up).

INTERVIEWER Really? If ……………… ¹⁶ (you/give up) acting, what ……………… ¹⁷ (you/do)?

PAUL Well, if ……………… ¹⁸ (I/decide) to stop being an actor, I think ……………… ¹⁹ (I/become) a teacher. If ……………… ²⁰ (I/work) with young people, ……………… ²¹ (I/teach) them from my own experience and I think ……………… ²² (they/learn) a lot.

F Different possibilities

Write the questions using the words given and the conditional form in brackets. When you have completed the exercise, answer the questions.

0 you/get married/what kind of person/you/marry? (first)
   If you get married, what kind of person will you marry?

1 you/can change your appearance/what/you/change? (second)

2 you/watch TV tonight, what/you/watch? (first)

3 you/go out tonight/where/you/go? (first)

4 you/can live in another country/where/you/live? (second)

5 you/have a lot of money/what/you/buy? (second)

6 you/learn to speak English well/how/you/use the language? (first)

OVER TO YOU Now go to page 124.

17 Connecting future sentences
Conditional clauses

1. Some examples of **conditional clauses for the future**:
   If you leave now, you won't be late.
   Unless you leave now, you'll be late.
   You won't be late *as long as you leave* now.
   You'll be late *even if you leave* now.

2. We use **unless**, **as long as** and **even if** to talk about the future in the pattern:

   > unless/as long as/even if + present simple

3. We use **unless** with a positive verb with the meaning 'if …. not':
   Unless I borrow some money, I can't go out tonight.
   (= if I don't borrow …)

4. We can use **as long as** with the meaning 'if …':
   We'll have a picnic *as long as the weather is* good.
   (= if the weather is good)

5. We can use **even if** for emphasis:
   Even if we score a goal, we won't win the game.

6. We also use **in case** + **present simple** to talk about the future, with the meaning 'because it might happen':
   Take my phone number *in case you need* to contact me tomorrow. (= because you might need to contact me)

Grammar in action

1. We use **unless** to talk about something that is necessary in the future, and to talk about the result if this does not happen:
   I won't go on that ride unless you come with me. (= if you don't come with me)

2. We use **as long as** to emphasize that something is only possible in the future if another thing happens or doesn't happen:
   As long as you drink plenty of water during the race, you'll be fine.

3. We use **even if** to emphasize that a possible future action or event will not change the future result:
   Even if we work all night, we won't finish on time. (= because there is too much to do)

4. We use **in case** to talk about possible future situations and problems, and actions that someone takes or can take because these situations and problems are possible. We often use **in case** when we give advice:
   Take a jumper in case it gets cold later.

A Music lessons

A music teacher is talking to a group of students in their first lesson. Rewrite what he says, using *unless*.

0. You won't improve if you don't practise regularly.
   You won't improve ……*unless you practise regularly.*……

1. If you don't pay attention, you won't learn.
   ……………………………………………………………, you won't learn.

2. You won't enjoy the lessons if you don't concentrate.
   You won't enjoy the lessons ……………………………………………………

3. If you don't make a mistake, I won't tell you to stop playing.
   ……………………………………………………………, I won't tell you to stop playing.

4. You won't be able to join the orchestra if you don't reach a high standard.
   You won't be able to join the orchestra ……………………………………………………

5. If your parents don't buy an instrument for you, you'll have to borrow one.
   ……………………………………………………………, you'll have to borrow one

6. If I'm not late for some reason, lessons will always start at 2.30.
   ……………………………………………………………, lessons will always start at 2.30.

B Exam advice

Some parents are talking to their children before they take an exam.
Complete what they say, using *as long as* or *even if*.

0 *As long as you concentrate* (you/concentrate), you'll be fine.
1 .... (you/not panic), you'll be OK.
2 .... (you/not pass), I won't be angry with you.
3 .... (you/write clearly), everything will be fine.
4 .... (you/not know all the answers), you'll pass.
5 .... (some of the questions/be/hard), you'll do well.
6 .... (you/do your best), I'll be proud of you.

C Packing for the trip

Carl and Rick are packing their suitcases before they go on holiday to another country.
Complete their conversation using *in case* and the words in the box.

| we/need   we/not be   one of us/start   ~~we/spend~~   we/have   it/get |

CARL OK, what are we going to take?
RICK Well, I've packed all my clothes. I've put in all my beach things *in case we spend* ⁰
a lot of time sunbathing. But I've also put in a raincoat .... ¹ lucky
with the weather. And I've put in a jumper .... ² cold at night.
CARL Good idea. I think I'll do that. Now, I'm going to take various things
.... ³ problems during the trip. I'm putting in various medicines
and tablets .... ⁴ to feel ill. And I've made a list of various phone
numbers .... ⁵ to contact someone in an emergency.

WORD FOCUS

Find words in the conversation that describe:
A clothes (x2)
....
....
B things you take when you are ill (x2)
....
....

D Kathy's party

Complete this email about a party, using *unless*, *as long as*, *even if* or *in case* and
the words in brackets. You will need to use some negative verbs.

Are you going to Kathy's party at the Friends night club next weekend? My Dad says I can
go *as long as I don't go* ⁰ (I/go) on my own, so will you come with me? He also says that I
can't go .... ¹ (I/get) a taxi home, so you could come back with me and stay at
our house. He's going to give me plenty of money for the taxi .... ² (it/be) very
expensive late at night, so you won't have to pay for it. Oh, and my Dad also says it's OK for
me to go .... ³ (I/get) home by midnight.
The usual crowd from college won't be there. Kevin says he doesn't want to go, so
.... ⁴ (he/change) his mind, he won't be there. And Dana won't be there. She's
been ill, but .... ⁵ (she/get) better, she won't be able to go because her parents
won't let her. And Robin won't go .... ⁶ (his girlfriend/agree) to go too – and
she doesn't like night clubs. But .... ⁷ (we/know) many people, I'm sure we'll
have a great time. .... ⁸ (the music/be) good, we'll be able to dance and enjoy
ourselves. So, please come with me. I'm going to phone you tonight .... ⁹ (you/
see) this message before then.

Verb forms and structures | 67

17 Connecting future sentences
Time clauses

7 We can use **when/before/after/until/as soon as + present simple** to talk about the future:
  When I get home tonight, I'm going to take it easy.
  Stay here until I get back.

8 We do not use *will* to talk about the future with these words:
  NOT *When I'll get home tonight* …

9 We can also use **when/before/after/until/as soon as + present perfect** to talk about the future:
  When you've taken these pills, you'll start to feel better.
  She won't be happy until she's found a good job.

> **TIP**
> We usually use the present simple with **before** and the present perfect with **after**:
>   *Wait! Wash your hands before you eat.*
>   *After you've washed your hands, you can start eating.*

Grammar in action

5 We use the **present simple** with these words for an action or situation that happens at a particular point in the future. Here, someone is ill and not at work:
  I'll go back to work when I feel better. (= at the time when I feel better)

6 We use the **present perfect** with these words to make it clear that one future action will or must be complete before a second action happens:
  I'm going to go diving when I've finished my meal.

7 We use **until** to talk about a point in the future when an action ends. Here, an adult is telling some children what happens in a game:
  In this game, you dance until the music stops. (= you stop at exactly the time the music stops)
  Here a boss is talking to an employee:
  You can't go home until you've finished all your work. (= you must finish your work first, then you can go)

8 We use **as soon as** to emphasize that something will or must happen a very short time after something else happens:
  As soon as the fire alarm rings, leave the building. (= immediately after the alarm starts to ring)

E Directions

Phil is going to drive to another town to visit his friend Dave. Phil has never made the journey before. Phil and Dave are talking on the phone. Complete their conversation using the correct phrases from the box. You will need to use capital letters sometimes.

> when you arrive   ~~before you set off~~   until the barrier lifts
> when I get there   when I'm   until I reach   as soon as you turn
> as soon as you pass   until you see   before you get   when you come

DAVE   OK, Listen, I'll give you some directions *before you set off* ⁰ on the journey.
PHIL   Right. I know that I have to go on the motorway .... ¹ junction 7.
DAVE   That's right. .... ² at junction 7, leave the motorway and you'll come to a roundabout. Go straight on at the roundabout .... ³ a sign saying 'Town Centre'. .... ⁴ that sign, you'll come to a crossroads.
PHIL   What will I do .... ⁵ at the crossroads?
DAVE   Turn left and go along Slack Road. You'll go past the hospital .... ⁶ to the end of that road. At the end of the road, turn right into Albert Street. .... ⁷ into Albert Street, you'll find my apartment block. It's the first building.
PHIL   Will I be able to park .... ⁸?
DAVE   Yes. .... ⁹ to the building, you'll find the entrance to the car park on the left. Press the button and wait .... ¹⁰. Then you can drive in.

68 | Verb forms and structures

F Cookery book instructions

Complete these instructions from a cookery book, using the words in brackets and the present perfect.

0 *When you've boiled* the water, put the pasta into the pan. (When/you/boil)
1 Wait ………………………… before slicing it. (until/the meat/cool down)
2 ………………………… the carrots, add them to the dish. (When/you/chop)
3 Fry the meat ………………………… brown. (until/it/go)
4 ………………………… the sauce, pour it over the meat. (After/you/prepare)
5 Put the food in ………………………… the required temperature. (when/the oven/reach)
6 Don't take it out of the oven ………………………… properly. (until/it/cook)
7 ………………………… salt and pepper, leave the dish to cook for 40 minutes. (After/you/add)
8 ………………………… in the oven for an hour, it will be ready to serve. (After/the dish/be)

G Advert for climbing courses

Complete this extract from a brochure, using the words in the box and the correct verb tenses.

> case/something/go   long/you/obey   when/you/stand   after/you/complete
> soon/you/do   when/you/learn   unless/you/try   before/you/move
> even/a climb/seem   ~~before/they/take~~   until/you/feel

CLIMBING FOR BEGINNERS

Beginners are welcome on our climbing courses. *Before they take* ⁰ one of our courses, lots of people think they'll never be good climbers. They're amazed at what they achieve.

If you come on one of our courses, you'll receive full training from our qualified and friendly staff. ………………………… ¹ how to do the basics, you'll be able to experience the excitement of real climbing. You'll start on small climbs ………………………… ² onto bigger ones. You won't have to do any serious climbing ………………………… ³ confident enough to do it.

………………………… ⁴ impossible at first, don't worry. ………………………… ⁵ to do it, you'll never know what you're able to achieve. And on our climbing courses, an instructor will be with you at all times ………………………… ⁶ wrong. If you want to come down, just pull on the rope. You'll be able to come down safely ………………………… ⁷ that. Climbing is exciting, but at our centre, it's not dangerous. ………………………… ⁸ the safety instructions, you won't have any problems.

………………………… ⁹ at the top after your first real climb, you'll feel great. And ………………………… ¹⁰ the course, you'll get a certificate to prove that you really did it!

OVER TO YOU Now go to page 125.

18 Articles
A/an and the

1 Some examples of sentences with **a/an** and **the**:
   *They live in **a big house**.*
   *They live in **the big house** on the corner.*

2 We can use **a/an** with a **singular noun**:
   *I bought **a ticket**.*

3 We can use **the** with **singular and plural nouns**:
   *I put **the ticket** in my pocket.*
   *I paid for **the tickets** with my credit card.*

4 We often use an adjective after **a/an** or **the** and before a noun:
   *I bought **a cheap ticket**.*
   ***The cheap tickets** have sold out.*

Grammar in action

1 We use **a/an** to talk about something for the first time. Here the speaker introduces something (a T-shirt) that she has not mentioned before:
   *I saw Alison yesterday. She was wearing **a new T-shirt**.*

We use **the** with a singular noun to talk about something we have already mentioned. Here, the speaker gives more information about something:
   Alison was wearing a new T-shirt.
   ***The T-shirt** had blue stripes.*

2 We use **a/an** to talk about one thing or person when there are many and we are not specifying which one. We are not interested in which one or we don't know which one:
   *I bought this jacket in **a shop** last week.*
   (= the jacket is important, not the shop)

We use **the** when we are specifying which thing or person we are talking about. We use **the** because which one we are talking about is important:
   *I bought this jacket in **the shop** next to the library.*
   (= which shop is important information)

To specify which one we are talking about, we often use a relative clause (see p. 110) after **the**:
   *I'm going to wear **the jacket** that/which I bought last week.*

3 We use **the** when it is clear what we are talking about and there are no other possibilities:
   ***The players** are coming onto **the court**.* (= the players in this match and the court for this match)

> **TIP**
> We use **a/an** before a type of job:
>   *My brother is **a doctor**.* (NOT *... is doctor.*)
>
> We use **the** for a specific job or job title that only one person has:
>   *His father is **the Managing Director** of a small company.*

A Birthday presents

Complete this description of a birthday by putting *a* or *the* into the gaps.

Last week it was my Dad's 50th birthday. In the morning ___the___⁰ postman brought him some cards and in the evening we took him for _____¹ meal in _____² restaurant. When he got up, Mum gave him _____³ very big parcel. We all wondered what was in _____⁴ parcel and when Dad opened it, we saw that it was _____⁵ new bike. Dad said that it was _____⁶ surprise and that he was very pleased with it. I bought him _____⁷ jumper and my brother gave him _____⁸ book about art. When he put _____⁹ jumper on, I could see that there was _____¹⁰ hole in it. He didn't see _____¹¹ hole because it was at _____¹² back, but I saw it. I got _____¹³ jumper from _____¹⁴ shop near here and I'm going to take it back to _____¹⁵ shop and get _____¹⁶ different one. In the afternoon, Dad went for _____¹⁷ ride on _____¹⁸ bike and then he read _____¹⁹ book from my brother. Then we went to _____²⁰ restaurant. We had _____²¹ good meal and Mum made _____²² short speech after _____²³ meal. I think Dad had _____²⁴ good day but I'm angry about _____²⁵ jumper.

B John's plans

John's parents are talking in the kitchen at home. Circle the correct articles in their conversation.

DAD   Where's John and what's he doing?
MUM   He's in a/(the)⁰ living room. He's watching a/the¹ programme on TV.
DAD   Oh, OK. What's he doing later?
MUM   He's going to see a/the² film. He's going to a/the³ cinema in Brook Street, I think. He's going to see a/the⁴ new James Bond film that came out last week.
DAD   Who's he going with?
MUM   Ah, well, he's going with a/the⁵ girl. But he doesn't want to say who a/the⁶ girl is.
DAD   It's probably a/the⁷ girl he told us about last week. You know, a/the⁸ girl he met at a/the⁹ college party last Saturday.
MUM   Ah, you're probably right. Anyway, he wants to take a/the¹⁰ car.
DAD   I suppose that's OK. He can park it in a/the¹¹ car park at the cinema.
MUM   I think he's excited about a/the¹² evening. He's even wearing a/the¹³ clean shirt!
DAD   Wow! It must be an/the¹⁴ important occasion for him!

C Restaurant questions

These are questions commonly asked by waiters and customers in restaurants. Put a tick (✓) if the article is correct and change the article if it is incorrect.

WAITER
0 Have you booked a ✓ table?
1 Would you like to leave your coats in the .... cloakroom?
2 Would you like a .... drink in the .... bar?
3 Can I recommend a .... chef's special?
4 Would you like a .... wine list?
5 Would you like a .... dessert?

CUSTOMER
0 Could I have ~~the~~ a clean knife, please?
6 Could we have the .... table for 6 people?
7 Can I see a .... menu, please?
8 Can we have a .... jug of water?
9 Could I speak to the .... manager?
10 Could I have a .... bill, please?

D My home life

Complete this blog by putting a, an or the into the gaps.

I live in a ⁰ big city in .... ¹ centre of Britain. .... ² city is called Coventry and I live in .... ³ area that is quite close to .... ⁴ city centre. I live in .... ⁵ old house in .... ⁶ quiet street. I'm .... ⁷ student at .... ⁸ local university, which is called Warwick University. .... ⁹ university is .... ¹⁰ modern one and it's .... ¹¹ good university. It has .... ¹² arts centre, which has .... ¹³ good programme of films and concerts. I'm doing .... ¹⁴ three-year course there.
My father works in .... ¹⁵ office. He's .... ¹⁶ Sales Director at .... ¹⁷ company that makes sports equipment. My mother is .... ¹⁸ nurse and she works at the new hospital that has just been built outside .... ¹⁹ city. I also have .... ²⁰ brother – he's .... ²¹ doctor and he works at .... ²² same hospital.

18 Articles
A/an, the, and no article

5 Some examples of sentences with **a/an**, **the** and **no article**:
   *That's **a nice song**.*
   *I like **the music** in that film.*
   *I like listening to **music**.*

6 We can only use **a/an** with a **countable noun**. A countable noun can have a plural form and describes something that exists in separate, individual forms:
   *Clive has **a very old car**.* ('car' is a countable noun.)

   We cannot use **a/an** with an **uncountable noun**. An uncountable noun has no plural form and describes something that does not exist in individual examples that can be 'counted' e.g.: *music, education, politics, food, water, weather, work, meat, rice, bread*
   NOT *I listened to a music.* (It is not possible to talk about different 'musics'.)

7 We can use **the** with singular and plural **countable nouns**:
   The teacher arrived and spoke to the students.

   We can use **the** with **uncountable nouns**:
   The food was good and I really liked the bread.

Grammar in action

4 We use **a/an** with countable nouns to talk about one thing or person, when many different ones exist:
   This is a vegetable.

5 We use **the** with a plural noun to talk about specific things or people:
   I like the vegetables in this dish.
   (= these particular vegetables)

We do not use an article before a plural noun when we are talking about things or people in general:
   Young children often don't like vegetables. (= young children in general and vegetables in general)

6 We use **the** with an uncountable noun to talk about a particular type or example of something:
   I put the money into my bag. (= particular money)

We do not use an article with an uncountable noun when we are talking about something in general:
   Money is a very important part of life. (= money in general and life in general)

7 **We do not use the** with:
- the names of most countries (except *the US* and *the UK*)
  She comes from Ireland and she lives in the US.
- the names of continents or languages:
  She comes from Africa. (NOT *the Africa*)
  Do you speak Spanish? (NOT *the Spanish*)
- types of music, but we can use **the** with musical instruments:
  He likes classical music. (NOT *the classical music*)
  He plays (the) saxophone in a band.
- meals, subjects for study, sports and games:
  What did you have for breakfast? (NOT *the breakfast*)
  She's very good at maths. (NOT *the maths*)
  I don't know how to play chess. (NOT *the chess*)

E Politics

WORD FOCUS
Find nouns in exercise E to complete this table:
adjective: *healthy*
noun: ....
verb: *elect*
noun: ....
verb: *employ*
noun: ....
noun: *politics*
person: ....
verb: *educate*
noun: ....

Read this short article. Put a tick (✓) if the underlined parts are correct and change them if they are incorrect.

I think that <u>politics</u> ✓ ⁰ is <u>interesting subject</u> *an interesting subject* ⁰. <u>Young people</u> ....¹ often aren't interested in <u>a subject</u> ....² but I am. In fact, I'd quite like to be <u>politician</u> ....³. At the moment in this country, <u>the subjects</u> ....⁴ that people are talking about are <u>education</u> ....⁵ and <u>health</u> ....⁶. And of course <u>the employment</u> ....⁷ is <u>big subject</u> ....⁸ too. There will be <u>an election</u> ....⁹ soon but lots of people don't vote in <u>elections</u> ....¹⁰ here. They say that they don't trust <u>politicians</u> ....¹¹ because they tell <u>the lies</u> ....¹² and they don't know anything about <u>lives</u> ....¹³ of <u>ordinary people</u> ....¹⁴. But <u>the attitudes</u> ....¹⁵ like that are wrong in my opinion. If you want to see <u>the changes</u> ....¹⁶ in the world, you have to do something. If you want the laws _____17 that the government _____18 introduces to be the good ones _____19, you have to be active. I'd like to be successful politician _____20, not because I want power _____21 but because I want the peace _____22 in world _____23 and I want to find answers _____24 to the problems _____25 that exist at the moment.

F Impressions of a new country

Tania has come to live in a new country. Complete her postcard to a friend at home about her feelings about the new country by putting *the* or — into the gaps. Put — if no article is required.

I've never been to ___the___⁰ UK before, but I've been to _____¹ France and to lots of countries in _____² Europe. There are lots of things in this country that are new to me. As you know, I like _____³ sport but _____⁴ sports they play in _____⁵ England are different. I don't understand _____⁶ cricket and I don't know much about _____⁷ rugby but I'm going to find out about them.
Some people have _____⁸ silly ideas about _____⁹ food that people eat in _____¹⁰ Britain. They don't really eat _____¹¹ fish and chips very much and they don't always have _____¹² bacon and eggs for _____¹³ breakfast. These are _____¹⁴ very old-fashioned ideas from _____¹⁵ past. These days, they eat _____¹⁶ pasta and _____¹⁷ curry and _____¹⁸ Chinese food and all kinds of things from all over the world.
I really like _____¹⁹ old buildings that they have here. I'm very interested in _____²⁰ architecture and I like reading about _____²¹ history of buildings I've visited. _____²² History is one of my favourite subjects, but I also want to learn about _____²³ culture of the country. I must say that I don't like _____²⁴ weather here. But _____²⁵ people that I've met have been nice and I've found it easy to make _____²⁶ friends. So I'm glad that I came here.

G Reader profile

This is an announcement in an international magazine. Readers who want to get into contact with other readers send their details to the magazine. Circle the correct choices.

In touch | *keeping readers connected*

This week's reader is Kathryn Hunt. Kathryn's (*a*)/*the*⁰ student at *a*/*the*¹ college in Canada, where she's studying *the*/–² Business and Economics. She wants to start *a*/–³ company that organizes *the*/–⁴ special events when she leaves college. Kathryn likes *the*/–⁵ rock music and *the*/–⁶ jazz and she often goes to *the*/–⁷ concerts. She can't play *a*/–⁸ musical instrument but she's planning to learn to play *a*/*the*⁹ trumpet! She also likes *the*/–¹⁰ reading and she particularly likes *the*/–¹¹ novels, especially *a*/–¹² crime fiction. Kathryn is *a*/*the*¹³ vegan, which means that she doesn't eat *a*/–¹⁴ meat and she also doesn't eat *the*/–¹⁵ dairy products such as *the*/–¹⁶ eggs or *a*/–¹⁷ cheese. She likes learning *the*/–¹⁸ foreign languages and at the moment she's learning *the*/–¹⁹ Mandarin in her spare time. If you want to write to Kathryn, write to *the*/–²⁰ Contacts Page of *the*/–²¹ magazine at *an*/*the*²² address below.

OVER TO YOU Now go to page 125.

19 Pronouns and possessives
Subject and object pronouns; possessive adjectives and pronouns

1 Some examples of sentences with **subject and object pronouns**:
   *I don't know **her**.*
   ***They** live near **us**.*

Some examples of sentences with **possessive adjectives and pronouns**:
   *This is **my** bag.*
   *Is this bag **yours**?*

2 We form these **pronouns** and **adjectives** in this way:

SUBJECT PRONOUN	OBJECT PRONOUN	POSSESSIVE ADJECTIVE	POSSESSIVE PRONOUN
I	me	my	mine
you	you	your	yours
he/she/it	him/her/it	his/her/its	his/hers/its
we	us	our	ours
they	them	their	theirs

***She** has lots of friends. Everybody likes **her**.*
*This isn't **my** passport. It's **yours**.*

Grammar in action

1 We use a **subject pronoun** as the subject of a verb, when it is clear which person or thing we are talking about:
   *In the shop, I spoke to an assistant. **She** (= the assistant) was helpful.*

We do not use a subject pronoun after a subject:
   NOT *An assistant she served me in the shop.*

2 We use an **object pronoun** as the object of the verb, when it is clear which person or thing we are talking about:
   *Mr Bruce is the Science teacher at school and I don't like **him**. (= Mr Bruce).*

3 We use a **possessive adjective** to talk about:
   - things that we own, such as our clothes, cars, gadgets, etc.:
     *Is this **your** coat?*
   - family members and friends:
     ***My** brother lives in Canada.*
     *Did **your** friends agree with you?*
   - parts of the body:
     *He broke **his** leg. (NOT the leg)*
   - things that are connected with us:
     *At **my** school, we have to work hard.*

4 We use a **possessive pronoun** to talk about something that belongs to us or is connected with us, without saying the noun:
   *The blue tennis racquet is **mine**. (= my racquet)*

We use a possessive pronoun when we know which thing we are referring to:
   *My computer is three years old. How old is **yours**?*
   (= your computer)

A The tourist information office

Complete this description of a job by putting in the correct subject or object pronouns.

............I............ ⁰ work in a tourist information office. Three other people work with ....¹. ....² are called Mandy, Rosemarie and Robert. Mandy is a very funny girl and ....³ always makes jokes. Rosemarie is an older woman and I don't know ....⁴ very well. Robert is a friendly man and everyone likes ....⁵ because ....⁶ 's very helpful. ....⁷ sit in seats at the counter and people come in and ask ....⁸ questions. ....⁹ try to help ....¹⁰ but sometimes ....¹¹ ask silly questions and ....¹² don't know the answers. But ....¹³ 's a good job and I enjoy ....¹⁴.

74 | Nouns, pronouns, determiners

B The good students

Two school students are talking about homework. Complete their conversation by putting in the correct possessive adjectives and possessive pronouns.

ANN   I've done _my_ ⁰ (I) homework. Have you done _____ (you)¹?
NICK Yes, I did _____ ² (I) two days ago.
ANN   What about Carl? Has he done _____ ³ (he)?
NICK I don't know. He usually does _____ ⁴ (he) late, doesn't he? He doesn't care about _____ ⁵ (he) school work.
ANN   Yes, and it's the same for Ruth.
NICK Mmm, I'm sure she hasn't done _____ ⁶ (she) yet. She's always out with _____ ⁷ (she) boyfriend.
ANN   We always try to do _____ ⁸ (we) work on time but other people don't do _____ ⁹ (they). That's why they get into trouble at school and we don't.
NICK But they probably have more fun than us.

C Childhood memories

An adult is remembering his childhood. Decide if the underlined words are correct or incorrect. Put a tick (✓) if they are correct and write the correct word if they are not.

0 My sister was born when I was 3. <u>Hers</u> _Her_ birthday is in June.
1 We didn't have a computer in <u>our</u> _____ house when I was little.
2 When he was 4 years old, my brother broke <u>his</u> _____ leg.
3 My sister and I had little bikes. <u>My</u> _____ was yellow and <u>hers</u> _____ was blue. I've still got <u>my</u> _____ .
4 My best friends were Dave and Paul. Sometimes they played at <u>my</u> _____ house and sometimes I played at <u>theirs</u> _____ .
5 My friends had nice cars but <u>our</u> _____ was very old.
6 My mother enjoyed <u>its</u> _____ job but my dad didn't like <u>his</u> _____ .

D On the plane

A group of friends are getting onto a plane. Complete what two of the friends say by putting in the correct possessive adjectives and possessive pronouns.

TOM   This is _my_ ⁰ seat, row F, seat 28.
LYNN No, it isn't, it's _____ ¹. Look, my boarding card says F28. _____ ² is number 29.
TOM   Oh yes, you're right, I didn't look at _____ ³ card properly.
LYNN Where shall we put _____ ⁴ bags?
TOM   I can put _____ ⁵ under the seat, it's only small. You can put _____ ⁶ in the overhead compartment. It's quite big but if you put it on _____ ⁷ side it should go into the compartment. Oh, have you got _____ ⁸ passports?
LYNN No, you've got them, they're in _____ ⁹ bag.
TOM   Oh yes, I forgot. Now, where are Richard and Judy? Where are _____ ¹⁰ seats?
LYNN _____ ¹¹ are at the back of the plane. He's right at the back, I think _____ ¹² seat is in row W, and _____ ¹³ is in row T. She's a couple of rows in front of him.
TOM   Why are _____ ¹⁴ seats so far away from _____ ¹⁵ ?
LYNN Well, we were a bit late checking in so we couldn't all get seats together.

WORD FOCUS

In exercise D, find words and phrases connected with aeroplanes and flying with these definitions:

A place to put luggage
_____
B line of seats
_____
C document you show before getting on a plane
_____

19 Pronouns and possessives
Reflexive pronouns; *each other*

3 Some examples of sentences using **reflexive pronouns** and **each other**:
I enjoyed **myself** at the party.
We painted the flat **ourselves**.
Pam and Fiona don't like **each other**.

4 We form **reflexive pronouns** in this way:

SUBJECT PRONOUN	REFLEXIVE PRONOUN
I	myself
you (singular)	yourself
he/she/it	himself/herself/itself
we	ourselves
you (plural)	yourselves
they	themselves

5 We use **reflexive pronouns** with certain verbs, for example:

| enjoy | hurt | teach | paint | cook |
| do | make | build | organize | |

6 We sometimes use **reflexive pronouns** in this pattern:

subject + verb + reflexive pronoun

Everyone **enjoyed themselves** last night.

7 We sometimes use **reflexive pronouns** in this pattern:

subject + verb + object + reflexive pronoun

He **cooked** the meal **himself**.

8 We use **each other** in these patterns:

verb + each other

We've **known each other** for a long time.

verb + preposition + each other

They **speak to each other** on the phone every day.

Grammar in action

5 We use a **reflexive pronoun** immediately after certain verbs, to talk about actions or experiences that only affect the subject and not other people:
Don't do that! You'll hurt yourself!
I made myself a sandwich.
(= I made it for me to eat)
Help yourself. (= take something without asking for permission)
Behave yourself. (= act in the correct way, do not do bad things)

6 We use a **reflexive pronoun** after certain verbs and an object to emphasize that the subject does or did the action, not another person or other people:
They built the cupboards themselves. (= They built them, not another person; they didn't buy them or pay someone to build them)
She paid for the ticket herself. (= She used her money; another person didn't pay for her.)

7 We use **each other** in these ways:
Bill and Sue love each other very much. (= Bill loves Sue very much and Sue loves Bill very much.)
Bill and Sue often buy presents for each other. (= He buys presents for her and she buys presents for him.)

E School prizes

The head teacher at a primary school is giving prizes to some of the children. Complete what the head teacher says by putting in the correct reflexive pronouns.

OK, the first prize today goes to Julia for this excellent picture. She painted it ......*herself*......⁰ and it took her a long time. Well done, Julia. Next, we have a prize for Carl, who ran in the 10 kilometre race last weekend. I did that ....¹ last year and I know it's not easy. Well, done, Carl. Next, a prize for Natasha and Bella. They held a party to raise money for charity and they organized it ....². We enjoyed ....³ at that party, didn't we? Good work, girls. Now, a prize for George for this fantastic model of our school. He built it ....⁴ at home and then brought it into school. It's fantastic that you built the whole thing ....⁵, George, with no help from anyone. Well done! OK, children, behave ....⁶ and stop talking. I have some information to give you.

F The new home

Sue and Tony have just moved into a new home. Sue is showing the new home to her friend Jill. Complete their conversation using the words below it and the correct reflexive pronouns.

SUE Welcome to our new home.
JILL Wow, everything looks so new. Did you _decorate it yourselves_ [0]?
SUE Yes, we _____ [1], we didn't have enough money to pay someone to do it.
JILL Was it really hard work?
SUE Yes, it was but we _____ [2].
JILL Those shelves are nice.
SUE Yes, Tony _____ [3]. It was his first time and he _____ [4] a few times while he was putting them up. But he's very pleased with the results.
JILL And the curtains? They look great.
SUE That's my work.
JILL Really? Did you _____ [5]?
SUE Yes, I didn't know how to do it, but I _____ [6] from a book and I managed to _____ [7].
JILL Wow, I'm impressed. I really envy people who can _____ [8]. I'm no good at that kind of thing.

0	decorate it	3	built them	6	taught
1	did everything	4	hurt	7	put them together
2	enjoyed	5	make them	8	do things

G Tina and Susannah's party

Tina and Susannah are having a party. Complete what Tina says to different people at the party by putting *ourselves*, *yourselves*, *themselves* or *each other* into the gaps.

0 Do you like the food? We didn't cook it _ourselves_, of course.
1 Some of my old friends are here. We don't see _____ very often so it's great to see them.
2 Do you see that couple over there? That's Fiona and Paul. I think they're arguing. They argue with _____ all the time.
3 Please help _____ to some more food, there's plenty for everyone.
4 Some of the people here don't know _____ very well but everyone's being friendly with _____.
5 I hope you like the music. We chose it _____.
6 That's Elaine over there. She's one of my best friends and we phone _____ almost every day.
7 I think this a good party and people are enjoying _____.

OVER TO YOU Now go to page 125.

Nouns, pronouns, determiners | 77

20 Quantifiers
All, most, some, a lot of, any, a few, a little

1. Some examples of sentences with these **quantifiers**:
   I bought **some fruit** in the market.
   I ate **some of the apples** and I kept **a few of them**.
   We worked hard **all day**.

2. We can use **all**, **most**, **some**, **a lot of** and **any** in these patterns:

   + noun
   I bought **some new clothes** last week.

   + of + the/possessive + noun
   You haven't eaten **any of your meal**.

   + of it/them
   We looked for a hotel but **most of them** were full.

   > **TIP**
   > It is not necessary to use 'of' after **all** with a noun but we must use 'of' before 'it/them':
   > I got all (of) the questions right. / I got all of them right.

3. We use **a few** in these patterns:

   + plural noun
   I read **a few magazines** yesterday.

   + of + the/possessive + plural noun
   A few of the people in my class do judo.

   + of them
   There were a lot of good books in the shop and I bought **a few of them**.

4. We use **a little + uncountable noun**:
   I've only got **a little money** left.

5. We use **some** with **positive verbs** and **any** with **negative verbs** and in **questions**:
   Have you got **any milk** or sugar? ~ Well, I've got **some sugar** but I haven't got **any milk**.

6. We do not use these patterns:
   the most, etc. + noun: (NOT *The most people in my class are friendly.*)
   the most, etc. of + noun: (NOT *I like the most of people in my class.*)
   most, etc. of + noun: (NOT *I like most of people in my class.*)
   In all these examples, we say *most people* or *most of the people*.

Grammar in action

1. We use **all**, **most**, **some**, **a lot of** and **any** to talk or ask about the amount or number of something when we don't give an exact amount or number:
   Have you done all (of) the ironing? ~ No, I've done most of it, but I've got some shirts to do.

2. We use the pattern **all day/morning/night/week/year**, etc. to talk about whole periods of time:
   It rained all night. (NOT *all the night*)

A Some facts about my job

Underline the correct words in what a young woman says about her job.

0   *Most/Most of* days I start at 7 a.m. but *some/some of the* days I don't start until 8 a.m.
1   I write *a lot/a lot of* reports and I've spent *most of/the most of* the day writing one.
2   Sometimes it's hard to do *all my/all of* work.
3   *Some/Some of* days are very difficult but sometimes I don't have *any/any of* problems.
4   I spend *a lot my/a lot of my* time talking on the phone.
5   I get on well with *all of/all the* people at work and *most them/most of them* are friends.
6   Sometimes I'm very busy and I don't have *any/some* lunch.
7   Sometimes I spend *all/all the* day in meetings.
8   If I don't have *any/any of* work to do, I can go home early.
9   Sometimes I have so much work to do that I can't do *all it/all of it* in a day.

B Author discussion

Bob and Terry are talking about an author and his books. Complete their conversation by putting in the missing words. Put one word in each gap.

BOB Have you read ..*any*..⁰ books by Malcolm Parker?
TERRY No, I've heard of him, but I can't remember the names of ………¹ his books. Tell me the names of some ………².
BOB *Dark Alley*, *Cold Water*, *The Long Journey* – that's a few ………³ but he's written ………⁴ of books.
TERRY Are all ………⁵ good?
BOB I think so. I'm reading *Dark Alley* at the moment. I've read most ………⁶, but I've still got ………⁷ pages to go.
TERRY I started reading that book ………⁸ weeks ago. I read a lot ………⁹, about 200 pages, but I didn't enjoy any ………¹⁰ so I gave up. I didn't like any ………¹¹ characters, I thought all ………¹² were totally unrealistic.
BOB Really? I'm enjoying it. I think he's a really good writer.

C What did you eat today?

Adam and Roger are discussing what they ate today. Complete their conversation by putting *a few*, *a little* or *a lot* into the gaps.

ADAM What did you have for breakfast?
ROGER I just had ..*a little*..⁰ cereal, I wasn't very hungry. What about you?
ADAM I had ………¹ pieces of toast – I was really hungry this morning. What did you have for lunch?
ROGER I just had ………² pasta - I don't like to have ………³ of food at lunchtime. What about you?
ADAM I had ………⁴ sandwiches and ………⁵ crisps and then I had ………⁶ chocolate, but not too much.
ROGER You eat ………⁷ of unhealthy things, don't you?
ADAM Yes, and I know I need to lose ………⁸ weight. I'm going to start by eating ………⁹ fruit and ………¹⁰ fresh vegetables instead of my usual things.

D Local information

Decide if the underlined phrases in these pieces of advice from a tourist information leaflet are correct or incorrect. If they are correct, put a tick (✓). Write the correct phrase if they are incorrect.

0 <u>Most of</u> *Most* hotels in the city stay open <u>all</u> ✓ year.
1 <u>Some</u> ………… hotels will exchange money for you.
2 The weekly tourist card can be used in <u>the most of</u> ………… the city's tourist attractions.
3 Try <u>some of the</u> ………… local specialities – you'll love them!
4 <u>The most</u> ………… restaurants offer a children's menu.
5 Public transport into and out of the city centre runs <u>all the</u> ………… night.
6 <u>All</u> ………… museums and art galleries in the city are free.
7 If you haven't been to <u>any of the</u> ………… magnificent parks, you should visit them.
8 This is a very exciting city and you should see <u>all</u> ………… it!

Nouns, pronouns, determiners

20 Quantifiers
Much, many, none, no

5 Some examples of sentences with these **quantifiers**:
She hasn't got **many friends**.
There's **no food** in the cupboard.

6 We can use **many** and **much** with **negative verbs** and in **questions**, in these patterns:

> **many + plural noun**

I don't want **many potatoes**, thanks.

> **many of + the/possessive + plural noun**

Did you know **many of the people** at the party?

> **many of + them**

There were lots of people but I didn't know **many of them**.

> **much + uncountable noun**

I haven't got **much money** at the moment.

> **much of + the/possessive + singular/uncountable noun**

I haven't read **much of this book**.
I haven't got **much of my money** left.

> **much of + it**

It's a very long book and I haven't read **much of it**.

7 We can use **no** and **none** with **positive verbs**, in these patterns:

> **no + plural/uncountable noun**

There were **no hotels** here 30 years ago.
There was **no tourism** in this area 30 years ago.

> **none of + the/possessive + plural/uncountable noun**

None of my friends wanted to come with me.
None of the food was very nice.

> **none of + them/it**

I asked my friends but **none of them** wanted to come with me.

Grammar in action

3 We use **many** to talk about a number of things, and **much** to talk about an amount of something:
I didn't take many clothes, so I didn't have much luggage.

(For questions with **how much** and **how many**, see p. 28.)

4 **no** with a **positive verb** is the same as **any** with a **negative verb**:
There are no good night clubs in this town = There aren't any good night clubs in this town.

> **TIP**
> Remember to use **none** with a **positive verb**:
> *None of the tables in the restaurant were full.* (NOT ~~weren't full~~).
>
> We use **no** (NOT ~~none~~) before a **noun**:
> *There were no people in the street.*
>
> We use **none of** (NOT ~~no of~~):
> *None of the photos are good.*

E We don't travel

Val and Eva are talking about travelling. Complete their conversation by putting in *much*, *many*, *much of*, or *many of*.

VAL Have you been to ....*many*....⁰ countries?

EVA No, I haven't done ....¹ travelling. What about you? Have you had ....² experience of travelling?

VAL No, I never have ....³ money so I don't have ....⁴ holidays. And there aren't ....⁵ places that I'd like to visit. I guess I don't have ....⁶ interest in doing that.

EVA I went to Scotland once, but I didn't see ....⁷ the country because the weather was so awful. There are lots of mountains and lakes there but I didn't see ....⁸ them.

VAL Don't they eat something called haggis there?

EVA Yes, I tried some once but I didn't like it so I didn't eat ....⁹ it.

VAL   I went to Paris once, but I didn't see _____ 10 the sights. And I didn't know _____ 11 the language so I couldn't really talk to people.

EVA   Well, I guess we're just not good travellers, are we?

VAL   No!

F My unhappy friend

Complete this description of a friend by putting in *no* or *none of*.

My friend Simon has got a lot of problems. He's at college but he's got ___*no*___ 0 friends. There are lots of people in his class but _____ 1 them like him. _____ 2 the girls want to go out with him. They say he's very rude – he's got _____ 3 manners and _____ 4 charm. He's also got _____ 5 money and _____ 6 nice clothes. I tried to give him some advice but _____ 7 it helped him. He paid _____ 8 attention to what I said and it made _____ 9 difference to him. I've got _____ 10 sympathy for him now.

WORD FOCUS

Match phrases 1–4 from exercise F to definitions A–D:
1 have manners
2 have charm
3 pay attention
4 make a difference

A listen
B be polite
C be important
D have an attractive personality

G A bad shopping trip

Complete these sentences about a shopping trip by putting in the correct words and phrases from the box. Use each of the words and phrases in the box only once.

| many | any | a lot | none | a little |
| ~~some~~ | all | most | much | no | a few |

0 I went to the shopping centre because I wanted to buy ___*some*___ clothes.
1 I need some new things because _____ my clothes are quite old now.
2 I tried on a lot of clothes but I didn't buy _____ of them.
3 I saw a lot of clothes I liked but _____ of them fitted me.
4 I couldn't buy anything expensive because I didn't have _____ money.
5 It was a quiet day and there were only _____ people in the shops.
6 I was looking for bargains but I didn't see _____ of them – only one or two cheap things.
7 I got tired because I spent _____ of time going round the shops.
8 I spent _____ of my money on other things and I only had _____ money left when I came home.
9 I was unhappy when I came home because I had _____ new clothes to wear.

OVER TO YOU   Now go to page 125.

Nouns, pronouns, determiners | 81

21 Pronouns and determiners
One, ones; another, other, others

1 Some examples of sentences with these **pronouns and determiners**:
   *I like those cars and I want **one**.*
   *We can come back here on **another** day.*
   *I couldn't go last night because I had **other** things to do.*

2 We use **one** and **the one** to refer to a singular noun:
   *Would you like a drink? ~ No, thanks, I don't want **one** (= a drink) at the moment.*
   *I was looking for a particular book but I couldn't find **the one** (= the book) I wanted.*

   We use **ones** and **the ones** to refer to a plural noun:
   *Which trousers are you going to wear? ~ My new **ones**. (= trousers)*
   *These photos are **the ones** (= the photos) I took at the wedding.*

   We can use **one** in the pattern **one of + the/possessive + plural noun**:
   One of the people in my class has left the college.
   One of my friends has gone to live in the US.

3 We use **another** with singular nouns and **other** with plural nouns:
   *Would you like **another** sandwich?*
   *She never thinks of **other** people.*

   We use **the other** and **my/your** etc. **other** with singular or plural nouns:
   *You can have **my other** sandwich.*
   The other people at the interview seemed so clever.

   We use **the other (one)** in place of a singular noun and **the others** in place of a plural noun:
   *I didn't like the beef sandwich, but I liked **the other (one)**. (= the other sandwich)*
   *One of the interviewers seemed nice. **The others** didn't. (= the other interviewers)*

Grammar in action

1 We use **one**, **the one**, **ones** and **the ones** instead of repeating a noun that has been mentioned and is therefore understood:
   Would you like to borrow my pen? ~ No, it's OK, I've got one.

2 We use **which one** and **which ones** to ask someone to specify a particular thing or particular things:
   There are lots of good hotels. Which one shall we book?

3 We use **one of** to talk about one person or thing when there are many:
   One of the flowers has died.

4 We use **another** with the meaning 'one more':
   Could I have another cup of coffee, please.

5 We use **another** and **other** with the meaning 'a different' and 'different':
   James has left the company. He's found another job.
   Have you got these shoes in other sizes?

6 We use **the other (one)** and **the others** when it is clear which thing(s) we mean:
   I've got one sock but I can't find the other one. (= the other sock)
   Two of the burglars got away. The others (= the other burglars) were arrested.

A The new bike

Nicola and Guy are talking about Guy's new bike. Complete their conversation using *one, the one, ones, the ones* or *one of*. For some gaps you must also use the word in brackets.

NICOLA That's a nice bike. Is it <u>a new one</u>⁰ (new)?
GUY Yes, my ....¹ (old) stopped working.
NICOLA Well, ...² (that) looks expensive. It's ....³ (the new) XT7 models, isn't it?
GUY No, I couldn't afford ....⁴ (those). No, ...⁵ (this) is an RP75. It was ....⁶ (only) in the shop that I liked and that I could afford.
NICOLA Really?

GUY   Yes, I looked at lots of really nice bikes, but all of .... ⁷ I wanted were too expensive for me. .... ⁸ I really wanted was the XT7 but it costs a lot.
NICOLA   Well, I've got .... ⁹ but it wasn't very expensive. I got it in a shop in the city centre.
GUY   .... ¹⁰ (which)?
NICOLA   Collier's. It's a .... ¹¹ (really good). It's got a fantastic range of bikes from .... ¹² (cheap) to .... ¹³ (very expensive). I got an XT7 there and it didn't cost too much.
GUY   Oh well, I'm happy with .... ¹⁴ I've got.

B Lots of luggage

Complete this description from a novel by putting the correct phrase from the box in each gap. Use each phrase at least once.

> another   the other   the other one   other   the others

When Chris arrived back from Greece, he was carrying a lot of luggage. He had a big suitcase in one hand and *another* ⁰ suitcase and some small bags in .... ¹ hand. And there was .... ² bag on his shoulders. When he got home, he had a cup of coffee and unpacked all the bags. The big suitcase contained all his clothes and .... ³ suitcase contained things that he bought while he was away. First of all, he took out his clothes from the big suitcase. Some of them were clean but .... ⁴ needed to be washed, so he put them in a pile on the floor. He put that suitcase away and then he unpacked .... ⁵. It contained souvenirs and .... ⁶ things from local shops in Greece. He put that bag away and then he unpacked all .... ⁷ bags. They contained presents for his family and for .... ⁸ people. He put some of them in a cupboard and he left .... ⁹ on his bed. Then he sat down and had .... ¹⁰ cup of coffee.

WORD FOCUS

Find phrases in exercise B beginning with *in* or *on* which are connected with:

A a piece of furniture
....

B part of a room
....

C a number of things on top of each other
....

D part of the body
....

C In the shoe shop

Complete this conversation in a shop by putting in the correct word or phrase, using *one*, *ones*, *another* and *other*. Put one word in each gap.

CUSTOMER   I'd like to get some boots, please. I need to get some strong *ones* ⁰.
ASSISTANT   OK, ... ¹ would you like? We have several different kinds.
CUSTOMER   I'd like .... ² in the window, the brown .... ³ called Trekkers.
ASSISTANT   OK, what size are you?
CUSTOMER   Well, ... ⁴ my feet is bigger than .... ⁵. I'll try a size 9 but I might need a 10.
ASSISTANT   OK, here's the size 9. I've also brought the size 10.
CUSTOMER   Thanks. Ah, this .... ⁶ fits OK, but .... ⁷ feels too small. Can I try .... ⁸ pair, please?
ASSISTANT   Yes, here you are.
CUSTOMER   Ah, these are fine. But they're light brown. .... ⁹ in the window are dark brown.
ASSISTANT   Oh, I'm afraid we've sold out of the dark brown .... ¹⁰. We're expecting to get some more soon. If you come back on .... ¹¹ day, we might have them.
CUSTOMER   No, it's OK, I'll take these.

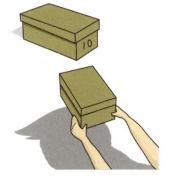

21 Pronouns and determiners
Something, everybody, nowhere, anyone, etc.

5 Some examples of sentences with these **pronouns**:
*I want to tell you **something**.*
***Everybody** knows what happened.*
*Did you eat **anything** for breakfast?*

6 We use **something**, **somebody/someone** and **somewhere** with positive verbs:
***Something** has made her unhappy.*
***Someone** phoned you while you were out.*

7 We use **everything**, **everybody/everyone** and **everywhere** with positive verbs:
***Everything** is fine at the moment.*
*I've looked **everywhere** but I can't find it.*

8 We use **nothing**, **nobody/no one** and **nowhere** with positive verbs:
*There was **nothing** in the cupboard.*
***Nobody/No one** spoke.*

9 We use **anything**, **anybody/anyone** and **anywhere** with negative verbs and in questions:
*She didn't tell **anyone**.*
*Did you find **anything** at the shops?*

Grammar in action

5 We use **something**, **somebody/someone** and **somewhere** with the meanings 'a thing', 'a person', and 'in a place'. We use these words when we are not saying, or don't know, which thing, person or place:
***Somebody** rang you, but she didn't leave a message.*

6 We use **everything**, **everybody/everyone** and **everywhere** with the meanings 'all things', 'all people', and 'in all places':
*He took **everything** out of his bag.*

7 We use **nothing**, **nobody/no one** and **nowhere** with the meanings 'no things', 'no people' and 'in no places':
***Nobody/No one** lives there.*

8 We use **anything**, **anybody/anyone** and **anywhere** with negative verbs with the meanings 'a thing', 'a person' and 'in or to a place':
*I can't see **anything** – it's very dark in here.*

9 We can use **else** in the phrases **something else**, **anybody else**, etc. with the meanings 'a different thing', 'another person', etc. Here, someone is talking to a friend in a very crowded place:
*Let's go **somewhere else**.*

10 We can use an **adjective** after **something**, **anything**, etc.:
***Something** strange is happening to me!*

D The missing notebook

Complete this conversation by putting in *something, anything,* **etc.**

ANNE You look worried. What's the problem?
TIM   I've lost ....*something*.... ⁰.
ANNE What?
TIM   My notebook. I've looked .... ¹ for it but I can't find it .... ².
ANNE Perhaps you left it .... ³ at college. Is it in your locker, for example?
TIM   No, there's .... ⁴ in my locker, it's completely empty.
ANNE Well, maybe .... ⁵ took it by accident.
TIM   No, I've asked .... ⁶ in my class but .... ⁷ has got it.

ANNE Well, there must be .... ⁸ you can do. Have you checked in all your pockets?

TIM Of course I have. Oh, just a minute, there's .... ⁹ in this pocket. I don't usually keep .... ¹⁰ in there. Ah, guess what it is!

E My news

Complete this email from Monica to her friend Sarah by putting in *something*, *anything*, etc. If there is a word in brackets, also use that word.

Hi Sarah,

I've got *something interesting* ⁰ (interesting) to tell you but you mustn't tell .... ¹ (else) because it's a secret. Clare has split up with Michael and she's seeing .... ² (new). His name's Toby and she says he's a builder, but she hasn't told me .... ³ (else) about him. That's a surprise isn't it? She didn't say .... ⁴ to me about problems with Michael before this happened and .... ⁵ (else) was expecting it to happen – we were all very surprised.

Well, apart from that, ... ⁶ (else) is normal and .... ⁷ (unusual) has happened since I last wrote to you. I haven't been .... ⁸ (exciting) and I haven't done .... ⁹ (different) from the usual routine. .... ¹⁰ is quite boring in my life. I hope .... ¹¹ (good) happens soon.

Love to .... ¹² in your family.

Monica

F Student mistakes

Antonio is a student in England, living with a host family. Correct these things he says to his host family by changing the underlined words and phrases.

0 I went to some nice shops today but I didn't buy <u>nothing</u> *anything* in them.
1 I don't want <u>nothing else</u> .... to eat, thank you.
2 I spoke in English but nobody <u>didn't understand</u> .... what I said.
3 I went to a café and I went to <u>another</u> .... places too.
4 I'm not going to go <u>nowhere</u> .... tonight, I'm going to stay here.
5 I like these biscuits more than the <u>one</u> .... we have at home.
6 I met <u>anyone</u> .... today who has been to my home town.
7 I don't usually buy a newspaper but I bought <u>a one</u> .... today.
8 We had <u>other</u> .... teacher today because our usual teacher was ill.
9 I think I said <u>wrong something</u> .... when I was in the shop.
10 <u>There isn't</u> .... nothing to watch on TV tonight.

OVER TO YOU Now go to page 126.

22 There, it, this, that, etc.
There and it

1 Some examples of sentences with **there** and **it** as the subject of a sentence or clause:
There's a hotel and there are three shops nearby.
It's very beautiful in this part of the country.

2 We always use **there** in these patterns:

> **there + be (singular/plural) + noun**

There's a big park in this area of the city.
There have been some problems at work.
There might be a lot of traffic.

> **there + be + number + of + object pronoun**

There were fifteen of us in the restaurant.

3 These are some examples of common patterns beginning with **it**:
It's nearly 5.30 p.m.   It's Friday.
It was a long way from the station to the hotel.
It won't be a sunny day tomorrow.
It's important for you to get some exercise.
It was nice of them to buy me a present.
It was good to meet/meeting you.
It's lucky that we found this hotel.

Grammar in action

1 We use **there** to say that something exists. We can use **there** to talk about something that exists physically:
There's some orange juice in the fridge.

We can also use **there** to talk about things that happen and situations:
There was an accident on the motorway.
There were no spaces in the car park.

2 We can use **there** for a number of people or things:
There are four people in my band.
There are four of us in the band. (NOT ~~We are four in the band~~ …)

3 We use **it + be** to say the time, day, month, date, etc.:
It's nearly five o' clock.

We use **it** to say a distance from one place to another:
It's 120 kilometres (from here) to Paris.

We use **it + be** or **it + verb** to talk about the weather:
It was sunny. / It was a sunny day. / It rained all day.

We can also use **there + be + noun** to talk about the weather:
There was a lot of rain here last month.

4 We use **it + be + for + me/him**, etc. **+ to infinitive** to describe someone's situation:
It was hard for him to find a job.

We use **it + be + of + me/him**, etc. **+ to infinitive** to describe someone's behaviour. In this example, the speaker is thanking someone:
It was kind of you to help me.

We use **it + be + adjective + to infinitive / -ing form** to describe feelings about experiences. Here, the speaker is meeting someone:
It's great to see/seeing you again.

We use **it + be + adjective + that** … to give opinions about situations:
It's obvious that he's angry.

A   Postcard from Venice

Anita is visiting Venice. Circle the correct words in her postcard to a friend.

Greetings from Venice. *There's/(It's)* ⁰ really good to be here and I'm enjoying myself. *There's/It's* ¹ a good time of year to come to this place because *there aren't/it isn't* ² many tourists. *There are/It's* ³ so many things I want to see here, but *there/it* ⁴ won't be possible to see all of them because *there/it* ⁵ isn't enough time. *There's/It's* ⁶ lunchtime now and I'm writing this outside a café. The weather hasn't been very good. *There/It* ⁷ hasn't been much sunshine, *there's/it's* ⁸ been mostly cloudy, but *there/it* ⁹ hasn't rained and *there's/it's* ¹⁰ quite warm. *There's/It's* ¹¹ interesting to sit here and watch all the people go by. *There's/It's* ¹² a very good atmosphere in this place and I'm glad I came.

86 | Nouns, pronouns, determiners

B Let's go to the cinema

Bill and Eric are discussing what to do. Complete their conversation by putting *there* or *it* into the gaps.

BILL   What shall we do this afternoon? __It__ ⁰ 's boring sitting here with nothing to do.
ERIC   Well, _____¹ 's a new film on at the cinema called *Red Alert*.
BILL   Mmm, _____² 's been a few weeks since I saw a film. Is it any good?
ERIC   Well, _____³ 's a good review of it in today's paper. It starts at 5 p.m.
BILL   OK, let's go and see it. What time is _____⁴ now?
ERIC   _____⁵ 's just after 4 p.m.
BILL   Well, _____⁶ 's not far to the cinema. _____⁷ 's plenty of time for us to get there.
ERIC   OK, we'll go.

C Good neighbours!

In this description of some neighbours, decide if the underlined words and phrases are correct or incorrect. If they are correct, put a tick (✓). If they are incorrect, write the correct word or phrase in the gap.

~~It's~~ __There's__ ⁰ a group of students who live in the house next to mine. They are six _____¹ and they are all studying to be doctors. It's _____² always parties at that house and it's _____³ always very noisy when they have a party. There's _____⁴ impossible to sleep and it's _____⁵ annoying for the neighbours. But there's _____⁶ great for me. They always invite me to their parties and I really enjoy them. It's _____⁷ lots of people at those parties and it's _____⁸ always music and dancing.

D Thanks for inviting me, but …

Jack's friend Steve has invited Jack to stay with him at his house. Complete Jack's email to Steve using the words below to fill each gap. Use short forms of verbs if possible.

__It was great to hear__ ⁰ from you and _____¹ me to come and stay with you. However, _____² in June. _____³ a conference that month and I have to go to it. _____⁴ have to go there at that time but it's a very big event. _____⁵ from my company at the conference. _____⁶ someone to go instead of me and so _____⁷ to you. I'm sorry about that. _____⁸ won't be able to see each other then. _____⁹ any other dates when I could come? _____¹⁰ some time with you. Please let me know.

0 was great/hear
1 was very good/you/invite
2 will be difficult/me/come
3 is
4 is unfortunate/I
5 will be /five
6 is too late/me/find
7 is impossible/me/come
8 is a pity/we
9 are
10 is always great/spend

22 There, it, this, that, etc.
This, that, these, and those

4 Some examples of sentences with **this**, **that**, **these** and **those**:
   I like **this** jacket but I don't like **that** one.
   These suits are cheap but **those** are very expensive.

5 We use **this** and **that** in these patterns:

   this/that + singular/uncountable noun

   I like **this** café but I don't like **that** music they're playing.

   this/that (pronoun)

   Have you done **this** before?
   I've already explained **that**.

6 We use **these** and **those** in these patterns:

   these/those + plural noun

   These flowers are nice and **those** trees are beautiful.

   these/those (pronoun)

   I've received a lot of emails. I've replied to **these** but I haven't read **those** yet.

   one of these/those (+ plural noun)

   She lives in **one of these** houses, but I'm not sure which one.
   Could I have **one of those**, please?

Grammar in action

5 We use **this** and **these** to talk about something that is physically near or in front of us when we are speaking, and **that** and **those** to talk about something that is a distance away when we are speaking:
   I'm really enjoying **this** book. (The speaker is holding a book.)
   Could you bring me **that** book, please? (The speaker is pointing to a book.)

6 We use **this**, **that**, **these** and **those** as pronouns with the meaning 'this/that thing/person/place' or 'these/those things/people/places'. Here, someone is holding a friend's book:
   Can I borrow **this**? ~ No, you can't borrow **that**, I haven't finished it yet.

7 We use **this** and **these** with a noun or as a pronoun to talk about things that exist or happen in the present, and **that** and **those** to talk about things that existed or happened before now:
   This is going to be a wonderful meal. It looks delicious.
   That was a fantastic meal. I really enjoyed it.

   These problems are difficult to solve.
   Those people behind us at the cinema last night were making a lot of noise.

8 We use **that** and **those** with a noun to refer to something that has been mentioned before:
   I like Wales. ~ I've never been to **that** country.
   I met Sam and Robin. ~ I don't know **those** people.

9 We use **that** as a pronoun to refer to something that has been mentioned before, with the meaning 'that fact' or 'that situation':
   Dave is leaving the company. ~ Oh, I didn't know **that**.

10 We use **that** and **those** with a noun to refer to things and people without identifying them specifically or saying what their names are:
   He's married to **that** woman who drives a big red car.
   She always buys **those** magazines that have lots of gossip about celebrities in them.

11 We use **one of these/those** to refer to one thing or person when there are many. Here, someone has chosen something in a shop:
   I'd like to buy **one of those** watches, please.

E   In the art gallery

A guide is talking to a group of visitors on a tour of an art gallery. Complete what he says, using *this*, *that*, *these* or *those*.

OK, now ___this___⁰ painting that we're now standing next to is one of the most famous paintings in the gallery. It's been in _____¹ gallery for over 100 years and people come from all over the world to see it. It's called *Sunrise*. The artist painted lots of wonderful scenes, but _____² is my personal favourite. Look at all _____³ details here, they're wonderful. In fact, in _____⁴ section of the gallery, there are many of his best paintings. _____⁵ are all from his early period and I like _____⁶ paintings more than any others of his. Now, if you look at _____⁷ painting over there, on the opposite wall, you'll see that it has a totally different style. In fact, all of _____⁸, on _____⁹ wall, are from his later period. _____¹⁰ is called *Mechanics* by the way. Anyway, I'll talk about some of _____¹¹ paintings when we get there, but before that let's concentrate on _____¹², because it's a truly great work of art.

F The train journey

Caroline and Lucy are on a train journey. Complete their conversation by putting *this*, *that*, *these*, or *those* into the gaps.

CAROLINE   ...This...⁰ journey is quite boring, isn't it?
LUCY   Yes, _____¹ trains are quite slow. But if you take one of _____² fast trains that only take two hours, it's quite expensive.
CAROLINE   Yes, I know _____³.
LUCY   Still, _____⁴ seats are OK, aren't they?
CAROLINE   Yes, they are. But I'm bored.
LUCY   Well, read _____⁵. I've finished reading it now and it's a good magazine. Here, you can have it.
CAROLINE   No, I don't want _____⁶. Where are _____⁷ biscuits we bought at the station?
LUCY   We ate _____⁸ when we got onto the train.
CAROLINE   Oh yes, I'd forgotten about _____⁹.
LUCY   Here, have one of _____¹⁰ sweets, they're very nice.
CAROLINE   No, I don't like _____¹¹, they're horrible. I think I'll go to the buffet car and buy some of _____¹² chocolate I really like.
LUCY   Yes, _____¹³ is a good idea. Could you get me some of _____¹⁴ too? And some more of _____¹⁵ sweets, I've nearly finished _____¹⁶.
CAROLINE   OK, I'll go in a minute.

G Competition announcement

Complete this announcement by a TV presenter about a competition by putting *there*, *it*, *this* or *that* into the gaps.

OK, ...this...⁰ is the moment you've all been waiting for – _____¹ is now competition time. _____² is a fantastic prize for the winner, and _____³ is it – the TB6 multi-media unit that you can see on your screen now. OK, to win this fantastic prize, _____⁴ is just one question that you have to answer and _____⁵ is the question: Where were the first TV broadcasts made? OK, _____⁶ was the question, and if you can answer it, _____⁷ is easy to enter the competition. _____⁸ is the number you need – 345231. _____⁹ won't be expensive to call, as local rates will apply. I'm sure that _____¹⁰ will be many thousands of entries for this competition and I'll announce the winner next week. Good luck!

WORD FOCUS

When the presenter says *'local rates will apply'*, he/she is talking about:

A the place where the competition is happening.

B the number of people who enter the competition.

C the cost of phoning to enter the competition.

OVER TO YOU   Now go to page 126.

23 Comparison of adjectives
Comparative adjectives

1 Some examples of sentences with **comparative adjectives**:
   His wife is **older** than him.
   The weather is **better** today.
   My sister is **more intelligent** than me.

2 We form **comparative adjectives** in this way:

   short adjectives (with one syllable):
   ▶ add **-er**

   high → high**er**   small → small**er**

   short adjectives ending with one vowel and one consonant (except 'w'):
   ▶ double the consonant and add **-er**

   big → bi**gg**er   hot → ho**tt**er   low → low**er**

   short adjectives ending with **-e**:
   ▶ add **-r**

   nice → nice**r**   late → late**r**

   long adjectives (with two or more syllables):
   ▶ **more** + adjective

   useful → **more** useful
   interesting → **more** interesting

   adjectives ending with **-y**:
   ▶ change to **-ier**

   dirty → dirt**ier**   easy → eas**ier**

   irregular adjectives:

   good → better   bad → worse
   far → farther/further

3 We often use this pattern to compare:

   comparative adjective + than

   My new car is **faster than** my old one.
   This question is **more difficult than** the others.

Grammar in action

1 We use **comparative adjectives** to say that two or more things or people are different in a way.

   We can use comparative adjectives to give facts and opinions:
   Nathan is taller than Carl.
   I like that painting but I think this one is better.

2 When we are comparing people, we often use an object pronoun (*me*, *him*, etc.) after **than**:
   Clare was happier than me about the news.

   When we are comparing things belonging to people, we often use a possessive pronoun (*mine*, *yours*, etc.) after **than**:
   Dave's car is smaller than mine.

> **TIP**
> We can use **get** with a **comparative adjective** to talk about a change. To emphasize that a change continues to happen, we sometimes repeat the comparative adjective:
> She got angrier and angrier/more and more upset.

A Possessions

Clive is talking about his possessions. Complete what he says, using the comparative forms of the adjectives in brackets.

0 My bike's quite slow and I want to get a ___faster___ (fast) one.
1 I want to get a _____ (expensive) camera than the one I've got.
2 I've got an old computer and I want one that's _____ (modern).
3 My games console is OK but I want a _____ (good) one.
4 I'd really like to have a _____ (nice) guitar.
5 My phone isn't very good and I want a _____ (advanced) one.
6 I need new exercise equipment because I want to get _____ (fit).
7 My music system is getting _____ (bad) and I need a new one.
8 I want a car that's _____ (powerful) than the one I've got.

B Which film?

Alice and Brenda are discussing which film to see. Complete their conversation using the comparative forms of the adjectives in brackets. Sometimes you must also use *than*.

ALICE   I want to see *Moonlight*, I think it'll be _more exciting than_ ⁰ (exciting) *Dark Woods*.
BRENDA Yes, but it'll be _____ ¹ (scary). And you get _____ ² (frightened) me in horror films, don't you?
ALICE   That's true. You're _____ ³ (brave) me, and you're always _____ ⁴ (calm).
BRENDA I think we should see *Dark Woods*. The reviews say that it's _____ ⁵ (funny) *Moonlight*.
ALICE   Yes, but *Moonlight* is _____ ⁶ (popular), everyone's talking about it.
BRENDA I know, but it'll be _____ ⁷ (easy) to get tickets for *Dark Woods*. _____ ⁸ (Few) people want to see it.
ALICE   But I think *Moonlight* will be _____ ⁹ (entertaining).
BRENDA OK, we'll see *Moonlight*.

C Comparing Tom and me

David is talking about his schoolfriend Tom. Complete his comparative sentences, using a comparative adjective and an object pronoun or a possessive pronoun.

0 He's not very tall. I am.   I'm _taller than him_.
1 He's good at maths. I'm not.   He's _____.
2 He lives in a big house. I don't.   My house is _____.
3 His family is rich. My family isn't.   His family is _____.
4 He lives near the school. I don't.   He lives _____.
5 He wears very fashionable clothes. I don't.   His clothes are _____.
6 I'm quite thin. He isn't.   I'm _____.
7 His parents are quite young. My parents aren't. His parents are _____.

WORD FOCUS

Which of the adjectives in exercise D describes something that causes someone to be unhappy?

_____

Which of the adjectives in exercise D describes a feeling of unhappiness?

_____

D Working at home

Complete this text about working at home, using the comparative forms of the adjectives in brackets. Sometimes you must also use *than*.

Some people say that working at home is _better than_ ⁰ (good) going out to work. They say that people who work at home are _____ ¹ (free), their hours are _____ ² (flexible) and they are able to live _____ ³ (relaxed) lives. They're _____ ⁴ (happy) people who work in offices, and if they want, they can be _____ ⁵ (lazy) too.
But other people say that working at home can be _____ ⁶ (difficult) going out to work. They say that for some people, working at home is _____ ⁷ (stressful). People who do it are _____ ⁸ (lonely) people who can talk to colleagues at work, and they also have to be _____ ⁹ (organized).
Working at home instead of going out to work is getting _____ and _____ ¹⁰ (common) in many parts of the world. But it doesn't suit everyone.

23 Comparison of adjectives
As … as; superlative adjectives

4 Some examples of sentences with **as … as**:
I'm not **as clever as** you.
I don't spend **as much money as** him.

5 We can use **(not) as … as** for comparing in these patterns:

> **(not) as + adjective + as**

My computer **is(n't) as good as** yours.

> **(not) as much + uncountable noun + as**

I **(don't) earn as much money as** Anna.

> **(not) as many + plural noun + as**

I **(don't) buy as many clothes as** Anna.

6 Some examples of sentences with **superlative adjectives**:
This is **the oldest** building in the city.
That's **the worst** meal I've ever had!
He is **the most popular** singer in this country.

7 We form **superlative adjectives** in this way:

short adjectives (with one syllable):
▶ add **-est**

> high → the high**est**   small → the small**est**

short adjectives ending with one vowel and one consonant (except 'w'):
▶ double the consonant and add **-est**

> big → the b**iggest**   hot → the hot**test**

short adjectives ending with **-e**:
▶ add **-st**

> nice → the nice**st**   late → the late**st**

long adjectives (with two or more syllables):
▶ **the most** + adjective

> useful → **the most** useful
> interesting → **the most** interesting

adjectives ending with **-y**:
▶ change to **-iest**

> easy → the eas**iest**

irregular adjectives

> good → the **best**   bad → the **worst**
> far → the **farthest/furthest**

Grammar in action

3 We use **as + adjective + as** to say that things or people are the same or not the same in a way:
I'm not **as strong as** him.

We use **as + much/many + as** to say that amounts or numbers are the same or not the same. Here, two people are in an airport:
I'm carrying **as many bags as** you.
I'm carrying **as much luggage as** you are.

4 We use a **superlative adjective** with the meaning 'more … than all others'. For example, 'the most expensive tickets' = 'more expensive than all other tickets':
Harry is **the tallest** person in the team.

E Comparing you and me

Helen is talking to her friend Clare and comparing herself with Clare. Complete the rewritten comparisons, using as … as.

0 Your family is big. My family isn't. → My family *isn't as big as* yours.
1 Your watch was very expensive. My watch wasn't. → My watch ……………………… yours.
2 You do a lot of work. I do a lot of work too. → I ……………………… you.
3 You've got lots of qualifications. I haven't. → I ……………………… you.
4 You're very brave. I'm not. → I ……………………… you.
5 You're happy. I'm happy too. → I ……………………… you.

6 You earn a lot of money. I don't. → I .... you.
7 Your bike is very good. My bike isn't. → My bike .... yours.
8 You go to lots of parties. I don't. → I .... you.

F Interview with a travel writer

Complete the questions asked in an interview with a travel writer, using superlative forms of the adjectives in brackets.

0 What's ....*the best*.... (good) place you've ever been to?
1 Tell me about .... (exciting) trip you've ever made.
2 What do you think is .... (beautiful) place you've visited?
3 Which hotel is .... (nice) one you've ever stayed in?
4 What are .... (difficult) parts of your job?
5 What's .... (funny) thing that's ever happened to you?
6 Which city is .... (clean) and which one is .... (dirty)?
7 Tell me about .... (hot) place you have ever been to and .... (cold) place.
8 What's .... (bad) experience you've ever had on your travels?
9 What's .... (interesting) thing that's happened to you?
10 Which country has .... (friendly) people, in your opinion?

G The company I work for

Adam is talking about his job. Complete what he says, using the words in brackets in the correct comparative or superlative forms and patterns.

This year I got a new job, and my new job is ....*better than*.... ⁰ (good) my old one. I now work for .... ¹ (big) company in this area, and my company is .... ² (successful) any other company in our industry. Our products are .... ³ (popular) the ones other companies sell and other companies don't have .... ⁴ (employees) us. This year was .... ⁵ (good) year in the company's history. Our sales were .... ⁶ (high) last year and the company is getting .... and .... ⁷ (big).

My job is .... ⁸ (interesting) job I've ever had. My office is .... ⁹ (far) from my home than my previous one, so my journey to work is .... ¹⁰ (long), but my previous job was not .... ¹¹ (challenging) this one and I didn't earn .... ¹² (money) I earn now. I'm very happy now. My colleagues are .... ¹³ (nice) people I've ever met and I'm working for .... ¹⁴ (fine) company in this area.

OVER TO YOU Now go to page 126.

24 Adverbs
Adverbs of manner; comparison of adverbs

1. Some examples of sentences with **adverbs of manner**:
   *She smiled **happily**.*
   *The children played **quietly**.*

2. We form adverbs in this way:

   most adjectives
   ▶ add **-ly**:

   | quick → quick**ly**   careful → careful**ly** |

   adjectives ending with **-y**:
   ▶ change to **-ily**

   | eas**y** → eas**ily** |

   adjectives ending with **-ble**:
   ▶ change to **–bly**

   | comforta**ble** → comforta**bly** |

   irregular adverbs:

   | good → **well**   fast → **fast**   hard → **hard** |
   | late → **late** |

   > Some common adverbs of manner are:
   > slowly quickly badly happily efficiently
   > angrily carefully correctly

3. Some examples of sentences with **comparative adverbs**:
   *Try to do your work **more carefully** in future.*
   *You work **harder** than me.*

4. We form **comparative adverbs** in this way:

   | more + adverb (+ than) |

   *She works **more efficiently than** him.*

   Some very common **comparative adverbs** are irregular:

   | well → **better**   fast → **faster** |
   | hard → **harder**   late → **later** |

   *She cooks **better than** me.*
   *They arrived **later than** me.*

5. We can also make comparisons in this pattern:

   | (not) as + adverb + as |

   *I **don't** learn things **as quickly as** you.*
   *I **can** cook **as well as** her.*

Grammar in action

1. We use **adverbs of manner** with verbs to describe how someone or something does an action:
   I didn't write the address clearly and I couldn't read it.

2. We use **comparative adverbs** to talk about doing things in a different way:
   You should cycle more carefully.

   We use **comparative adverbs + than** to compare how people and things do actions and to say that they are different. We can compare how we do something with how a friend does something, for example:
   Lana can run faster than me.

3. We use **as + comparative adverb + as** to compare how people and things do actions and to say that they are or are not the same:
   I can draw as well as Tony but I can't paint as well as him.

A School report

Complete this school report by Julie's teacher by forming the correct adverbs from the adjectives in brackets.

Julie is an excellent member of the class. She does all her work ___quietly___ ⁰ (quiet) and _____ ¹ (efficient) and she checks it all _____ ² (careful) before handing it in. She always comes to school _____ ³ (punctual) and she never arrives _____ ⁴ (late) for a class. She works _____ ⁵ (good) with the other members of the class and she learns _____ ⁶ (quick). She speaks to her teachers _____ ⁷ (polite) and she concentrates _____ ⁸ (hard) when she is in class. In my opinion, she will pass her exams at the end of the year _____ ⁹ (easy), and she will complete her studies very _____ ¹⁰ (successful).

B Our horrible boss

Complete this description of a boss by putting in the adverb forms of the correct adjectives from the box.

> quick   easy   ~~bad~~   secret   late   good   busy   incorrect   nervous
> angry   immediate

Our boss behaves ____badly____ ⁰ at work. He doesn't treat us _____ ¹ and he often shouts at us _____ ². When he comes to speak to us, we look at each other _____ ³, because we think he's going to tell us off. He likes to see that we are working _____ ⁴, because he always wants us to complete every piece of work very _____ ⁵. If we do something _____ ⁶, we get into bad trouble with him and he often makes us work _____ ⁷ without extra pay. We talk about him _____ ⁸ and he doesn't know we call him 'The Monster'. We'd all like to leave this company _____ ⁹ but we can't find other jobs _____ ¹⁰, so we have to stay.

C The tennis match

Complete this newspaper report of a tennis match by putting in the comparative adverb forms of the adjectives in brackets. You may also need to use *than*.

Lewis through to final

Lewis was very nervous at the beginning of the match. Franklin started the match ____more calmly____ ⁰ (calm) and was playing _____ ¹ (good) him. He was hitting the ball _____ ² (hard) Lewis and he was running around the court _____ ³ (fast). But after a while, Lewis started to play _____ ⁴ (confident) and to hit the ball _____ ⁵ (accurate). The crowd began to support him _____ ⁶ (loud) and he began to score points _____ ⁷ (easy) Franklin. Lewis started to play _____ ⁸ (impressive) as the game continued and he hit some very good shots. Franklin started to behave _____ ⁹ (unpleasant) and he shouted at the umpire several times. Lewis played _____ ¹⁰ (intelligent) him and finally won an easy victory.

D Comparing Laura and Wendy

Laura and Wendy often disagree. Complete Wendy's replies to what Laura says about her, using the correct adverbs.

0 You're a dangerous driver. ~ I don't drive ____as dangerously____ as you.
1 You wear fashionable clothes. ~ I don't dress _____ you.
2 You're a good piano player. ~ I don't play the piano _____ you.
3 You're a careful planner. ~ I don't plan things _____ you.
4 You're a clear speaker. ~ I don't speak _____ you.
5 You're a healthy eater. ~ I don't eat _____ you.

24 Adverbs
Adverbs of degree

6 Some examples of sentences with **adverbs of degree**:
   I'm **extremely** tired.
   It was a **fairly** good result.
   I feel **much** better today.
   She's **a lot** older than him.

7 We use an **adverb of degree** before an adjective or adverb:
   I was **very/extremely/really** excited.
   We played **very** badly.
   That idea is **completely/absolutely/totally** stupid!
   The tickets were **fairly** expensive.
   He finished his work **quite** quickly.

We can also use an **adverb of degree** before an adjective and a noun:
   It was a **fairly/very** interesting book.

But we use the pattern **quite + a/an + adjective + noun**:
   It's **quite an interesting book**.

8 We use the adverbs **much**, **far**, **a lot** and **a bit** to make comparisons in this pattern:

> much / far / a lot / a bit + comparative adjective / comparative adverb (+ than)

Your computer is **much more expensive than** mine.
Jack is a good player but Dave is **far / a lot better**.
Try to do your work **a bit more carefully** in future.

Grammar in action

4 We use **very**, **extremely**, **really** to make adjectives and adverbs stronger:
   His clothes were **very/extremely/really** dirty.
   They played **extremely** well.

We use **completely**, **absolutely**, **totally** for emphasis, with the meaning 'very, very' or 'as … as possible':
   The dustbin was **completely/absolutely/totally** full.

We use **fairly**, **quite** with the meaning 'not very':
   His hair is fairly/quite long.
   She's got a fairly big dog. / She's got quite a big dog.

5 We use **much**, **far**, **a lot** with comparative adjectives and adverbs to say that the difference between people, things or actions is very big:
   Your room is **much/far/a lot** tidier than mine.
   You can run **much** faster than me.

We use **a bit** with comparative adjectives and adverbs to say that the difference between people, things or actions is not very big:
   This saucepan is **a bit** bigger than that one.
   He's doing his work **a bit** more efficiently now.

E Martin's holiday

Martin has been on holiday. Complete what he tells his friends about it by putting in suitable adverbs of degree. Sometimes more than one adverb is suitable in a gap.

0 I've just had an ......*extremely*...... pleasant holiday. It was great!
1 The weather was .... nice but it wasn't wonderful.
2 It got .... cold in the evenings and I had to put on lots of warm clothes.
3 The hotel was .... a long way from the beach and it took a .... long time to get there.
4 The beach was .... nice and I had a wonderful time there.
5 I went to the beach .... frequently but there were lots of days when I didn't go there.
6 Local people spoke to me .... politely and treated me .... well – they were lovely.
7 I was .... amazed by some of the wonderful things I saw.
8 It was an .... fantastic holiday – the best I've ever had.

Adjectives and adverbs

F Job candidates

Bella and Lisa have interviewed candidates applying for a job at their company. Complete their conversation using the words in brackets.

BELLA Well, those interviews lasted _much longer than_ ⁰ (much/long) I was expecting.
LISA True, and the candidates were ....¹ (lot/young) the people we saw yesterday.
BELLA Well, I thought Frank Spencer was ....² (far/good) Edith Green.
LISA Really, I thought Edith was ....³ (bit/suitable) Frank.
BELLA Well, she is ....⁴ (bit/old) him.
LISA Yes, and she's ....⁵ (much/experienced).
BELLA But Frank spoke ....⁶ (far/confident) her.
LISA That's true. But she thought about her answers ....⁷ (bit/careful) him.
BELLA Yes, but Frank seemed to be ....⁸ (much/ambitious). And he seemed ....⁹ (lot/keen) to work for us.
LISA Well, I'd be ....¹⁰ (much/happy) if we chose Edith. Let's discuss it again later.

WORD FOCUS

Which of the adjectives in brackets has these meanings?

A very interested in doing something
....

B having the required qualities
....

C wanting to be very successful
....

G In the library

Complete this story by putting in the correct words from the box.

> more   quite   absolutely   far   well
> silently   lot   hard   ~~extremely~~   bit
> slowly   fairly   quickly

It was _extremely_ ⁰ quiet in the library. Everybody was sitting ....¹ and working ....² on their studies. I was walking ....³ to some shelves to look for a book when someone said 'Pssst!' I looked round and I was ....⁴ amazed to see Don. 'I thought you were in South America', I said. 'No, I've been back for ....⁵ a long time,' he said. 'Oh, what happened?' I asked. 'Well, things didn't go ....⁶,' he said. 'I had a ....⁷ good job when I first went there, but I lost it and things became ....⁸ more difficult for me. So I came home as ....⁹ as I could. I've had a bad time, but things are a ....¹⁰ better now and I'm very happy.' 'Let's meet a ....¹¹ later,' I said, 'and you can tell me all about it. Meet me at the entrance to the building in 20 minutes. We can speak ....¹² easily if we're not in here.'

OVER TO YOU   Now go to page 126.

25 Prepositions (1очно)
Prepositions of place

1 **In**, **at**, and **on** are the most common **prepositions of place**: words we use to say where something or someone is.
>I was **in** the garden when you phoned.
>I'll be **at** home from seven this evening.
>The keys are **on** the kitchen table.

2 Here are some more examples of **prepositions of place**:

>I was **outside** the building.
>I could see people **inside** it.
>Your keys are **under** the table.

>There were clouds **above** us.
>A man in a suit was sitting **next to/beside** me and a girl was sitting **opposite** me.
>There's a tree **in front of** the house.

>The drummer was **behind** the other musicians.
>We live **near (to)** the sea.
>The sugar is **between** the tea and the coffee.

Grammar in action

1 We use **in** with streets, cities, districts and regions and countries:
>She lives in Roland Street / in Oxford / in England.

We use **in the** with regions (the north, etc.):
>They live in the south of Spain.

We use **at** with addresses:
>I live at 47, George Street.

2 We use **in the** with rooms:
>in the kitchen / in the toilet

We use **in a/the/my**, etc. with other enclosed places:
>in an envelope / in the cupboard / in my pocket

We use **on the** with surfaces:
>on the floor / on the ceiling / on the pavement

We use **on the** second **floor**, etc. to talk about part of a building:
>My flat is on the third floor.

3 We use **at home**, **at work**, **at school**, **at university** to talk about being in the place where we live, work, or study:
>I was at work / at home yesterday.
>Jane is at university and she's taking her exams soon.

But we say **in hospital**, **in prison** to talk about being a patient or prisoner in the place:
>Jack is very ill and he's in hospital.

> **TIP** Notice that we do not say ~~at the work~~, ~~at the school~~, etc. with this meaning.

4 We use **at the** to describe being in or using a building:
>Some friends met me at the airport.
>You can buy this at the supermarket.

A Where I work

An office worker describes the place where she works. Complete her description by putting in the correct prepositions.

I work ....in....⁰ Cardiff, which is the capital city of Wales. It's ....¹ the south of Wales. The place where I work is ....² the centre of the city. To be exact, it's ....³ 526, Broad Street. My office is ....⁴ the 12th floor of a big office block. When I'm ....⁵ work, I usually stay ....⁶ my office doing my work on my computer. ....⁷ my desk, I've got my computer, some photos of my family, and various other things. I also keep a lot of things ....⁸ the drawers of my desk and ....⁹ a cupboard. I usually have lunch ....¹⁰ the office canteen – the food is really good there.

B Party in my street

Complete this description of a party by putting in the correct prepositions from the box.

> in front   under   inside   behind   near   above   outside   ~~opposite~~   next

There was a party going on at the house __opposite__ ⁰ ours. When I looked at the windows, I could see that there were lots of people _____ ¹ the house. There were also lots of people _____ ² it, in the street. Some of them were talking and some of them were dancing. Someone had put an enormous pair of speakers in the little garden _____ ³ of the house and loud music was coming from them. _____ ⁴ to the speakers, there was a barbecue. Someone was standing _____ ⁵ the barbecue cooking food and smoke was rising into the air _____ ⁶ the barbecue. It's very difficult to sleep when there's so much noise happening _____ ⁷ to you. I put my head _____ ⁸ the covers but I couldn't sleep.

C Meeting Nikki

Marie is on the phone to her friend Linda. Complete their conversation by putting in the correct prepositions. Also use *the* when it is required.

MARIE   Yesterday, while I was __at the__ ⁰ supermarket, I met Nikki. I didn't see her at first because she was standing _____ ¹ me in the queue. A voice said 'Hi, Marie' and I turned round and it was her.

LINDA   Really? I thought she was _____ ² university in Paris. What's she doing here?

MARIE   Well, she's living _____ ³ home again now. She gave up her course. It's a long story, but she's had a lot of bad luck. She was _____ ⁴ hospital for two weeks and then she decided to come home.

LINDA   What was the problem?

MARIE   Well, she fell over something _____ ⁵ pavement and hurt her head.

LINDA   Oh, dear. So is she going to stay _____ ⁶ this town now?

MARIE   She's not sure. At the moment she's working _____ ⁷ a shop.

LINDA   Which one?

MARIE   The clothes shop _____ ⁸ ground floor of that new building _____ ⁹ State Street.

D0

D1

D2

D Holiday photos

Brian has been on a trip to a city in another country. He is showing his photos to a friend. Complete what he says about each photo using the correct prepositions.

0 This is me __in__ our hotel room.
1 I took this _____ the airport when we arrived.
2 These are some people sitting _____ a café.
3 This is John with his hands _____ his pockets.
4 This is a painting _____ the ceiling of a church.
5 This is me standing _____ one of the bridges.
6 This is John standing _____ a famous statue.
7 This is a picture of the city from a hill _____ it.
8 That's our hotel _____ those two tall buildings.

D3

D5

D7

D4

D6

D8

Prepositions | 99

25 Prepositions (1)
Prepositions of movement

3 Look at the pictures and read the sentences about **movement**:

He walked **out of** his house.
He got **into** his car.
He drove **across** the bridge. / He drove **over** a river.

He drove **under** a bridge.
He drove **through** a tunnel.
He drove **along** the motorway.

He drove **up** a hill.
He drove **down** the hill.
He drove **round** the corner.

He drove **onto** a ferry.
He drove **off** the ferry.
He drove **towards** the city.

He drove **past** some hotels.
He drove **to** the airport.
He parked **between** two buses.

Grammar in action

5 We use these phrases to talk about **transport and travelling**:

> **by car/train/plane/boat/bike/bus/taxi**

I go to work by car.
We went home by bus.

> **on foot**

I decided to go on foot because I didn't want to drive.

> **in the/my**, etc. **car**

We went to the station in the car/in our car.

> **on my**, etc. **bike**

He goes to work on his bike.

> **on the train/plane/boat/bus**

She travelled to London on the train.

> **in a taxi**

She went there in a taxi.

E   My journey to work

An office worker is describing her journey from home every morning. Complete her description by putting in the correct prepositions. You may need to use the same preposition more than once.

I walk ___to___ ⁰ work every day. Most of the people I work with go _____ ¹ car, but I prefer to go _____ ² foot, because it's healthier. I come _____ ³ the door of

100 | Prepositions

my apartment and then I take the lift _____⁴ to the ground floor. I walk _____⁵ my apartment block and then I go _____⁶ the road to the corner. I walk _____⁷ the corner and then I go _____⁸ a shopping centre until I reach the other side of it. Then I come _____⁹ some traffic lights. I go _____¹⁰ the road to the other side. Then I reach a bridge that goes _____¹¹ the main road. I go _____¹² the steps and _____¹³ the bridge. At the other side of the bridge is my office building. I go _____¹⁴ the building _____¹⁵ the main entrance. And then I start work.

F Travelling every day

Different people describe the way they travel to and from work every day. Decide if the underlined parts of each sentence are correct or incorrect. If they are correct, put a tick (✓) and if they are incorrect, write the correct word or phrase. There may be more than one possible answer.

0 I always go to work in car _by car/in the car/in my car_.
1 It's quicker for me to get to work on my bike _____.
2 When I work late, I sometimes go home by a taxi _____.
3 When I'm on the train _____ home from work, I sometimes fall asleep.
4 I take the train that goes under of _____ the ground.
5 I usually go to work by my bike _____.
6 I go to work by the bus _____ and I get out _____ the bus near of _____ my office.

G Celebrity report

Complete this magazine report about a film star by putting in the correct prepositions from the box.

> round   outside   into   in front   on (x2)   ~~at~~   next   behind   towards
> past   in (x2)   along   out of   between

Hollywood *extra*

Donna Winter arrived ____at____⁰ the cinema for the premiere of her latest film _____¹ a limousine. She got _____² the car and walked quickly _____³ the cinema entrance. She was _____⁴ two bodyguards. Then she walked _____⁵ the red carpet that was _____⁶ the entrance for the stars. She went _____⁷ all the photographers and reporters who were _____⁸ a barrier but she didn't stop. _____⁹ of the cinema, hundreds of fans were waiting _____¹⁰ the pavement to see her. She heard them shouting her name, and she turned _____¹¹ and went to speak to some of them. She signed her name _____¹² their autograph books and _____¹³ pictures they gave to her, and she let them take pictures of her standing _____¹⁴ to them. Then she went _____¹⁵ the cinema for the film.

Find these things in the picture:
bodyguards ....
fans ....
red carpet ....
limousine ....
barrier ....

WORD FOCUS

OVER TO YOU   Now go to page 125.

26 Prepositions (2)
In, with, by, without

1 Some examples of sentences with **in**, **by**, **with** and **without**:
He goes to work in a suit.
A man with a beard came into the room.
By banking online, you can use your account without paying a fee.

Grammar in action

1 We use **in** with clothes to describe what somebody is wearing:
He went out in a T-shirt and jeans.
She went to the party in her new dress.

2 We use **with** to talk about part of a person's body or part of an animal's body:
She's a little girl with blonde hair and blue eyes.
A giraffe is an animal with a very long neck.

We use **with** to talk about part of an object or one thing that is included in something:
I've got a suitcase with wheels.
The room was full of shelves with books in them.

We use **with** to talk about using something in order to do an action:
I cleaned my teeth with my electric toothbrush.
He cleaned the floor with a cloth.

3 We use **by + -ing** to talk about how people do things, and actions that produce particular results:
You can change the temperature by turning this knob.

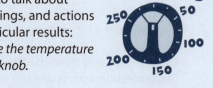

4 We use **without + -ing** to talk about not doing something. We often use **without + -ing** to say that we are surprised that an action does not happen because we expect it to happen:
She left the house without closing the door. (= and she didn't close the door)

A The meal

This is the beginning of a story called 'The Meal'. Put *in* or *with* into the gaps to complete it.

A man ......**with**......⁰ an angry face walked down the street. He was ....¹ an old overcoat and he was wearing shoes ....² holes in them. He was carrying a bag ....³ a long handle. He came to a house ....⁴ a green door. He opened the door ....⁵ a key that he took out of his pocket. A woman ....⁶ blonde hair was waiting for him. She was sitting at a table ....⁷ lots of food on it. She was ....⁸ a very smart dress ....⁹ shiny jewels on it. 'Where have you been?' she said.

B Playing the guitar

Complete the rewritten sentences about how someone learnt to play the guitar. Use *by* or *without*.

0 He looked in lots of shops and he found a good guitar.
   He found a good guitar ......**by looking**...... in lots of shops.
1 He didn't spend a lot of money but he found a good guitar.
   He found a good guitar .... a lot of money.
2 He used a book and he learnt how to play.
   He learnt how to play .... a book.

102 | Prepositions

3 He didn't have any lessons but he learnt how to play the guitar.
He learnt how to play the guitar _____ any lessons.
4 He practised a lot and he improved.
He improved _____ a lot.
5 He played with other people and he became more confident.
He became more confident _____ with other people.
6 He played at the school concert and he didn't feel nervous.
He played at the school concert _____ nervous.

C Teacher's instructions

A teacher is giving instructions to a class about a trip to a museum they are going to take the next day. Complete what the teacher says, using the correct prepositions.

0 Come ____with____ a packed lunch.
1 Come _____ warm clothes because it's going to be a cold day.
2 I want you to travel on the coach _____ making a lot of noise.
3 We're going to go round the museum _____ a guide.
4 The guide will be someone _____ a white jacket _____ a blue badge on it.
5 There will be a quiz _____ 20 questions in it.
6 You'll answer the questions _____ finding the information in the museum.
7 _____ answering all the questions correctly, you might win a prize.
8 I'm going to give you a sheet _____ more information on it now.

> **WORD FOCUS**
> A *packed lunch* is a meal that you:
> A buy in a shop.
> B make at home.
> C order in advance.

D My cousin's job

Complete the rewritten facts about someone's job. Use *in*, *with*, *by* or *without* at the beginning of each answer.

0 My cousin has a very interesting job.
My cousin is a person ____with a very interesting job____.
1 When he goes to work, he wears a suit.
He goes to work _____.
2 He works for a company. It has about 50 employees.
He works for a company _____.
3 He has an office. It has a view over the city.
He has an office _____.
4 Sometimes he works all day and he doesn't stop for lunch.
Sometimes he works all day _____.
5 His company creates advertisements for other companies and it makes a lot of money.
His company makes a lot of money _____.
6 My cousin's job has a good salary.
My cousin has a job _____.
7 He does research with customers to plan the advertisements.
He plans the advertisements _____.

Prepositions | 103

26 Prepositions (2)
Prepositional phrases

2 Some examples of sentences with common **prepositional phrases**:
*He contacted me **by email at the end of** last week.*
***In the past** I was away **on business** a lot, but now I don't travel much.*

Grammar in action

5 We use **at** in some common phrases connected with **time**:

We use **at first** to talk about a situation or feeling that changed later:
***At first** I was nervous but then I relaxed.*

We use **at last** to say that we are pleased that something has happened because we have waited for it for a long time:
***At last** someone is coming to rescue me!*

We use **at the beginning/end (of)** to talk about the beginning and end of a period of time or something that lasts for a period of time:
***At the end of** the match, the winners celebrated.*
***At the beginning** (of the film), someone was murdered.*

6 We use **by** in some common phrases connected with **communications**:
*You can contact me **by phone** or **by email**.*

We use **by credit card** and **in cash** to talk about ways of **paying for things**:
*I paid for the shopping **by credit card**.*

7 We use **on** in some common phrases connected with **travelling**:
*Adam is **on holiday** at the moment.*
*My father is in Japan **on business**.*
*I'm going **on a trip** to Italy next week.*

We use **on** in some common phrases connected with **media**:
*I watched the news **on TV**, and then I listened to a programme **on the radio**.*

We use **on** in some common phrases connected with using **technology**:
*She was talking **on her mobile phone**.*
*I looked for the information **on the internet** and I found it **on a website**.*

8 We use **in** in these common phrases connected with **the past and the future**:
*I'll be back **in ten minutes**. (= 10 minutes after now)*
*I'm hoping to visit Australia **in the future**. (= at some time in the future)*
*I won't drive so fast **in future**. (= in all of the future)*
*Did you book a table **in advance**? (= before the time when something happens or before an event)*
***In the past**, this was a very successful football club.*

> **TIP**
> We use **by** with the latest time in the future when something will or can happen:
> *I have to do this work **by Friday**.*
> *(= not later than Friday)*

We use **in** in some common phrases connected with **writing and speaking**:
*This book was originally written **in French**.*
*You must apply **in writing**. (= by letter, not by phone, email, etc.)*
*I made a note **in pencil**.*
*Please fill in your details **in capitals / capital letters**.*

E Test advice

A teacher is talking to a group of students about a test they are going to take. Complete the teacher's advice, using the correct prepositions.

0 Write your answers ....*in*.... pen in the spaces provided.
1 Put your name .... capitals at the top of the paper.
2 You might be nervous .... first, but don't worry.
3 When you're .... the end of the test, check your answers.
4 The results of the test will be ready .... the end of July.
5 You'll be able to find your results .... the website.

F **Holiday plans**

Eddie is telling his friend Megan about a holiday he is going to have. Complete their conversation with the correct prepositions.

EDDIE   I'm going ....on.... holiday soon. ....¹ last I'm going to have a break after all this hard work!

MEGAN   Oh, when are you going?

EDDIE   ....² the beginning of June. ....³ about three weeks.

MEGAN   That sounds great. Where are you going?

EDDIE   Spain. I found a fantastic villa ....⁴ the internet.

MEGAN   Was it easy to organize that?

EDDIE   Yes, I contacted the owner ....⁵ email and then I spoke to her ....⁶ the phone. Some of the details were ....⁷ Spanish and I didn't understand them. But the owner spoke good English, so that was OK.

MEGAN   Did you have to pay for it ....⁸ advance?

EDDIE   Well, I've paid a deposit ....⁹ credit card and I'll pay the rest ....¹⁰ cash when I get there.

MEGAN   That sounds good. I think I'll book my holidays that way ....¹¹ future.

G **The past and the present**

These are some sentences that students wrote when they were asked to compare the past with the present. Complete them by putting in the correct prepositions.

- ....In.... the past, people worked ....¹ their hands and built things ....² tools, but now a lot of these jobs are done by computers.
- Today, people have much more access to news and information ....³ TV and ....⁴ the radio.
- Air travel has increased a lot and today lots of people can easily go ....⁵ trips to distant countries, for holidays or ....⁶ business.
- People don't communicate ....⁷ writing very much and they don't speak to each other so much because they're always ....⁸ their mobile phones. Lots of young people prefer to communicate ....⁹ sending texts to each other.
- It's hard to live in the modern world ....¹⁰ knowing anything about computers and all the other technology.

OVER TO YOU   Now go to page 127.

27 Reported speech
Say and tell

1. Some examples of **reported speech** sentences with **say** and **tell**:
   I **said that** I wanted two tickets.
   I **told him** he was wrong.

2. When we report things that people say, we often use the past simple form **said** and change the tense of the verb the speaker used, in this way:

ACTUAL WORDS	REPORTED SPEECH
present simple 'I **need** a drink.'	**past simple** He said (that) he **needed** a drink.
present continuous 'I**'m feeling** ill.'	**past continuous** She said (that) she **was feeling** ill.
past simple / present perfect 'I **enjoyed** the party.'	**past perfect** (**had** + past participle) He said (that) he **had enjoyed** the party.
will 'I**'ll phone** later.'	**would** She said (that) she **would phone** later.
am/is/are going to 'I**'m going to buy** it.'	**was/were going to** He said (that) he **was going to buy** it.
can 'I **can't come**.'	**could** She said (that) she **couldn't come**.

   > **TIP** It is not necessary to use **that** in a reported speech sentence.

3. We use **say** and **tell** in these patterns:

say (that) …	She **said (that)** she was leaving.
tell + object pronoun (that) …	She **told me (that)** she was leaving.

   We cannot use an object with **say**:
   NOT ~~She said me (that) she was leaving.~~

   We must use an object with **tell**:
   NOT ~~She told (that) she was leaving.~~

Grammar in action

1. We use **reported speech** when we are speaking or writing about something that another person said:
   I saw Tom yesterday. He said (that) he was enjoying his new job.

2. We use **said** when we are simply reporting someone's words. We use **said** when it is clear or not important who the person was speaking to:
   I saw Helen yesterday. She said that she wasn't going out with Liam any more. (= we know that she said this to 'me')

HELEN — I'm not going out with Liam anymore. — AMY

We use **told + object pronoun** when we want to make clear who the person was speaking to:
Helen told Amy that she wasn't going out with Liam any more. (= Helen told another person and this is an important piece of information)

A Train problem

A train stopped in a tunnel and it didn't move for a long time. Report what the people said, using the correct reported speech forms of the words in brackets.

0. The driver said that ……*he was*…… sorry for the delay. ('I'm sorry')
1. The driver said that ……………… the cause of the problem. ('I don't know')
2. The woman next to me said ……………… it. ('I can't believe')
3. I said that ……………… . ('I'm going to complain')
4. The man opposite me said that ……………… late for a meeting. ('I'll be')
5. Some children said ……………… to get out. ('We want')

6 Another passenger said that _____ to get angry. ('I'm beginning')
7 Someone said _____ for 20 minutes. ('The train hasn't moved')
8 Another passenger said that _____ on her last journey. ('The same thing happened')

B Carol's new job

Two old friends, Carol and Alex met in the street one morning. Report what they said to each other, using the correct reported speech verb forms.

ALEX   Hi Carol. How are you?
CAROL I'm really happy. I've started a new job and I'm having a great time there. The work is interesting and the people are very friendly.
ALEX   What's the job?
CAROL I'm doing market research. I love it.
ALEX   I'm pleased for you. Listen, I have to go, but we can meet soon. It'll be nice to have a long chat about things.
CAROL Yes, I haven't seen you for ages. How about next week?
ALEX   We can't meet next week because I'm going to be away. I won't be back until Friday.
CAROL Well, I'll give you a ring on Saturday.
ALEX   Great. I'll wait for you to call me.

> **WORD FOCUS**
> Which word in exercise C is used in two phrases connected with relationships? If you are going _____ with someone, you are someone's boyfriend/girlfriend. If you ask someone _____, you ask someone to go somewhere with you because you want to start a relationship as boyfriend/girlfriend.

Carol said the she ___was___ ⁰ really happy. She said that she _____ ¹ a new job and that she _____ ² a great time there. She said that the work _____ ³ interesting and that the people _____ ⁴ very friendly.
Carol said that she _____ ⁵ market research and she _____ ⁶ it. Alex said that he _____ ⁷ pleased for her. He said that he _____ ⁸ but that they _____ ⁹ soon. He said that it _____ ¹⁰ nice to have a long chat about things. Carol said that she _____ ¹¹ Alex for ages.
Alex said that they _____ ¹² next week because he _____ ¹³ away. He said that he _____ ¹⁴ back until Friday. Carol said she _____ ¹⁵ him a ring on Saturday. Alex said he _____ ¹⁶ for her to call him.

C Student gossip

Some students were talking about each other in the college café. Report what they said using *told* and the correct reported speech verb forms. Use *that* in each sentence.

0 Anne _told me that she wasn't going out_ with Ian any more.
1 I _____ surprised to hear that.
2 Wendy _____ well in the exams.
3 Mary _____ studying hard.
4 George _____ a girlfriend.
5 Elaine _____ her out.
6 Diane _____ a new dress.
7 Oliver _____ her.

I'm not going out with Ian any more.
I'm surprised to hear that.

Neil won't do well in the exams.
Neil is going to start studying hard.

Kate has bought a new dress.
Kate's new dress doesn't suit her.

Bruce can't get a girlfriend.
Bruce asked me out.

27 Reported speech
Tell and ask

4 Some examples of **reported speech** sentences with **tell** and **ask**:
  I **told them what** I wanted.
  She **asked me what** my name was.
  I **asked him whether** he was feeling ill.
  She **told me to wait** for her.

5 We can use **tell** and **ask** in this pattern:

> **tell/ask + object + question word + subject + reported speech verb**

She **told her friends where** she was going.
I **asked the assistant how much** it cost.

Notice that after *what, when, where, how*, etc. we use the pattern of a statement (*she was going, it cost*), not the pattern of a question (NOT *was she going, did it cost*).

6 We can use **ask** in this pattern:

> **ask + object + if/whether + subject + reported speech verb**

She **asked me whether** I was enjoying my course.

Notice that after *if/whether* we use the pattern of a statement (*I was enjoying*), not the pattern of a question (NOT *was I enjoying*).

7 We can use **tell** and **ask** in this pattern:

> **tell/ask + object (+ not) + to infinitive**

The teacher **told them to be** quiet.
The teacher **told them not to make** a noise.

Grammar in action

3 We use **tell + object + question word** to report what someone said when answering a question or to report information that someone gave:
  I told my teacher why I was late.
  (= I said: 'I'm late because ...')

4 We use **ask + object + question word** to report questions that ask for information:
  The taxi driver asked me where I wanted to go.
  (= He said: 'Where do you want to go?')

5 We use **ask + object + if/whether** to report questions that ask for the answer **Yes** or **No**:
  He asked me if/whether I could hear him.
  (= He said: 'Can you hear me?')

6 We use **tell + object + to infinitive** to report an order or an instruction:
  His father told him to go and play outside.
  His father told him not to play computer games all day.

7 We use **ask + object + to infinitive** to report a request:
  She asked him to listen. She asked him not to speak.
  (= She said: 'Please listen. Please don't speak.')

D The job interview

Report what happened in this job interview, using question words (*what, where, when*, etc.) and the correct reported speech verb forms.

Things the interviewer asked me:
Why did you apply for the job?
When can you start work?
What are your ambitions?
How much are you earning in your present job?

Things I told the interviewer:
I saw the advert in the local paper.
I won't be able to start until September because I'm going on holiday.
I'm going to get back from my holiday on 2 September.

0 He asked me _why I had applied_ for the job.
1 He asked me .... work.
2 He asked me ....
3 He asked me .... in my present job.

4 I told him .... the advert.
5 I told him .... start until September.
6 I told him .... from my holiday.

E Tourist enquiries

Rosemarie works in a tourist office. She is reporting questions that tourists asked her at work. Complete what she says, using *if/whether* or a question word and the correct reported speech verb forms.

Questions people asked me today:

Can you find a hotel for me?
0 Someone asked me *if/whether I could find* a hotel for him.

What time does the museum open?
1 Someone asked me ....

Will the shops be open on Sunday?
2 Someone asked me .... open on Sunday.

How much does a travel card cost?
3 Someone asked me ....

Did I leave my umbrella here earlier?
4 Someone asked me .... her umbrella here earlier.

Has the festival started?
5 Someone asked me ....

Where can I find a good restaurant?
6 Someone asked me .... a good restaurant.

Is it going to stop raining soon?
7 Someone asked me .... raining soon.

Do you like dealing with tourists?
8 Someone asked me .... dealing with tourists!

F Problems with a neighbour

Complete the rewritten story about an argument between neighbours, using the correct reported speech forms. Use *say (that) …*, *tell + object (that) …*, *ask + object + to* infinitive, or *tell + object + to* infinitive.

My neighbour was having a party and the music was very loud. I said 'Please turn the music down. It's causing me a problem. I can't sleep because of it.' He said 'Shut up!' I said 'Don't be so unpleasant. And please don't make so much noise.' He said 'I'm not going to turn it down.' I said 'I'll call the police.' He said 'I don't care. Go away.' I phoned the police and said 'Please come.' They knocked on his door and said 'Don't disturb the neighbours.' He smiled and said 'I don't want to upset anyone.' He turned the music down and I went to sleep. I'm not going to talk to him again.

My neighbour was having a party and the music was very loud. I asked *him to turn* ⁰ the music down. I told *him (that) it was causing* ⁰ me a problem. I said .... ¹ because of it. He told .... ². I told .... ³ so unpleasant. Again, I asked .... ⁴ so much noise. He told .... ⁵ it down. So I told .... ⁶ the police. He said .... ⁷. He told .... ⁸. I phoned the police and asked .... ⁹. They knocked on his door and asked .... ¹⁰ the neighbours. He smiled and said .... ¹¹ to upset anyone. He turned the music down and I went to sleep. I'm not going to talk to him again.

OVER TO YOU Now go to page 127.

28 Relative clauses
Who, which, that

1 Some examples of sentences with **relative clauses**:
   My father works for a company **which/that** makes computer parts.
   The person **who/that** answered the phone was very polite to me.

2 We can form **relative clauses** with this pattern:

   noun + which/that/who + verb

   We use **which** or **that** to talk about things:
   I caught **the bus which/that goes** to the city centre.

   We use **who** or **that** to talk about people.
   Irene is **a girl who/that lives** in my street.

   In this kind of relative clause, the noun before **which**, **who** or **that** is the subject of the verb after **which**, **who** or **that**: *the bus* is the subject of *goes*; *a girl* is the subject of *lives*.

   > **TIP**
   > Notice that we do not use a subject pronoun before the verb:
   >   NOT *the bus which it goes to* …
   >   NOT *the girl who she lives* …

Grammar in action

1 We use this kind of **relative clause** to give information about the thing or person we are talking about. The purpose of the sentence is to give the information in the relative clause:
   He has a car which/that cost a lot of money.

   The main point of this sentence is that the car cost a lot of money, not simply that he has a car.

2 We use this kind of **relative clause** to say or explain which thing or person we are talking about:
   He's the player who scored the winning goal.

3 We can also use this kind of **relative clause** in questions to specify which thing or person we are asking about:
   What's the name of the woman who works in reception?

A My friend in Australia

Complete this description of a friend's life in Australia by joining each pair of sentences, using *who* or *which*.

0 I have a friend. He has gone to live in Australia.
   ....I have a friend who has gone to live in Australia.................

1 He works for a company. It sells sports equipment.
   ....

2 He has relatives. They have been in Australia for many years.
   ....

3 He has a wife. She got a job as a teacher at a local school.
   ....

4 They live in a nice house. It is very close to the beach.
   ....

5 They have three children. The children love living in Australia.
   ....

B **What's her name?**

Jane and Matt are talking about an actress. Complete their conversation, using the phrases in the box.

> who does   that started   who helps
> who's always   that show   who also works
> that happen   who starred   that won
> that's just finished   who plays

JANE What's the name of that actress _who's always_ ⁰ on TV? You see her all the time. You know, the one ....¹ a detective in that series.

MATT Are you talking about the series ....²? The one ....³ lots of awards.

JANE No, I'm talking about a series ....⁴ a couple of weeks ago. It's about a private detective ....⁵ as a fashion model. She has a boyfriend ....⁶ her and together they solve crimes ....⁷ in the world of fashion.

MATT Ah, I know! She's that actress ....⁸ adverts for shampoo.

JANE That's right, those adverts ....⁹ her sitting on a luxury yacht.

MATT Yes, of course I know her. She's the one ....¹⁰ in a really good series about doctors last year. But I don't know her name.

C **While you're staying in my apartment …**

Fiona has travelled to Paris to stay in her friend's apartment while her friend is away. Her friend has left a message for her giving her advice and information for her stay in the apartment. Complete what her friend has written by joining each pair of sentences. Use *who* for people and *that* for things.

0 Two buses go to the city centre. They are numbers 26 and the 78.
   The buses _that go to the city centre are_ numbers 26 and 78.

1 A woman lives in the next apartment. She will help you.
   The woman .... you.

2 A shop sells basic groceries. It's at the end of the road.
   A shop .... at the end of the road.

3 A man owns the shop. He speaks good English.
   The man .... good English.

4 A takeaway does really good food. It's just round the corner.
   A takeaway .... just round the corner.

5 A woman cleans the apartment. She comes every Thursday.
   The woman .... every Thursday.

6 A brochure tells you all about events in the city. It's on the kitchen table.
   A brochure .... on the kitchen table.

WORD FOCUS

Find words with these meanings in exercise C:

A food you buy at a shop or supermarket
 ....

B a shop selling food to eat; a meal you buy from a shop and eat in another place
 ....

Building sentences | 111

28 Relative clauses
Which, that, who, where, when, whose

3 Some examples of another type of **relative clause**:
   *The computer **which/that** I bought last week doesn't work very well.*
   *He's a singer **who/that** I really like.*

4 We can form **relative clauses** with this pattern:

> noun + which/that/who + second subject + verb

   *The book **which/that** I'm reading is great.*
   *She's **a person who/that** everyone likes.*

In this kind of relative clause, there is another subject after **which**, **who** or **that**: *I* is the subject of *'m reading*; *everyone* is the subject of *likes*.

> **TIP**
> Notice that we do not use an object pronoun after the verb:
>   NOT *the book that I'm reading it* …
>   NOT *a person who everyone likes her* …

5 We can use **where** and **when** in this kind of relative clause:
   *It's **a café where a lot of young people** meet each other.*
   *1999 was **the year when I** first travelled abroad.*

6 We can use **whose** + **noun** with or without a second subject:
   *He's an actor **whose films are** always very popular.*
   *He's an actor **whose films I** really like.*

Grammar in action

4 We use this kind of **relative clause** to give information that involves another thing or person in addition to the person or thing we are talking about:
   The book that she was reading was very boring.

This sentence gives information both about 'the book' – it was boring – and about 'she' – she was reading it.

5 We use **where** to give information about a place. Here, the speaker is showing someone their home town:
   This is the house where I spent my childhood.

6 We use **when** to give information about a time or a period of time. We might use it to explain what happens on a certain day:
   5 September is the day when the school year starts.

7 We use **whose** + **noun** as a possessive form, instead of 'my', 'his', 'her', etc. to give information about people's possessions, family members, names, organizations, or creations:
   She's a writer whose books have sold millions.
   (= her books have sold …)

D   The birthday party

Kate and Anna are talking before they go to a birthday party for their friend Carmen. Complete their conversation, using *who* or *which* and the phrases in the box.

> she knows   ~~you've never met~~   I always enjoy   she didn't like   you showed
> I haven't seen   nobody else will get   I bought   I'm sure

KATE   Will I know many of the people at Carmen's party?
ANNA   Most of them, I think. But there will be some people *who you've never met* ⁰ before. There will be people ....¹ from work.
KATE   What have you bought her?
ANNA   I've bought her something ....² her. It's a piece of jewellery ....³ she'll like.
KATE   Are you going to wear that dress ....⁴ me the other day?
ANNA   No, I'm going to wear the jacket ....⁵ last week.
KATE   Will Jerry be there? He's someone ....⁶ for ages.
ANNA   I don't know. He said something to Carmen ....⁷. I don't think they're friends any more.
KATE   Oh that's a shame. He's a funny guy ....⁸ meeting. Anyway, let's go …

E My holiday photos

Anthony is showing his holiday photographs to a friend. Correct the underlined parts of what he says.

0 These are some photos <u>that I took them</u> *that I took* on holiday.
1 This is someone <u>who we met him</u> .... at the hotel.
2 I took this on the day <u>which we went</u> .... to the cathedral.
3 That's a photo of us <u>that another guest at the hotel he took</u> ....
4 This is the hotel <u>that we stayed</u> ....
5 Those are some people from our group <u>whose their names I can't remember</u> ....
6 That's me in a hat <u>that I bought it</u> .... in a souvenir shop.
7 Those are some people <u>who we made friends with them</u> .... in a restaurant one night.
8 That's the man <u>which bag got lost</u> .... at the airport.

F General knowledge quiz

Rewrite these questions for a general knowledge quiz, using relative clauses. When you have done the exercise, answer the questions or try to find the answers.

0 Name this writer. She wrote the Harry Potter books.
   Name the writer *who wrote the Harry Potter books.*
1 Name this building. It's the tallest in the world.
   Name the building ....
2 Name this instrument. Louis Armstrong played it.
   Name the instrument ....
3 Name this singer. People called him 'The King'.
   Name the singer ....
4 Name this sport. William Webb Ellis invented it.
   Name the sport ....
5 Name this building. The President of the US lives there.
   Name the building ....
6 Name this director. He made the Star Wars films.
   Name the director ....
7 Name this decade. The Beatles became famous then.
   Name the decade ....
8 Name this scientist. He discovered penicillin.
   Name the scientist ....
9 Name this country. Its capital city is Helsinki.
   Name the country ....

OVER TO YOU Now go to page 127.

29 Conversational English
Short answers and short questions; question tags

1 Some examples of **short answers**:
   Are you watching this programme? ~ **Yes, I am.**
   Did you watch that programme last night? ~ **No, I didn't.**

2 We form **short answers** with positive or negative forms of the verb tense used in the question, in these patterns:

   | Yes, + subject + positive be/auxiliary/modal |

   | No, + subject + negative be/auxiliary/modal |

   Are you OK? ~ **Yes, I am. / No, I'm not.**
   Will they win? ~ **Yes, they will. / No, they won't.**

   Notice that we use the full form in positive short answers (*Yes, I am* NOT *Yes I'm*).

3 Some examples of **short questions**:
   I don't like this music. ~ **Don't you?**
   I'm very angry. ~ **Are you?**

4 We form **short questions** with positive or negative forms of the verb tense used in the statement by another person, in these patterns:

   | positive statement → positive be/auxiliary/modal + subject |

   | negative statement → negative be/auxiliary/modal + subject |

   I'm going to leave. ~ **Are you?**
   I haven't been here before. ~ **Haven't you?**

5 Some examples of **question tags**:
   It's a nice day today, **isn't it?**
   You haven't met Brenda, **have you?**

6 We form **question tags** after statements in this way:

   | positive statement + negative be/auxiliary/ modal + subject |

   | negative statement + positive be/auxiliary/ modal + subject |

   You enjoyed the film, **didn't you?**
   You can't hear me, **can you?**

Grammar in action

1 We use **short answers** when we are saying **Yes** or **No** to answer a question. We often do not simply answer 'Yes' or 'No', we also add a subject and the first part of a verb. This makes the answer more polite:
   Did you win? ~ **No, we didn't.**

2 We use **short questions** to react to what someone says. We use short questions after a statement if we are surprised by what someone says or because we want to check that what someone says is really true:
   I'm cold. ~ **Are you?** (= I'm surprised)

3 We use **question tags** to check that what we are saying is true or correct. Here someone is talking to a member of staff at a railway station:
   This train stops at Brussels, **doesn't it?**

A **Mum and Edward**

Edward is a 12-year-old schoolboy. Complete the short answers he gives to his mother and the short answers his mother gives to him when they are at home.

MUM   EDWARD
0 Have you finished your homework?   Yes, _I have_. It was easy.
1 Are you feeling OK?   No, _____. I feel ill.
2 Did you have a good day at school? No, _____. It was awful.
3 Are you going to play football today? Yes, _____. It's Thursday.

EDWARD   MUM
4 Can I have something to eat?   No, _____. It's nearly dinner time.
5 Did you read this letter from the school? Yes, _____. It's interesting.
6 Will you help me with my homework? Yes, _____. Wait a minute.

B The new girlfriend

Steve and Billy are talking about their friend, Nick. Put in the short questions.

STEVE
I've just heard something interesting.
Well, Nick has got a new girlfriend.
Yes, she's called Martha Brown.
Well, she lives near you.
.... ⁴ Well she isn't very nice.
She doesn't like Nick's friends.
Nick told me.
Last night. We were talking on the phone.

BILLY
Have you? ⁰ Tell me about it.
.... ¹ I didn't know that.
.... ² I don't know her.
.... ³ Well, I haven't met her.
.... ⁵ What's wrong with her?
.... ⁶ How do you know that?
.... ⁷ When did he say that?
.... ⁸ Tell me what he said.

WORD FOCUS

Which of these is another way of asking the question '*What's wrong with her?*'?

A What mistake has she made?
B What's her problem?
C Why is she wrong?

C Party time

Bella and Sharon are at a party. Complete their conversation by putting in the short questions and short answers.

BELLA
I've met lots of interesting people.
.... ¹ I'm enjoying myself.
.... ² I want to stay.
.... ³ I'm not working tomorrow.
Well, come and dance for a few minutes.
.... ⁵ I love it.

SHARON
Have you? I haven't. ⁰ I'm bored.
Well, I want to go home now.
Well, I can't have a late night.
.... ⁴ You're lucky.
I don't like dancing.
Well, you go and dance. I'm leaving.

D A difficult interview

Complete this extract from a TV interview with an actress called Helen by putting in the question tags.

INTERVIEWER	You're one of the top actresses in the world, _aren't you?_ ⁰
HELEN	Yes, I suppose I am.
INTERVIEWER	And you've been in some fantastic films, ... ¹
HELEN	Yes, that's true.
INTERVIEWER	But you haven't won an Oscar, ... ²
HELEN	No. I don't know why. I've nearly won a few times.
INTERVIEWER	But you will win this year, ... ³
HELEN	I don't know, but I think I've got a good chance.
INTERVIEWER	Your most recent film, *Dandelion*, was very popular, ... ⁴ And the critics liked it, ... ⁵
HELEN	Yes, it did very well and the public loved it.
INTERVIEWER	Now, you don't like talking about your private life, ... ⁶
HELEN	No, I don't. I like to keep it private.
INTERVIEWER	So you won't talk about your new boyfriend, ... ⁷
HELEN	No, I'm not going to discuss that.
INTERVIEWER	He isn't an actor, ... ⁸
HELEN	No, but I'm not going to talk about him.

29 Conversational English
Short responses: *so, too, neither/nor, either*

7 Some examples of **short responses** with **so**, **too**, **neither**, **nor**, and **either**:
I like this song. ~ **So do I.** / **I do too**.
I can't ski very well. ~ **Neither/Nor can I.** / **I can't either**.

8 We use **so** after a positive statement in this pattern:

so + positive *be*/auxiliary/modal + subject

I'm hungry. ~ **So am I.**
I've been to Spain. ~ **So have I.**

We use **too** after a positive statement in this pattern:

subject + positive *be*/auxiliary/modal + too

I'm hungry. ~ **I am too.**
I've been to Spain. ~ **I have too.**

9 We use **neither** or **nor** after a negative statement in this pattern:

neither/nor + positive *be*/auxiliary/modal + subject

She doesn't eat meat. ~ **Neither/Nor does he.**
I can't sing. ~ **Neither/Nor can I.**

We use **either** after a negative statement in this pattern:

subject + negative *be*/auxiliary/modal + either

She doesn't eat meat. ~ **He doesn't either.**
I can't sing. ~ **I can't either.**

> **TIP**
> We often use the informal, spoken phrase **Me too**, instead of *So do I, So am I*, etc. and instead of *I am too, I have too*, etc.
> *I'm getting tired.* ~ **Me too.** (= *So am I.*)

Grammar in action

4 We use **so**, **too**, **neither/nor** and **either** in these patterns when we are agreeing with a statement or saying that our situation or experience is the same:
I'm hot. ~ **So am I.** (= and I'm hot)
I've bought a ticket for the concert. ~ **I have too.**
(= and I've bought a ticket)
I can't remember his name. ~ **Neither/Nor can I.**
(= and I can't remember his name)
I don't want to go tonight. ~ **I don't either.**
(= and I don't want to go)

5 We can also use **so**, **too**, **neither/nor** and **either** with **possessive subjects**. Here, people are comparing things they own:
My car is very old. ~ **So is mine.** / **Mine is too.**
My phone doesn't work. ~ **Neither does mine.** / **Mine doesn't either.**

6 We use **so**, **too**, **neither/nor** and **either** in full sentences linked with **and** to say that something is true for both people/things. Here, people are talking about shared exercises:
I enjoyed the film and so did my girlfriend.
I enjoyed the film and my girlfriend did too.

Kate didn't like the food and neither did Nick.
Kate didn't like the food and Nick didn't either.

E A bad trip

John and Chris are on a backpacking trip to various countries and having a lot of problems. Complete their responses, using *So* or *Neither/Nor* and the words in brackets.

0 I don't like this place.   (I)   Neither/Nor do I.
1 I'm homesick.   (I)   ....
2 I didn't like that food.   (I)   ....
3 My bag's too heavy.   (mine)   ....
4 I couldn't sleep on that train. (I)   ....
5 I feel ill.   (I)   ....
6 I've spent too much money.   (I)   ....
7 Your hair looks terrible.   (yours)   ....
8 I'm not enjoying this trip.   (I)   ....

F Me, my friends and music

Miranda is talking about her friends and their interest in music. Complete what she says using *so, neither/nor, too* or *either*.

0   I'm very keen on music and most of my friends *are too*.
1   I like rock music and most of my friends ....
2   I'm going to a festival in July and .... Tessa and Molly.
3   I couldn't go to that festival last year and Molly ....
4   I haven't been to many festivals. Tessa and Molly ....
5   I'm taking guitar lessons and Tessa ....
6   I can't play the guitar very well and .... Tessa.
7   I want to form a band. Tessa ....
8   I can't sing. Tessa ....
9   But I'm not nervous about performing and .... Tessa.
10 I like being creative and .... Tessa.

G Travel discussion

Two friends, Michael and Alice, are discussing travel. Fill each gap in their conversation with a short question, a short answer, a question tag, or a pattern with *so, neither/nor, too* or *either*.

MICHAEL I'm going to London next month. Have you been there?
ALICE   No, *I haven't* 0. I don't like big cities.
MICHAEL .... 1 I think they're really exciting. Paris is great and Rome and Madrid .... 2. I've been to all of them. I really like travelling and discovering new places.
ALICE   .... 3 I. But I don't like noise and crowds and .... 4 my husband. We prefer to go to quieter places. We like to relax on holiday.
MICHAEL Me .... 5. But I find the big cities very relaxing. For example, they've all got really nice parks.
ALICE   .... 6 I don't know much about them. And anyway, I don't have much money to spend on holidays.
MICHAEL .... 7 I. I always stay in cheap hotels and I don't go to expensive restaurants.
ALICE   But it's hard to find those places, ... 8 No, it's the countryside for us. I like going for walks and .... 9 my husband.
MICHAEL My wife .... 10. We do lots of walking in the cities we visit.
ALICE   Well, I can't wait for my next holiday.
MICHAEL I .... 11. I'm really looking forward to it.

OVER TO YOU   Now go to page 127.

30 Clause and sentence building
Still, only, also

1 Some examples of sentences with **still**, **only** and **also**:
   It's **still** raining now.
   I've **only** read 20 pages of the book.
   She's polite and she's **also** very clever.
   I'm studying French and **I'm also learning** Italian.
   I've spoken to Carl and **I've also phoned** Ted.
   I can speak French. **I can also speak** Italian.

2 We can use **still** with verbs in these patterns:

   subject + still + positive/negative verb

   I **still like** her.
   It **still hasn't arrived**.

   subject + be/modal + still + verb

   I'm **still thinking** about it.
   I'm **still not feeling** well.
   I **can still remember** exactly what happened.

3 We can use **only** in these patterns:

   only + number/amount

   Only 15/a few people came to the party.

   subject + only + verb

   It **only happened** once.

   subject + be/auxiliary/modal + only

   Don't get angry, I'm **only joking**.
   I've **only been** to one foreign country.
   I **can only stay** for 10 minutes.

4 We can use **also** with verbs in these patterns:

   subject + also + verb

   I tidied my room and I **also did** the washing-up.

   subject + be/auxiliary/modal + also

Grammar in action

1 We use **still** to say that something continues to happen or to be true. We use **still** when we want to emphasize that something has not stopped or changed:
   He **still hasn't cut** his hair.

2 We use **only** to say that a number or amount is small:
   There's **only** one sandwich left on the plate.

   We use **only** with verbs with the meaning 'not more than':
   He was **only wearing** a T-shirt and it was a cold day.

   We use **only** to say that something is not important, serious or interesting. Here, someone is giving a present to a friend:
   Don't get excited, it's **only** something cheap!

3 We use **also** to say that there is something more than what we have said before. We can use **also** like this:
   He's got a nice car and he's **also got** a motorbike.
   He's got a nice car. He's **also got** a motorbike.
   He's got a nice car. **Also**, he's got a motorbike.

   We use **too** with the same meaning as **also** but we use **too** at the end of a sentence:
   He's got a nice car and he's got a motorbike **too**.

A Nothing has changed

Complete this letter using the phrases below it and *still*. Make sure that you put *still* in the right place in each gap.

Well, nothing has changed here since the last time I wrote to you – <u>everything is still</u> ⁰ the same. _____ ¹ in the same place – _____ ² the same job and _____ ³ it! Last month, they told me that I was going to have a pay rise but _____ ⁴ happy about the place. As you know, I really want to get a better job. _____ ⁵ for other jobs but unfortunately _____ ⁶ one. Anyway, I hope _____ ⁷ me next Friday.

   0 everything is   3 I don't like   6 I haven't found
   1 I'm working   4 I'm not   7 you can meet
   2 I have   5 I'm applying

118 | Building sentences

B The visitor

Alicia is visiting Britain and she is at a party. Someone asks her some questions. Decide if the underlined parts of Alicia's replies are correct or not. Put a tick (✓) if the underlined part is correct. If it is not correct, write the correct phrase using *only*.

0 Are you living here? ~ No, <u>I only am visiting</u>.   *I'm only visiting.*
1 Have you been here many times? ~ No, <u>I've been only</u> here once before.   ....
2 Have you been here long? ~ No, <u>I only arrived</u> two days ago.   ....
3 Do you know many people here? ~ No, <u>I only know</u> a few people.   ....
4 Are you going to stay here for long? ~ No, <u>I'm going only to stay</u> for a week.   ....
5 Are you here to learn English? ~ No, <u>I'm only</u> on holiday.   ....
6 Can you speak English very well? ~ No, <u>I can speak only</u> it a bit.   ....

C Job applications

These are extracts from letters of application for jobs. Decide if the underlined parts are correct or not. Put a tick (✓) if the underlined part is correct. If it is not correct, write the correct phrase using *also* or *too*.

0 I've worked in shops before. I <u>have also</u>   *also have*   experience of bar work.
1 My computer skills are good and I <u>am also</u>   ....   a good organizer.
2 I like reading. <u>Too,</u>   ....   I'm interested in politics.
3 My main hobby is music and <u>I also like</u>   ....   playing a variety of sports.
4 I'm studying for a Business degree. I <u>also am learning</u>   ....   Spanish.
5 I've worked in tourism before. I <u>have travelled also</u>   ....   a lot.
6 I have good telephone skills and I <u>also can type</u>   ....

D Come to the theatre

Two friends are discussing a trip. Complete their conversation using *still*, *only*, *also* or *too*.

HELENA Are you coming on the theatre trip on Saturday?
ANITA   I don't know. I'm *still* ⁰ thinking about it. I haven't decided yet.
HELENA I think it's going to be good and it'll .... ¹ be a nice change for you. You've been working too hard.
ANITA   Yes, but I've .... ² got lots of work to do. I've .... ³ done a bit of the latest project and there are .... ⁴ three days left before we have to hand it in.
HELENA Come on, you .... ⁵ have plenty of time to do that. The trip is .... ⁶ going to take a few hours. .... ⁷, it'll give you a break from all the work.
ANITA   I know, but the problem isn't .... ⁸ that work. I've got lots of other things to do .... ⁹.
HELENA Like what?
ANITA   Well, I .... ¹⁰ haven't replied to the emails I've had recently.
HELENA Come on, it .... ¹¹ takes a few minutes to do that. You can .... ¹² come to the theatre with us.
ANITA   Oh … OK, I'll come.

30 Clause and sentence building
Because, so, so that; instead; apart from, except; although/though

5 Some examples of sentences with these words:
*The lights were red **so** I stopped.*
***Apart from** June, it was a miserable summer.*
***Although** the café was shut, there were people inside.*

6 We use **because** in these patterns:

> **because + subject + verb**

*She apologized **because she was late**.*

> **because of + noun**

*She was late **because of a traffic jam**.*

7 **So** and **so that** are followed by **subject + verb**:
*We went outside **so that we could enjoy** the sunshine.*

8 We use **instead of**, **apart from**, and **except (for)** before a noun/pronoun or -ing form. We can also use **instead** at the end of a clause:
***Instead of going** to the meeting, Chris went home.*
***Instead of him**, Sapna came to the meeting.*
*Chris couldn't come. Sapna **came instead**.*

9 We use **although** and **though** at the beginning of a clause. We can also use **though** at the end of a clause.
***Although** she's very poor, she's happy.*
*She's very poor – she's happy, **though**.*

Grammar in action

4 We use **because** and **so** to link a cause with a result.
We use **because** before the cause of something:
*I fell on the floor **because** the chair broke.*

We use **so** before the result of something:
*The chair broke **so** I fell on the floor.*

5 We use **so that** to talk about the purpose of an action.
We use **so that** before the intended result of an action.
For future intentions, we often use the present simple after **so that**:
*I'm writing the date in my diary **so that** I don't forget it.*

For past actions, we often use **would** and **could** after **so that**:
*I came in quietly **so that** she wouldn't wake up.*

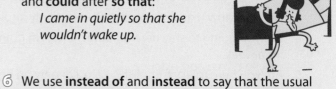

6 We use **instead of** and **instead** to say that the usual or expected action does not happen and a different action happens or is preferred. We use **instead of** before the action that doesn't happen, or **instead** after the action that does happen:
***Instead of** taking the lift, I walked up the stairs.*
*I didn't take the lift. I walked up the stairs **instead**.*

7 We use **apart from** and **except (for)** to say that a statement is not true for every person or thing. We use **apart from / except (for)** before the person or thing that the statement is not true for:
***Apart from** me, everyone was smiling.*
*Everyone was smiling **except (for)** me.*

8 We use **although/though** to link two contrasting facts or opinions which are both true:
***Although/Though** she's tall, she couldn't reach the top shelf.*

> **Although/Though** are quite formal. We use **but** in informal sentences:
> *She's tall **but** she couldn't reach the top shelf.*

E A success story

Complete this story about someone who succeeded in life, by linking the sentences with *because, because of, so,* or *so that*.

0 Stefan was popular with his teachers ...... *because* ...... he was a good student.
1 He studied hard .... he would be able to get good qualifications.
2 He decided to leave his home .... he couldn't find a job there.
3 He found a job in another country easily .... his qualifications.
4 He took classes before he left .... he would be good at the language.
5 He was a good worker, ... he did well in his new job.
6 He made a lot of new friends, ... he was happy in his new country.
7 People liked him .... his personality.
8 He was happy in his new country .... he had friends and money.

F Bad behaviour on the museum trip

Complete the rewritten statements about a class trip to a museum, using the linking words in brackets.

0 The trip was well-organized but I didn't enjoy it. (although)
   Although the trip was well-organized, I didn't enjoy it.

1 Some students didn't go on the trip. They stayed at college. (instead)
   Some students didn't go on the trip. They ....

2 The guided tour was short but we got bored. (though)
   ...., we got bored.

3 People didn't listen to the guide. They talked and laughed. (instead)
   People talked and laughed ....

4 The interactive exhibits were the only things that were interesting. (except)
   Nothing was interesting ....

5 I was the only person who bought souvenirs in the shop. (apart)
   ...., nobody bought souvenirs in the shop.

6 I didn't learn a lot but I had fun with my friends. (although)
   ...., I had fun with my friends.

WORD FOCUS

Find words with these meanings in exercise F:

A things you can see
   ....

B things you can get
   ....

G Elena's course

Jenny and Michael are talking about their friend Elena. Complete their conversation, using the correct words and phrases from the box. Use each choice once.

| still   only   also   too   ~~because~~   because of   so   so that   instead of |
| instead   apart   except   although |

JENNY   Have you seen Elena recently?
MICHAEL Yes, I see her quite regularly *because*⁰ because we go to the same gym.
JENNY   Is she ....¹ doing that course in media studies?
MICHAEL No, she's given it up. She decided to do something different ....² .
         She felt it wasn't the right course for her, ...³ she's stopped doing it.
JENNY   Really? She ....⁴ started that course last year, didn't she?
MICHAEL Yes. ....⁵ she liked it at the beginning, she decided that it wasn't
         what she wanted to do. She didn't like the college. ....⁶ , she felt that
         it wasn't a very good course.
JENNY   What was wrong with it?
MICHAEL Well, ...⁷ from one or two of the assignments, she felt that it wasn't
         useful. ....⁸ doing practical work, she had lots of lectures about
         popular culture.
JENNY   And she gave up the course ....⁹ that?
MICHAEL Yes, but she changed her mind about her career ....¹⁰ . She's
         now applying for other courses ....¹¹ she can be a teacher.
JENNY   Wow! I don't know anyone ....¹² for Elena who would
         change their plans so quickly!

OVER TO YOU Now go to page 128.

Over to you

For examples of the kind of sentences you might say or write, see pp. 149–52 in the answer key.

01 Present continuous

Say or write down three things that are happening at this moment in the place where you are reading or studying this.

Say or write down three things that are happening in your life or in the world during this period of time but not at this exact moment.

Say or write down three things that are fixed and organized in your future.

02 Present simple

Say or write down three things that happen in a typical day for you.

Say or write down three things that will happen at particular times in the future.

Say or write down three things that you do regularly but that you are not doing now, making sentences with the **present simple** and the **present continuous**.

03 Past simple and past continuous

Say or write down three important events in your life in the past and say when they happened.

Say or write down three things that you were doing or that were happening in your life a year ago.

Say or write a sentence that begins a story, using the **past simple** and the **past continuous**. Then try to tell the rest of the story!

04 Present perfect

Say or write down three important or unusual things that you have done in your life, using the **present perfect**.

Say or write down three things that you have done today, but don't say when you did them.

Say or write down three things that you have done today, using **just** or **already**.

Say or write down three things that you haven't done but that you think you will do, using the **present perfect** and **yet**.

05 Past simple and present perfect

Say or write down three important or unusual things that you have done in your life, using the **present perfect** and say when you did them, using the **past simple**.

Say or write down three things that have not happened for a period of time. Use the **past simple** and **ago** and the **present perfect** and **for** or **since**.

06 The future

Say or write down three important things that you have decided to do in your life in the future, using **going to**.

Say or write down three things that you predict for the future about other people, using **going to**.

Say or write down three things that you believe about the future, using **will/won't**.

07 Question words

Think of a person you would like to interview – it doesn't have to be a famous person. Say or write down a series of questions you would like to ask that person. Create one question beginning with each of these words: **What**, **Who**, **Where**, **When**, **Why**, **How**, and **Which** and **Whose**. Use as many verb tenses as you can.

Imagine that you are going to visit a country or city that you have never been to before and that you are talking to someone from that country or city. Say or write down a series of questions to ask that person. Create one question beginning with each of the following: **How much**, **How many**, **How long**, **How far**, **How often**, **How + adjective**.

08 Subject and object questions

Say or write down three subject questions beginning with **Who** about people that you know. Use different verb tenses for each question.

Think of a famous person and say or write down three object questions about that person, one beginning with **Who**, one beginning with **What** and one beginning with **Which**. Use different verb tenses for each question.

Say or write down three subject questions and three object questions for a general knowledge quiz. Use as many verb tenses as you can, and begin at least one question with **Who**, **What**, **Which**, and **Whose**.

09 *Can, could,* and *would*

Say or write down three sentences about your abilities in the past in comparison with your abilities now. In each sentence use **can/can't** and **could/couldn't**.

Say or write down three things that are possible or impossible for you now or in the future, using **can/can't** and three things that were impossible for you in the past, using **couldn't**.

Say or write down three questions you might ask in a shop, using **Can I, Could I, Could you,** and **Would you?**

Say or write down three things that you are permitted to do at home, at school or at work and three things that you are not permitted to do, using **can, can't,** and **be allowed to**.

10 *May, might, could,* and *should*

Say or write down three things that are possible in the future for you using **may** and **might**. Use **may** for things that are not very possible and **might** for things that are really possible.

Say or write down three things that **may not/might not** happen in the future. Think of things that are not about you personally.

Say or write down three things that it is possible for you to do now or in the future, using **could**.

Say or write down two things that you believe probably will and probably won't happen in the future, using **should** and **shouldn't**.

11 *Must* and *have to*

Say or write down three things that you must do today, three things you must do in the future and three things you had to do in the past. Use both **must** and **have to** when it is possible to do so.

Say or write down two rules of a game you know. Use **mustn't** for one rule and **have to** for the other.

Say or write down three rules in the place where you work, study or live.

Say or write down three things that are not necessary in the place where you work, study or live.

Say or write down three things you recommend to a visitor to the place where you live.

12 *Should*

Say or write down three things that you believe are the right way of behaving or good ideas for you and three things that you do which you think are wrong or bad, using **should** and **shouldn't**.

Imagine that someone wants to start doing a sport or hobby that you do or know a lot about. Give that person three positive pieces of advice using **you should** or **I think you should** and three negative pieces of advice using **you shouldn't** or **I don't think you should**.

Imagine that you are talking to someone who has asked you to suggest what they can do during the summer. Suggest two things to this person using **should** and two things using **shouldn't**. Then suggest something you are less certain about, using **could**. Then suggest two things using **I'd** and two things using **I wouldn't**.

13 The infinitive

Say or write down six sentences that are true for you, using the verbs listed in Grammar in action 1–4 on page 50 and the *to* infinitive. Use a different verb in each sentence and use as many different verb tenses as you can. Use **not** + *to* infinitive in two of your sentences.

Say or write down four sentences using **want** which you know are true. Use **want** + *to* infinitive for two sentences and **want** + **object** + *to* infinitive for two sentences.

Say or write down three sentences that are true for you, using **modals**. Use a different modal in each sentence.

Say or write down two sentences using **make** + **object** + **infinitive without** *to* and two sentences using **let** + **object** + **infinitive without** *to* that are true for you. Describe a present fact in one sentence in each pair and a past situation in the other sentence in each pair.

14 The *-ing* form

Say or write down six sentences that are true for you, using the verbs listed in Grammar in action 1–4 on page 54 and the *-ing* form. Use a different verb in each sentence.

Say or write down four sentences using *-ing* as a subject and describing present and past facts or events in your life. Use an object after the *-ing* form in two of the sentences.

Say or write down three sentences using **would like** that are true for you. In the sentences, describe things that you want to do now or in the future.

Say or write down three sentences from your own experience using the *to* infinitive to describe the purpose of an action. Use the *to* infinitive at the beginning of one of the sentences.

15 The passive

Say or write down three sentences describing things that happened to you in the past, using the **past simple passive**.

Say or write down three sentences using different passive tenses and describing facts about your school. Create one sentence with the **present simple passive**, one sentence with the **present perfect passive** and one sentence with the **passive form** of **going to**.

Say or write down three sentences using **modal passive** forms that you might see in public information or in public places.

Say or write down three sentences using passive verb forms and **by** + **agent**, describing things created or produced by different people. Use a different tense or verb form in each sentence. Write the active form of each sentence after each passive sentence.

16 Conditionals

Say or write down three things that you believe are possible in your future, and three things that you believe are possible in the future in general, using **first conditional** sentences. Use negative verbs in some of the sentences.

Say or write down four things that are different from your present situation and imagine the results if these situations really existed. Create **second conditional** sentences. Use **could** in two of the sentences.

Imagine three things that you think are unlikely to happen in the future but that you would like to happen, using **second conditional** sentences.

17 Connecting future sentences

Say or write down four things that you the think will or won't happen in the future, using **unless**, **as long as**, **even if**, and **in case**. Create one sentence for each one.

Say or write down five things that you intend or plan to do in the future, using **when**, **until**, **as soon as**, **before**, and **after**. Create one sentence for each. Use the **present simple** in four of the sentences and the **present perfect** in one of the sentences.

18 Articles

Say or write down three pairs of sentences about things that you can see in the room you are in. Use **a/an** to mention something for the first time and **the** to say something more about it.

Say or write down three pairs of sentences about buildings. In the first sentence, do not specify which building you are talking about and use **a/an**. In the second sentence, specify which building you are talking about and use **the**.

Say or write down two sentences about food with **no article** in each sentence. Use a **plural noun** in one sentence and an **uncountable noun** in the other sentence.

Say or write down two sentences about the same food with **the** in each sentence. Use a **plural noun** in one sentence and an **uncountable noun** in the other sentence and specify particular food.

Say or write down a pair of sentences about an important aspect of life. Use **no article** in one of the sentences to say something general and **the** in the other sentence to be specific.

Say or write down a sentence including each of the following, using **the** or **no article**: a country, a continent, a language, a type of music, a musical instrument, a meal, a subject for study and a sport or game.

19 Pronouns and possessives

Say or write down three pairs of sentences about people you know. First of all, say who you are talking about. Then use a **subject pronoun** in one sentence and an **object pronoun** in the other.

Say or write down three sets of sentences about things that you possess and things that other people possess. In the first sentence in each set, mention the possession; in the second sentence use a **possessive adjective** and in the third sentence use a **possessive pronoun**.

Say or write down four sentences about things that you have done and that other people have done, using **reflexive pronouns**.

Say or write down two sentences using **each other**.

20 Quantifiers

Say or write down three sentences about the town, village or area where you live, using the pattern **quantifier + noun**. Use a different quantifier in each sentence.

Say or write down three sentences about your school or your job using the pattern **quantifier (+ of) + the/possessive + noun**. Use a different quantifier in each sentence.

Say or write down three sentences about your friends, using the pattern **quantifier (+ of) + my friends**. Use a different quantifier in each sentence.

Say or write down two sentences about things you ate or drank recently. Use **a few** in one sentence and **a little** in the other.

Say or write down two negative sentences using **many** and two negative sentences using **much** that are true for you.

Say or write down four sentences about experiences you have had, two using the pattern **quantifier + of it** and two using the pattern **quantifier + of them**. Use as many quantifiers as you can.

21 Pronouns and determiners

Say or write down five sentences about things that you like or want, using **one**, **ones**, **the one**, **the ones,** and **one of**. Use as many different patterns as you can.

Say or write down four sentences about your interests or hobbies using **another**, **the/my other**, **other,** and **the others**. Use a different pattern in each sentence.

Say or write down four sentences about your life in the recent past. In one sentence use a pronoun beginning with **some** (something, somebody, etc'), in one sentence use a pronoun beginning with **every**, in one sentence use a pronoun beginning with **no** and in one sentence, use a pronoun beginning with **any**.

Say or write down four sentences about your life in the recent past. In two sentences use the pattern **pronoun + adjective** and in two of the sentences use the pattern **pronoun + else**.

22 There, it, this, that, etc

Say or write down four sentences about the place where you study or work, using **there**. In three sentences, use as many verb tenses and forms as you can. In one sentence use a **number + of + pronoun**.

Say or write down five sentences beginning with **it** to talk about each of the following: the time, the day, the month, the date, a distance.

Say or write down two sentences about the weather. Use **it** in one sentence and **there** in the other.

Say or write down four sentences about things that have happened to you, beginning with the following: It was easy for me … It was kind of … It was great to … It was lucky that …

Imagine that you are showing a visitor round your home. Say or write down pairs of sentences you can tell the visitor about your home, using **this**, **that**, **these,** and **those**. In each pair of sentences, use a noun after **this**, etc in one sentence and use **this**, etc as a **pronoun** in the other sentence.

23 Comparison of adjectives

Say or write down five sentences comparing two people that you know and five sentences comparing two places. Use **comparative adjective + than** and use as many different kinds of adjective as you can.

Say or write down three sentences comparing yourself with someone else, using **as … as**.

Say or write down five sentences about places, using **superlatives**.

24 Adverbs

Say or write down five sentences describing actions you have seen recently, using **adverbs of manner**. Use a different adverb for each sentence.

Say or write down two sentences comparing the way you do or did something with the way another person does or did it. Use **comparative adverb + than** in one sentence and **as + comparative adverb + as** in one sentence.

Say or write down five sentences describing your own experiences and feelings. In one sentence use **extremely/very/really,** in one sentence use **fairly/quite + adjective**, in one sentence use **a fairly**, in one sentence use **quite a**, and in one sentence use **completely/absolutely/totally**.

Say or write down four sentences comparing people you know. Use **much** in one sentence, **a lot** in another, **far** in another, and **a bit** in the other. Use adjectives and adverbs.

25 Prepositions (1)

Say or write down three sentences about where you live, two using **in** and one using **at**.

Say or write down three sentences about where various things are in the place where you live or work, two using **in** and one using **on**.

Say or write down four sentences describing the place where various things are in the room that you are in now. In each sentence, use a different one of the following: **under, above, next to, beside, opposite, in front of, behind, near (to), between.**

Say or write down four sentences describing things that you do when you are on a journey that you know well. In each sentence, use a different one of the following: **out of**, **into**, **across**, **along**, **through**, **up**, **down**, **round**, **towards**, **past**.

Say or write down three sentences about different kinds of transport you use or have used. In each sentence use a different one of the following: **by**, **on**, **in**.

26 Prepositions (2)

Say or write down two sentences describing someone, one using **in** to describe the person's clothes and one using **with** to describe the person physically.

Say or write down one sentence describing something that you use frequently, using **with** to talk about something that it has.

Say or write down two sentences describing how you did something, one using **with** to talk about what you used and one using **by + -ing** to talk about how you did it.

Say or write down one sentence describing something that you didn't do, using **without + -ing**.

Say or write down three sentences about experiences you have had and things you have done, using a different **time prepositional phrase** with **at** in each one.

Say or write down three sentences about the past and the future, using a different **prepositional phrase** with **in** in each one.

Say or write down two sentences about paying for something, using a different **prepositional phrase** in each one.

Say or write down two sentences about communicating with someone and two sentences about technology, using a different **prepositional phrase** in each one.

27 Reported speech

Say or write down six things that people said to you recently. Use **say** in three of the sentences and **tell** in three sentences. Use a different verb form for each sentence.

Say or write down six questions that someone asked you recently. Use **ask + what**, **when**, **where**, **etc** for three of the reported questions and **ask + if/whether** for three reported questions. Use different verb forms.

Say or write down three reported requests and three reported orders or instructions that you have received or made recently. Use **ask** for the requests and **tell** for the orders or instructions.

28 Relative clauses

Say or write down three sentences describing people and three sentences describing things, using relative clauses with the same subject as the rest of the sentence. Use **who** for three of the sentences and **which/that** for three of them.

Say or write down three sentences describing people and three sentences describing things, using relative clauses with different subjects from the rest of the sentence. Use **who** for three of the sentences and **which/that** for three of them.

Say or write down three sentences about your own personal experiences using relative clauses with **where**, **when** and **whose**. Create one sentence for each of them.

29 Conversational English

Write down three questions you might ask in a shop. Then write the three **short answers** to those questions. Use different verb forms.

Imagine three surprising things that a friend might say to you. Write what your friend says and the **short questions** that you use to express your surprise. Use different verb forms.

Choose a country and write three questions with **question tags** about that country. Use different verb forms.

Write three positive statements about a friend of yours that are also true for you. Write **short responses** with **so** and **too** after each statement. Use different verb forms. Then create single sentences with **and**.

Write three negative statements about a friend of yours that are also true for you. Write **short responses** with **neither/nor** and **either** after each statement. Use different verb forms. Then create single sentences with **and**.

30 Clause and sentence building

Say or write down four sentences containing facts about your life. Use **still** in the first sentence, **only** in the second, **also** in the third and **too** in the fourth.

Say or write down four sentences explaining actions that you did recently. Use **because** in the first sentence, **because of** in the second, **so** in the third, and **so that** in the fourth.

Describe a choice you have made recently. Describe what you did in one sentence using **instead of** and in a pair of sentences using **instead** in the second sentence.

Say or write down two sentences describing a fact that is true of only one person or place. Use **apart from** in one sentence and **except (for)** in the other.

Write down three pairs of facts about yourself that contrast. Write one sentence using **although** and one sentence using **though**.

Form tables

A Plural nouns

	SINGULAR	PLURAL
+ -s With most nouns we add **-s** to make them plural:	car mistake photo	car**s** mistake**s** photo**s**
+ -es With nouns that end with **-s**, **-ss**, **-sh**, **-ch** and **-x** we add **-es**:	bus glass wish beach box	bus**es** glass**es** wish**es** beach**es** box**es**
-f/-fe → -ves We change **-f/-fe** to **-ves** in the plural:	life knife *but* roof	li**ves** kni**ves** roof**s**
-y → -ies With nouns that end with a consonant* + **-y**, we change the **-y** to **-ies**:	story city family	stor**ies** cit**ies** famil**ies**
Irregular nouns	man person child	**men** **people** **children**

B Present simple

	I/YOU/WE/THEY	HE/SHE/IT
+ -s After **he/she/it**, we add **-s** to most present simple verbs:	work write say	work**s** write**s** say**s**
+ -es We add **-es** to verbs that end with **-ss**, **-sh**, **-ch**, **-o** or **-x**:	pass finish teach do mix	pass**es** finish**es** teach**es** do**es** mix**es**
-y → -ies We change **-y** to **-ies** with verbs that end with a consonant* + **-y**:	try marry fly	tr**ies** marr**ies** fl**ies**

---

* Consonants
b c d f g h j k
l m n p q r s t
v w x y z

Vowels
a e i o u

Syllables
|hit| = 1 syllable
|vi|sit| = 2 syllables
|re|mem|ber| = 3 syllables

C -ing forms

	INFINITIVE	-ING FORM
+ -ing		
With most verbs we add **-ing**:	walk	walk**ing**
	eat	eat**ing**
-e + -ing		
With verbs that end with a consonant* + **-e**, we delete the **-e** and add **-ing**:	make	mak**ing**
	come	com**ing**
	write	writ**ing**
-ie → -ying		
With verbs that end with **-ie**, we change **-ie** to **-ying**:	lie	l**ying**
	die	d**ying**
	tie	t**ying**
-t → -tting		
With verbs that end with one vowel* + one consonant (e.g. *get*, *hit*, *stop*), we double the consonant:	sit	si**tting**
	run	ru**nning**
	swim	swi**mming**
+ -ing		
But note that we do not double the consonant, 1) when it is **y** or **w** (e.g. *play*) 2) when the last syllable* is not stressed (e.g. *reMEMber*, *VISit*):	play	play**ing**
	happen	happen**ing**
	listen	listen**ing**
	remember	remember**ing**

D Regular verbs: past simple and past participle

	INFINITIVE	PAST SIMPLE	PAST PARTICIPLE
+ -ed			
With most verbs we add **-ed**	cook	cook**ed**	cook**ed**
	finish	finish**ed**	finish**ed**
+ -d			
With verbs ending with **-e**, we add **-d**	live	live**d**	live**d**
	close	close**d**	close**d**
-y → -ied			
With verbs that end with one consonant* + **-y**, we change the **y** to **-ied**:	study	stud**ied**	stud**ied**
	carry	carr**ied**	carr**ied**
	try	tr**ied**	tr**ied**
-p → -pped			
With verbs that end with one vowel* + one consonant (e.g. *stop*), we double the consonant:	stop	sto**pped**	sto**pped**
	plan	pla**nned**	pla**nned**
+ -ed			
But note that we do not double the consonant, 1) when it is **y** or **w** (e.g. *play*) 2) when the last syllable* is not stressed (e.g. *LISten*, *HAppen*, *Open*):	stay	stay**ed**	stay**ed**
	happen	happen**ed**	happen**ed**
	open	open**ed**	open**ed**
	visit	visit**ed**	visit**ed**
Note that in British English **l** is usually doubled, even if the syllable in unstressed (e.g. *travel*)	cancel	cance**lled**	cance**lled**
	travel	trave**lled**	trave**lled**

E Irregular verbs: past simple and past participle

INFINITIVE	PAST SIMPLE	PAST PARTICIPLE
be	was / were	been
become	became	become
begin	began	begun
break	broke	broken
bring	brought	brought
build	built	built
buy	bought	bought
catch	caught	caught
choose	chose	chosen
come	came	come
cost	cost	cost
cut	cut	cut
do	did	done
drink	drank	drunk
drive	drove	driven
eat	ate	eaten
fall	fell	fallen
feel	felt	felt
find	found	found
fly	flew	flown
forget	forgot	forgotten
get	got	got
give	gave	given
go	went	gone
grow	grew	grown
have	had	had
hear	heard	heard
hide	hid	hidden
hit	hit	hit
hold	held	held
hurt	hurt	hurt
keep	kept	kept
know	knew	known
learn	learnt/learned	learnt/learned
leave	left	left

INFINITIVE	PAST SIMPLE	PAST PARTICIPLE
lend	lent	lent
let	let	let
lose	lost	lost
make	made	made
meet	met	met
pay	paid	paid
put	put	put
read	read	read
ring	rang	rung
run	ran	run
say	said	said
see	saw	seen
sell	sold	sold
send	sent	sent
show	showed	shown / showed
shut	shut	shut
sing	sang	sung
sit	sat	sat
sleep	slept	slept
speak	spoke	spoken
spell	spelt / spelled	spelt / spelled
spend	spent	spent
stand	stood	stood
steal	stole	stolen
swim	swam	swum
take	took	taken
teach	taught	taught
tell	told	told
think	thought	thought
throw	threw	thrown
understand	understood	understood
wake	woke	woken
wear	wore	worn
win	won	won
write	wrote	written

F Comparative and superlative adjectives

	ADJECTIVE	COMPARATIVE	SUPERLATIVE
+ -er/-est			
We add **-er/-est** to short adjectives (one-syllable* adjectives):	warm	warm**er**	the warm**est**
	tall	tall**er**	the tall**est**
	young	young**er**	the young**est**
+ -r/-st			
We add **-r/-st** to adjectives that end with **–e**:	late	late**r**	the late**st**
+ -g → -gger			
With short adjectives that end with one vowel* and one consonant* (e.g. *big*), we double the consonant:	big	bi**gger**	the bi**ggest**
	hot	ho**tter**	the ho**ttest**
	wet	we**tter**	the we**ttest**
-w + -er / -est			
We don't double **w**:	low	low**er**	low**est**
more / most			
We use **more / the most** before adjectives of two or more syllables*:	expensive	**more** expensive	the **most** expensive
	famous	**more** famous	the **most** famous
	beautiful	**more** beautiful	the **most** beautiful
-y → -ier / -iest			
But note that with adjectives ending with **-y** (e.g. *happy*), we change **-y** to **-ier / -iest**:	happy	happ**ier**	the happ**iest**
	lucky	luck**ier**	the luck**iest**
	easy	eas**ier**	the eas**iest**
Irregular adjectives			
	good	**better**	the **best**
	bad	**worse**	the **worst**
	far	**further**	the **farthest**

G Adverbs

	ADJECTIVE	ADVERB
+ -ly		
With most adverbs, we add **–ly** to the adjective:	quick	quick**ly**
	correct	correct**ly**
	slow	slow**ly**
Exceptions:		
Adjectives that end with **–y** (y → **-ily**):	happy	happ**ily**
	lucky	luck**ily**
Adjectives that end with **–ble** (~~e~~ + **y**):	remarkable	remarka**bly**
Irregular adverbs:		
	good	**well**
	fast	**fast**
	hard	**hard**
	late	**late**

* Consonants
b c d f g h j k
l m n p q r s t
v w x y z

Vowels
a e i o u

Syllables
|hit| = 1 syllable
|vi|sit| = 2 syllables
|re|mem|ber| = 3 syllables

Verb tenses

infinitive: **cook**

	POSITIVE *full forms (short forms)*	NEGATIVE *full forms (short forms)*	QUESTIONS
Present simple			
I/you/we/they	cook	**do not** cook (you **don't** cook)	**Do** you cook?
He/she/it	cook**s**	**does not** cook (she **doesn't** cook)	**Does** he cook?
Present continuous			
I	**am** cook**ing** (I**'m** cooking)	**am not** cooking (**I'm not** cooking)	**Am** I cooking?
You/we/they	**are** cook**ing** (we**'re** cooking)	**are not** cooking (**aren't** cooking)	**Are** you cooking?
He/she/it	**is** cook**ing** (it**'s** cooking)	**is not** cooking (**isn't** cooking)	**Is** she cooking?
Past simple			
I/you/he/she/it/we/they	cook**ed**	**did not** cook (**didn't** cook)	**Did** you cook?
Past continuous			
I/you/we/they	**was** cook**ing**	**was not** cooking (**wasn't** cooking)	**Was** he cooking?
You/we/they	**were** cook**ing**	**were not** cooking (**weren't** cooking)	**Were** you cooking?
Present perfect			
I/you/we/they	**have** cook**ed** (I**'ve** cooked)	**have not** cooked (**haven't** cooked)	**Have** they cooked?
He/she/it	**has** cook**ed** (he**'s** cooked)	**has not** cooked (**hasn't** cooked)	**Has** she cooked?
Present perfect continuous			
I/you/we/they	**have** been cook**ing** (I**'ve** been cook**ing**)	**have not** been cooking (**haven't** been cooking)	**Have** you been cooking?
He/she/it	**has** been cook**ing** (he**'s** been cook**ing**)	**has not** been cooking (**hasn't** been cooking)	**Has** she been cooking?
Past perfect			
I/you/he/she/it/we/they	**had** cook**ed** (she**'d** cook**ed**)	**had not** cooked (**hadn't** cooked)	**Had** they cooked?

Answer key

01 Present continuous

A
1 I'm drinking
2 We're leaving
3 The train's going
4 I'm travelling
5 are you doing
6 I'm making

B WORD FOCUS C
1 The sun's / is shining
2 The teams are running
3 The England players are wearing
4 Both teams are playing
5 The England fans are looking
6 The players are leaving
7 the players are celebrating
8 The referee is blowing

C
1 What's he doing
2 He's spending
3 He's learning
4 he's having
5 She's living
6 she isn't / she's not going out
7 they aren't / they're not talking
8 He's enjoying
9 He isn't / He's not sitting
10 He's taking

D
1 is getting
2 are moving
3 is causing
4 aren't / are not using
5 aren't / are not / 're not travelling
6 are going
7 are telling
8 aren't / are not listening
9 are talking
10 aren't / are not / 're not doing

E
1 I'm going
2 the Principal's giving
3 I'm attending
4 we're taking
5 we're going
6 we're leaving
7 we're arriving
8 I'm playing
9 I'm not doing
10 I'm cooking
11 We're eating
12 we're watching
13 I'm writing
14 I'm having
15 I'm going
16 I'm playing
17 I'm going
18 I'm not doing
19 I'm staying
20 I'm taking

F
1 I'm doing
2 I'm finding
3 are you doing
4 I'm getting
5 I'm leaving
6 The taxi's / The taxi is coming
7 I'm not going
8 Who's going
9 We're celebrating
10 A band's / A band is playing
11 people are coming
12 I'm staying
13 I'm working
14 I'm going

G
1 'm studying
2 'm having
3 's treating
4 'm making
5 'm not missing
6 'm doing
7 'm learning
8 'm practising
9 'm not studying
10 'm visiting
11 're taking
12 're going
13 'm looking
14 's happening

02 Present simple

A
1 ✓; don't understand
2 ✓; tries
3 ✓; ✓
4 catches; ✓
5 doesn't hit; ✓
6 ✓; ✓
7 last; ✓
8 don't like; ✓

B WORD FOCUS B
An office is a room where a person or people work.
A diary is a list of what someone has to do in the future at work. It is also a small book that is used for writing down what you did each day, after you did it.
A canteen is a restaurant in a place of work.
Conferences are large meetings of business people.

1 brings
2 tells
3 does
4 organizes
5 deals
6 have
7 discuss
8 don't agree
9 don't last
10 don't eat
11 go
12 stay
13 gets
14 finishes
15 don't go
16 work
17 travel

C
1 Do you visit
2 I don't come
3 do you do
4 I read
5 I borrow
6 do you borrow
7 The library has
8 Do other members of your family use
9 my daughter does

D
1 leaves
2 arrive
3 shows
4 go
5 have
6 attend
7 starts
8 finishes
9 get
10 return

E
1 She stars
2 she earns
3 She appears
4 know
5 love
6 are talking
7 are telling
8 doesn't usually discuss
9 wants
10 we're waiting
11 is opening
12 is coming

F
1 speak
2 want
3 think
4 go
5 're studying
6 'm working
7 need
8 like
9 don't like
10 don't play
11 don't watch
12 read
13 'm trying
14 take
15 don't play
16 works
17 travels
18 's travelling
19 buys
20 'm using
21 'm not making

G
1 Are you looking; has
2 Do you need; We're / We are taking
3 love; it's / it is becoming
4 We serve; come
5 's / is growing; we're / we are looking
6 opens; are selling

03 Past simple and past continuous

A
1 moved
2 opened
3 became
4 didn't / did not speak
5 arrived
6 learnt
7 ate
8 worked
9 made
10 was
11 went
12 did
13 passed
14 studied
15 got
16 set
17 sold
18 owned
19 lived
20 bought

B
1 came
2 didn't start
3 arrived
4 didn't say
5 was
6 shouted
7 started
8 drove
9 got
10 wanted
11 made
12 didn't go
13 didn't arrive
14 didn't stay
15 didn't speak
16 were

C
1 was
2 left
3 asked
4 Did you become
5 took
6 played
7 didn't / did not earn
8 Did you feel
9 enjoyed
10 had
11 wanted
12 did it happen
13 saw
14 offered
15 knew
16 helped
17 appeared
18 made
19 bought
20 happened

D
1 was studying
2 was trying
3 was doing
4 wasn't going out
5 were having
6 were going
7 were enjoying
8 was sitting
9 wasn't doing
10 was working
11 was getting
12 was coming
13 was feeling
14 wasn't enjoying
15 was going
16 were saving
17 was planning
18 was serving
19 was living

E **WORD FOCUS** A get lost B get married C get stuck
1 arrived; was speaking
2 was doing; asked
3 was talking; rang
4 came; weren't / were not working; were looking
5 stopped; went
6 was eating; came
7 were sitting; asked
8 was the boss talking; were sitting
9 went; was feeling; was smiling
10 were talking; offered

F
1 met
2 was sitting
3 came
4 asked
5 started
6 were chatting
7 discovered
8 had
9 were writing
10 were doing
11 didn't / did not like
12 became
13 were having
14 had
15 decided
16 were planning
17 continued
18 gave
19 started
20 were travelling
21 had
22 met
23 made
24 were having
25 came
26 wrote

04 Present perfect

A
1 I've worked; I haven't become
2 I've lived; I haven't lived
3 I've studied; I've learnt
4 I've bought; I haven't read
5 I've tried; I haven't found

B
1 he hasn't contacted
2 has he done / 's he done
3 He's decided
4 He's found
5 He hasn't said
6 He hasn't told
7 Has he planned
8 he's given
9 he's sold
10 he's bought

WORD FOCUS very surprised

C
1 's had
2 have joined
3 haven't done
4 hasn't come
5 haven't eaten; 've been

D
1 Helen has left / 's left
2 she's started
3 She's bought
4 Things have got
5 He's found
6 he's become
7 I haven't met
8 people have told
9 The weather has been / 's been
10 The rain hasn't stopped
11 You've made

E
1 ✓
2 ✓
3 We haven't been to that shop yet.
4 I've already bought lots of things.
5 Have you bought anything yet?
6 We've already been here for three hours.
7 I haven't looked in all the shops yet.
8 The shop over there has just opened.
9 ✓
10 ✓

F
1 I've already got my copy.
2 I've just bought it
3 I haven't listened to it yet
4 Have you heard it yet?
5 I've already played it
6 Have you bought tickets for his concert yet?
7 I've just phoned the box office
8 they've already sold out

9 I've already seen him
10 I haven't seen him yet
11 I've just phoned
12 He hasn't phoned back yet

G
1 I've never done
2 I've never jumped
3 I've never climbed
4 I've never dived
5 Have you ever wanted
6 I've never been
7 I've never understood
8 have you ever played
9 I've never been
10 I've never won
11 I've never scored
12 Have you ever tried
13 I've never succeeded
14 Sport has never been
15 Have you ever felt
16 it's never worried

05 Past simple and present perfect

A
1 I've cooked
2 Have you cooked
3 I've cooked
4 I haven't seen
5 did you learn
6 Someone taught
7 I was
8 did you live
9 I lived
10 I had
11 Have you lived
12 I've had
13 I worked
14 Did you enjoy
15 I had
16 I made
17 I enjoyed
18 I've finished

B
1 have you done
2 I've forgotten
3 I've left
4 I put
5 I decided
6 I didn't take
7 I haven't brought
8 did you book
9 I did
10 they sent
11 did you pay
12 I paid
13 Did they send
14 I've found
15 they've kept

C WORD FOCUS B
1 's / has played
2 's / has won
3 voted
4 hasn't been
5 left
6 got
7 worked
8 was
9 went
10 had
11 saw
12 chose
13 changed
14 've / have wanted

D
1 5 years ago
2 since April
3 3 months ago
4 since 1996
5 for 6 months
6 for 2 months
7 for 3 weeks

E
1. I've / I have known him since 2002.
2. Steve has / Steve's worked for the same company for five years.
3. I haven't / have not seen Steve for a couple of months.
4. Steve hasn't / has not phoned me since March.
5. We haven't / have not played tennis together for a long time.
6. Steve has / Steve's been very busy for several months.
7. Steve hasn't / has not had a holiday since last year.

F
1. did he go there
2. He went
3. Have you ever been there
4. I've never been there
5. I've been there
6. She's gone home
7. She's gone to bed
8. I've never been here
9. has she gone
10. she's gone outside

06 The future

A
1. I'm going to do; I'm going to get
2. I'm going to join; I'm going to run
3. I'm not going to sit; I'm going to go
4. I'm not going to spend; I'm going to save
5. I'm not going to watch; I'm going to read
6. I'm going to lose; I'm not going to eat
7. I'm going to be; I'm not going to shout
8. I'm going to learn; I'm going to prepare
9. I'm not going to worry; I'm going to enjoy

B **WORD FOCUS** A audience B refreshments C interval D show
1. are you going to get
2. I'm going to get
3. The rest of you are going to come
4. are the refreshments going to arrive
5. They're going to arrive
6. We're going to put
7. we're going to arrange
8. are people going to start
9. People are going to start
10. Robin and Thelma are going to organize
11. Pamela is / Pamela's going to collect
12. Alan is / Alan's going to help
13. is the timetable for the show going to be
14. The first part of the show is going to finish
15. Elaine and Frank are going to serve
16. The interval is / The interval's going to last
17. The second part of the show is going to begin
18. The show is / The show's going to finish
19. Are we going to stay
20. we're going to tidy

C
1. 's / is going to taste
2. 's / is going to fall
3. 's / is going to be
4. 're / are going to drop
5. isn't / 's not going to look
6. isn't / 's not going to work
7. 're / are going to ruin

D
1. I'll go
2. I'll keep
3. I'll tell
4. Will you wake
5. I won't forget
6. I'll bring you
7. Shall I cook
8. I won't have
9. you'll be
10. I'll leave
11. I'll be
12. you'll do
13. you'll get

E
1. Shall I meet
2. I'll walk
3. Will you find
4. it'll be
5. I won't get
6. Shall I send
7. I won't need
8. Shall I bring
9. that won't be
10. I'll put
11. You'll be
12. Shall I call
13. I'll wait
14. we'll have

F
1. 'll meet
2. 'll learn
3. 'll be
4. won't miss
5. won't be
6. 'll talk
7. 'll wonder
8. won't forget
9. Shall I write
10. will you contact
11. 'll keep
12. Will you tell
13. will you send
14. won't be
15. 'll come
16. 'll fix

07 Question words

A
1. Whose
2. How
3. When
4. Where
5. Why
6. Who
7. Which

B
1. Why did you buy a new dress?
2. Where did you buy it?
3. What is / What's the shop called?
4. Which street is the shop in?
5. Whose party is it?
6. Who is / Who's Stella?

C
1. Where does the London Marathon end?
2. Whose statue is
3. What do people buy
4. When did Heathrow Airport open?
5. Which street does the Prime Minister live in?
6. Why do people go

D
1. Why did you run away?
2. When did you last see the missing person?
3. How did the burglars get into your house?
4. Which window did the burglars break?
5. What did the burglars take?

E
1. How much
2. How long
3. How far
4. How many
5. How often
6. How good

F
1. How old is the building?
2. How long has it been a museum?
3. How popular is it?
4. How many tourists visit it every year?
5. How often are there special exhibitions?
6. How much does a season ticket for the museum cost?

G **WORD FOCUS** B
1. Whose assistant is he
2. What did he tell
3. Why is he leaving
4. When is he going to leave
5. Where is he going to work
6. Which company is he going to work for
7. How big is that company
8. How did he get
9. How much is he going to earn

08 Subject and object questions

A
1. Who knows the answer?
2. Who's / Who is going to hand out the books?
3. Who got every answer right?
4. Who's / Who is listening carefully?
5. Who left a pen here yesterday?
6. Who's / Who has finished the exercise?

B
1. Who's / Who is Elaine going out with?
2. Who did Mark sit next to on the bus?
3. Who do you like most in the class?
4. Who's / Who is going to be Ruth's partner next week?
5. Who's / Who has Eric invited to his party?
6. Who was Tom phoning in the break?

C **WORD FOCUS** B
1. Who killed Chris?
2. Who saw what happened?
3. Who's / Who is Harry trying to find?
4. Who's / Who is trying to find Olivia?
5. Who does Harry want to kill?
6. Who has / Who's left her husband?
7. Who's / Who is Sharon living with now?
8. Who's / Who is going to start a new life in Australia?
9. Who's / Who is in love with Sharon?
10. Who's / Who is Geoff in love with?

D
1. What's / What is your job title?
2. Who sits next to you in the office?
3. Who do you have lunch with most days?
4. Who runs the department?
5. What happened at work today?
6. What are you working on at the moment?
7. Who did you work with on that project?
8. What did the project involve?
9. Who applied to be the new boss?
10. Who did they appoint as the new boss?

E
1. What did Edward Jenner discover?
2. Which very famous character did the author JK Rowling create?
3. Who did John Wilkes Booth shoot in Washington in 1865?
4. What caused the Great Fire of London in 1666?
5. Who won the award for Best Actor at last year's Oscars?
6. Which king of England had six wives?
7. Who's / Who has had more Number 1 hits in Britain than any other singer?

F
1. won the painting competition?
2. painting won the painting competition?
3. did Daniel paint?
4. painting did the teacher choose?
5. did the teacher give the first prize to?
6. painting came second in the competition?
7. was the title of your painting?
8. painting did you like the most?

09 Can, could, and would

A
1. I can't hear
2. I can't get
3. I can't find
4. Can you speak up
5. I couldn't hear
6. I can't open
7. Can you remember
8. I can remember
9. I couldn't find
10. I can't explain
11. Can you wait
12. I can drive
13. I can open

B
1. couldn't speak
2. could understand
3. could go
4. couldn't have
5. can speak
6. can make
7. can do
8. can't remember
9. can think of
10. can understand

C
1 I can go / I'll be able to go
2 Can we discuss
3 we can arrange
4 Can we go / Will we be able to go
5 We can't use / We won't be able to use
6 Can you borrow / Will you be able to borrow
7 he can't lend / he won't be able to lend
8 Can we get / Will we be able to get
9 We can't take / We won't be able to take
10 we can get / we'll be able to get
11 I can look up
12 Can you do
13 I can phone / I'll be able to phone
14 I can tell / I'll be able to tell

D
1 were able to / managed to get
2 were able to / managed to arrive
3 couldn't find
4 were able to / managed to carry
5 were able to / managed to find
6 were able to / managed to book
7 were able to / managed to see
8 couldn't take
9 couldn't get
10 couldn't use
11 were able to / managed to find
12 were able to / managed to come

E
1 Could / Would / Can you show
2 Could / Would / Can you tell
3 Can / Could / May I recommend
4 Could / Can / May I order
5 Can / Could / May I take
6 Could / Can we move
7 Can / Could / May I change
8 Could / Would / Can you bring
9 Could / Can we have
10 Could / Would / Can you get

F
1 we can do
2 Can you watch
3 I'm not allowed to watch
4 can watch
5 I'm not allowed to do
6 I'm allowed to watch
7 I can't watch
8 Are you allowed to play
9 I can play
10 I can't play

WORD FOCUS   A speak   B look   C stay

G
1 could I book
2 Could you wait
3 May I have
4 Would you spell
5 Could you tell
6 Could I make
7 Could I stay
8 you can't smoke
9 Can I park
10 you can leave
11 can I use
12 you can go
13 could you give
14 would you send

10 May, might, could, and should

A
1 might see
2 might come
3 might be
4 might not enjoy
5 might find
6 might not think
7 might not be
8 might make
9 might have
10 might not get
11 might be
12 might want
13 might be
14 might have to
15 might be able to

B
1 might get;   might not be
2 might visit;   might not have
3 might travel;   might come
4 might read;   might not want
5 might not rain; might spend
6 might not do;   might take

C
1 may not arrive
2 may have to
3 may last
4 may not leave
5 may get
6 may not get back
7 may have
8 may not be able to

D
1 might not speak
2 might not be
3 might want
4 may book
5 may do
6 might organize
7 might get on
8 might offer
9 might not be able to
10 might forget
11 may not go
12 may not stay

E
1 might / could arrive
2 might / could make
3 might not be
4 might / could rise
5 might / could appear
6 might not last
7 might / could be
8 might not feel
9 might / could enjoy
10 might not rain

F **WORD FOCUS** A
1 might invite
2 might get
3 might do
4 could go
5 might do
6 could give
7 might stay
8 could have

G
1 it might not happen
2 I might fail
3 you shouldn't do
4 it shouldn't take
5 I should get
6 we might play
7 we might watch
8 we might not stay
9 we might decide
10 it should be

11 Must and have to

A (i)
1. must pay
2. must get
3. must arrive
4. must complete
5. must tell

(ii)
1. have to pay
2. have to get
3. has to arrive
4. have to complete
5. have to tell

B
1. I must meet / have to meet
2. she must speak / she has to speak
3. she must discuss / she has to discuss
4. I must hurry / I have to hurry
5. she had to borrow
6. I had to give
7. I must tell / I have to tell / I'll have to tell

C
1. have to get
2. have to leave
3. have to catch
4. had to walk
5. has to drive
6. has to have
7. 'll have to find

D
1. (really) must go
2. (really) must meet
3. (really) must eat
4. (really) must see
5. (really) must spend
6. (really) must look
7. (really) must take
8. (really) must bring

E
1. mustn't touch
2. have to get
3. have to win
4. has to jump
5. mustn't start
6. have to cross
7. mustn't kick

F WORD FOCUS A sensible B risks C fancy D disturb
1. mustn't
2. don't have to
3. mustn't
4. don't have to
5. mustn't
6. don't have to
7. don't have to
8. don't have to
9. mustn't
10. don't have to

G
1. I mustn't tell
2. you don't have to tell
3. Do you have to play
4. I don't have to do
5. Do you have to go
6. I won't / don't have to go
7. Did you have to get
8. I didn't have to do
9. You mustn't repeat
10. I mustn't say

12 Should

A
1. you should do
2. You should go
3. you shouldn't visit
4. I think you should walk
5. you should look for
6. You shouldn't spend
7. You should experience
8. Do you think I should hire
9. I don't think you should do
10. You should use
11. Should I get
12. you shouldn't travel
13. You should remember
14. you shouldn't try

B WORD FOCUS A up B for C away
1. shouldn't use
2. should walk
3. should cycle
4. shouldn't fly
5. shouldn't buy
6. shouldn't throw away
7. should recycle
8. should organize
9. should produce
10. shouldn't destroy
11. should look for
12. shouldn't use up
13. shouldn't wait
14. should take care

C
1. should come on
2. shouldn't make
3. should be
4. shouldn't appear
5. shouldn't look

D
1. you could start
2. I'd speak / I would speak
3. I wouldn't get
4. you could apologize
5. I wouldn't listen
6. I'd forget / I would forget
7. I'd eat / I would eat
8. I wouldn't feel

E
1. mustn't
2. must
3. should
4. might not
5. should
6. shouldn't
7. shouldn't
8. should
9. might not
10. might
11. should
12. might

F
1. wouldn't
2. shouldn't
3. 'd / would
4. could
5. must
6. mustn't
7. might not
8. might

13 The infinitive

A
1. to bring
2. to improve
3. to spend
4. to take
5. to go
6. to pay
7. to see
8. to arrive
9. to get in

B
1. refused to play
2. offered to take
3. agreed to bring
4. promised to be

C
1. 've / have agreed not to discuss
2. decided not to get
3. 'll / will try not to do
4. 'll / will remember not to go
5. promise not to scare

D **WORD FOCUS** A
1 didn't want her old boyfriend to go
  don't want him to be
2 wanted people to have
  don't want the food to run out
3 didn't want people to sit
  want everyone to dance

E
1 Can I use
2 Should I get
3 it might / it may be
4 They must be
5 You'll find / You can find

F
1 wouldn't / didn't let us go
2 made us do
3 lets people behave
4 makes everyone concentrate
5 lets us enjoy
6 won't / doesn't let students give
7 let us bring
8 made me read

G
1 describe
2 to take
3 to go
4 visit
5 me to meet
6 to have
7 everyone sing
8 to do
9 me miss
10 not to get
11 not to laugh
12 not to look
13 to pay
14 say
15 be
16 stay
17 to rent
18 to bring

14 The -ing form

A
1 to stop joining
2 doesn't like sitting
3 hates waiting
4 doesn't enjoy travelling
5 to keep doing
6 love listening
7 enjoy being
8 don't mind getting
9 finish / 've finished / have finished working
10 like spending

B
1 went skiing
2 go shopping
3 went dancing
4 go swimming
5 went skating

C
1 Understanding
2 Shopping
3 Travelling
4 parking
5 driving
6 crossing
7 being
8 Going
9 meeting
10 Leaving

D
1 don't like buying
2 Would / Do you mind coming
3 don't mind helping
4 go shopping
5 hate doing
6 don't like spending
7 don't enjoy being
8 Trying
9 Stop complaining
10 haven't finished / didn't finish telling
11 Would / Do you mind listening
12 keep talking
13 love shopping

WORD FOCUS A nice B special C boring D busy

E
1 I like spending
2 I'd like to go
3 I like coming
4 I like talking
5 I'd like to work
6 would you like to happen
7 I'd like to earn
8 I'd like to give up
9 I don't like being
10 I'd like to have

F
1 Getting
2 Phoning
3 to speak
4 to leave
5 to fix
6 Planning
7 making
8 To help
9 Doing
10 to stop

G
1 to take
2 To save
3 going
4 having
5 spending
6 to keep
7 dancing
8 to save
9 Choosing
10 to experience
11 seeing
12 finding out
13 To choose
14 to learn
15 to visit
16 staying
17 finding
18 to be
19 doing
20 To get
21 booking
22 Organizing
23 to help
24 to travel
25 to be

15 The passive

A
1 was being repaired
2 was told
3 was delayed
4 was put
5 were given
6 were searched
7 was taken out
8 was charged
9 wasn't shown

B
1 is going to be shown
2 is going to be completed
3 are going to be created
4 have been chosen
5 have been named
6 have been left

C
1 can be made
2 are accepted
3 will be delivered
4 must be provided
5 is being processed
6 has been sent

D
1 when was it taken
2 I wasn't invited
3 The party wasn't planned
4 lots of people weren't told
5 How many people were invited
6 Harry is being covered
7 I wouldn't be amused

E
1 Details of all our courses can be found
2 Lessons are not given
3 All course fees must be paid
4 New courses are being introduced
5 Tests are taken

F
1 stories are sent in by children
2 fantastic stories are being created by many of you
3 the competition was won by a story
4 that story was written by Ellie Stone
5 It was published by the teenage magazine
6 it was read by thousands of people
7 the competition is going to be judged by the film director
8 the top prize is being offered by a film studio
9 the winning story will be made into a short film by Marvin
10 That film will be shown by this channel

G **WORD FOCUS** A event B action C person
1 took
2 was being served
3 was grabbed
4 am / 'm being robbed
5 will be seen
6 will be asked
7 will be written
8 wasn't seen
9 appeared
10 ran
11 will help
12 might remember
13 contained
14 will throw
15 will be found
16 will be returned
17 has happened

16 Conditionals

A
1 don't do
2 won't be able to
3 'll do
4 aren't
5 'll save
6 find
7 'll be
8 don't see
9 doesn't improve
10 'll go
11 write
12 'll reply

B
1 we won't get
2 it won't matter
3 we're
4 will the others do
5 we're not
6 they won't panic
7 they have to
8 people will be
9 we don't turn up
10 you keep
11 everything will be
12 he makes
13 everyone will be
14 he wants
15 nobody will mind
16 he tells
17 we'll laugh
18 he talks
19 I'll have to

WORD FOCUS A turn up B hurry C panic; D mind E matter

C
1 d   4 f   7 a
2 g   5 h   8 c
3 b   6 e

D
1 used   wouldn't be
2 did   would help
3 wouldn't be   didn't eat
4 wouldn't suffer wasn't
5 wouldn't be   didn't like

E
1 would it be   12 I'd stand
2 I could be   13 I'd enjoy
3 I'd be   14 I stopped
4 I was   15 I'd give up
5 I could play   16 you gave up
6 it would be   17 would you do
7 would you play   18 I decided
8 you could choose   19 I'd become
9 I'd love   20 I worked
10 I'd join   21 I'd teach
11 I'd play   22 they'd learn

F
1 If you could change your appearance, what would you change?
2 If you watch TV tonight, what will you watch?
3 If you go out tonight, where will you go?
4 If you could live in another country, where would you live?
5 If you had a lot of money, what would you buy?
6 If you learn to speak English well, how will you use the language?

17 Connecting future clauses

A
1 Unless you pay attention
2 unless you concentrate
3 Unless you make a mistake
4 unless you reach a high standard
5 Unless your parents buy an instrument for you
6 Unless I'm late for some reason

B
1 As long as you don't panic
2 Even if you don't pass
3 As long as you write clearly
4 Even if you don't know all the answers
5 Even if some of the questions are hard
6 As long as you do your best

C **WORD FOCUS** A raincoat, jumper B medicines, tablets
1 in case we're not / we aren't
2 in case it gets
3 in case we have
4 in case one of us starts
5 in case we need

D
1 unless I get
2 in case it's / it is
3 as long as I get
4 unless he changes
5 even if she gets
6 unless his girlfriend agrees
7 even if we don't know
8 As long as the music's / music is
9 in case you don't see

E
1 until I reach
2 When you arrive
3 until you see
4 As soon as you pass
5 when I'm
6 before you get
7 As soon as you turn
8 when I get there
9 When you come
10 until the barrier lifts

F
1 until the meat has cooled down
2 When you've chopped
3 until it has gone
4 After you've prepared
5 when the oven has reached
6 until it has cooked
7 After you've added
8 After the dish has been

G
1 When you've learnt
2 before you move
3 until you feel
4 Even if a climb seems
5 Unless you try
6 in case something goes
7 as soon as you do
8 As long as you obey
9 When you stand
10 After you've completed

18 Articles

A
1 a
2 a
3 a
4 the
5 a
6 a
7 a
8 a
9 the
10 a
11 the
12 the
13 the
14 a
15 the
16 a
17 a
18 the
19 the
20 the
21 a
22 a
23 the
24 a
25 the

B
1 a
2 a
3 the
4 the
5 a
6 the
7 the
8 the
9 the
10 the
11 the
12 the
13 a
14 an

C
1 ✓
2 ✓✓
3 the
4 the
5 ✓
6 a
7 the
8 ✓
9 ✓
10 the

D
1 the
2 The
3 an
4 the
5 an
6 a
7 a
8 the
9 The
10 a
11 a
12 an
13 a
14 a
15 an
16 the
17 a
18 a
19 the
20 a
21 a
22 the

E **WORD FOCUS** health; election(s); employment; politician(s); education
1 ✓
2 the subject
3 a politician
4 ✓
5 ✓
6 ✓
7 employment
8 a big subject
9 ✓
10 ✓
11 ✓
12 lies
13 the lives
14 ✓
15 attitudes
16 changes
17 ✓
18 ✓
19 good ones
20 a successful politician
21 ✓
22 peace
23 the world
24 ✓
25 ✓

F
1 -
2 -
3 -
4 the
5 -
6 -
7 -
8 -
9 the
10 -
11 -
12 -
13 -
14 -
15 the
16 -
17 -
18 -
19 the
20 -
21 the
22 -
23 the
24 the
25 the
26 -

G
1 a
2 -
3 a
4 -
5 -
6 -
7 -
8 a
9 the
10 -
11 -
12 -
13 a
14 -
15 -
16 -
17 -
18 -
19 -
20 the
21 the
22 the

19 Pronouns and possessives

A
1 me
2 They
3 she
4 her
5 him
6 he
7 We
8 us
9 We
10 them
11 they
12 we
13 it
14 it

B
1 yours
2 mine
3 his
4 his
5 his
6 hers
7 her
8 our
9 theirs

C
1 ✓
2 ✓
3 Mine ✓ mine
4 ✓ ✓
5 ours
6 her ✓

D WORD FOCUS A overhead compartment B row C boarding card
1 mine
2 Yours
3 my
4 our
5 mine
6 yours
7 its
8 our
9 your
10 their
11 Theirs
12 his
13 hers
14 their
15 ours

E
1 myself
2 themselves
3 ourselves
4 himself
5 yourself
6 yourselves

F
1 did everything ourselves
2 enjoyed ourselves
3 built them himself
4 hurt himself
5 make them yourself
6 taught myself
7 put them together myself
8 do things themselves

G
1 each other
2 each other
3 yourselves
4 each other; each other
5 ourselves
6 each other
7 themselves

20 Quantifiers

A
1 a lot of; most of
2 all my
3 Some; any
4 a lot of my
5 all; the most of them
6 any
7 all
8 any
9 all of it

B
1 any of
2 of them
3 of them
4 a lot
5 of them
6 of it
7 a few
8 a few
9 of it
10 of it
11 of the
12 of them

C
1 a few
2 a little
3 a lot
4 a few
5 a few
6 a little
7 a lot
8 a little
9 a little
10 a few

D
1 ✓
2 most of
3 ✓
4 Most
5 all
6 ✓
7 ✓
8 all of

E
1 much
2 much
3 much
4 many
5 many
6 much
7 much of
8 many of
9 much of
10 many of
11 much of

F WORD FOCUS 1 B 2 D 3 A 4 C
1 none of
2 None of
3 no
4 no
5 no
6 no
7 none of
8 no
9 no
10 no

G
1 all
2 any
3 none
4 much
5 a few
6 many
7 a lot
8 most; a little
9 no

21 Pronouns and determiners

A
1 old one
2 that one
3 one of the new
4 one of those
5 this one
6 the only one
7 the ones
8 The one
9 one
10 Which one
11 really good one
12 cheap ones
13 very expensive ones
14 the one

B
1 the other
2 another
3 the other
4 the others
5 the other one
6 other
7 the other
8 other
9 the others
10 another

WORD FOCUS A in a cupboard; on his bed B on the floor C in a pile D on his shoulders

C   1 which ones
    2 the ones
    3 ones
    4 one of
    5 the other
    6 one
    7 the other one
    8 the other
    9 The ones
    10 ones
    11 another

D   1 everywhere
    2 anywhere
    3 somewhere
    4 nothing
    5 somebody / someone
    6 everybody / everyone
    7 nobody / no one
    8 something
    9 something
    10 anything

E   1 anybody / anyone else
    2 somebody / someone new
    3 anything else
    4 anything
    5 nobody / no one else
    6 everything else
    7 nothing unusual
    8 anywhere exciting
    9 anything different
    10 Everything
    11 something good
    12 everybody / everyone

F   1 anything / anybody else
    2 understood
    3 other
    4 anywhere
    5 ones
    6 somebody / someone
    7 one
    8 another
    9 something wrong
    10 There's / There is

22 There, it, this, that, etc.

A   1 It's
    2 there aren't
    3 There are
    4 it
    5 there
    6 It's
    7 There
    8 it's
    9 it
    10 it's
    11 It's
    12 There's

B   1 there
    2 it
    3 there
    4 it
    5 It
    6 it
    7 There

C   1 There are six of them
    2 There are
    3 ✓
    4 It's
    5 ✓
    6 it's
    7 There are
    8 there's

D   1 it was very good of you to invite
    2 it'll be difficult for me to come
    3 There's
    4 It's unfortunate that I
    5 There'll be five of us
    6 It's too late for me to find
    7 it's impossible for me to come
    8 It's a pity we
    9 Are there
    10 It's always great to spend / spending

E   1 this   5 These   9 that
    2 this   6 these   10 That
    3 these   7 that   11 those
    4 this   8 those   12 this

F   1 these   7 those   12 that
    2 those   8 those   13 that
    3 that   9 that   14 that
    4 these   10 these   15 these
    5 this   11 those   16 these
    6 that

G   1 it   6 that
    2 There   7 it
    3 this   8 This
    4 there   9 It
    5 this   10 there

WORD FOCUS   C

23 Comparison of adjectives

A   1 more expensive   5 more advanced
    2 more modern   6 fitter
    3 better   7 worse
    4 nicer   8 more powerful

B   1 scarier   6 more popular
    2 more frightened than   7 easier
    3 braver than   8 Fewer
    4 calmer   9 more entertaining
    5 funnier than

C   1 better at maths than me
    2 smaller than his
    3 richer than mine
    4 nearer the school than me
    5 more fashionable than mine
    6 thinner than him
    7 younger than mine

D
1 freer
2 more flexible
3 more relaxed
4 happier than
5 lazier
6 more difficult than
7 more stressful
8 lonelier than
9 more organized
10 more; more common

WORD FOCUS A stressful B lonely

E
1 wasn't as expensive as
2 do as much work as
3 haven't got as many qualifications as
4 'm not as brave as
5 'm as happy as
6 don't earn as much money as
7 isn't as good as
8 don't go to as many parties as

F
1 the most exciting
2 the most beautiful
3 the nicest
4 the most difficult
5 the funniest
6 the cleanest; the dirtiest
7 the hottest; the coldest
8 the worst
9 the most interesting
10 the friendliest

G
1 the biggest
2 more successful than
3 more popular than
4 as many employees as
5 the best
6 higher than
7 bigger; bigger
8 the most interesting
9 further / farther
10 longer
11 as challenging as
12 as much money as
13 the nicest
14 the finest

24 Adverbs

A
1 efficiently
2 carefully
3 punctually
4 late
5 well
6 quickly
7 politely
8 hard
9 easily
10 successfully

B
1 well
2 angrily
3 nervously
4 busily
5 quickly
6 incorrectly
7 late
8 secretly
9 immediately
10 easily

C
1 better than
2 harder than
3 faster
4 more confidently
5 more accurately
6 more loudly
7 more easily than
8 more impressively
9 more unpleasantly
10 more intelligently than

D
1 as fashionably as
2 as well as
3 as carefully as
4 as clearly as
5 as healthily as

E
1 quite / fairly
2 very / extremely / really
3 quite; fairly
4 really / extremely / very
5 fairly / quite
6 very / really / extremely; very / extremely / really
7 totally / completely / absolutely
8 absolutely

F
1 a lot younger than
2 far better than
3 a bit more suitable than
4 a bit older than
5 much more experienced
6 far more confidently than
7 a bit more carefully than
8 much more ambitious
9 a lot keener
10 much happier

WORD FOCUS A keen B suitable C ambitious

G
1 silently
2 hard
3 slowly
4 absolutely
5 quite
6 well
7 fairly
8 far
9 quickly
10 lot
11 bit
12 more

25 Prepositions (1)

A
1 in
2 in
3 at
4 on
5 at
6 in
7 On
8 in
9 in
10 in

B
1 inside
2 outside
3 in front
4 Next
5 behind
6 above
7 near
8 under

C
1 behind
2 at
3 at
4 in
5 on the
6 in
7 in
8 on the
9 in

D
1 at
2 outside
3 in
4 on
5 under
6 next to / beside
7 above
8 between

E
1 by
2 on
3 out of
4 down
5 out of
6 along
7 round
8 through / round
9 to
10 across
11 over
12 up
13 onto / across
14 into
15 through

F
1 ✓
2 by taxi / in a taxi
3 ✓
4 under
5 by bike / on my bike
6 by bus / on the bus; off; near

146 | Answer key

G **WORD FOCUS** 1 limousine 2 bodyguards 3 barrier
4 red carpet 5 fans
1 in   6 outside   11 round
2 out of   7 past   12 in
3 towards   8 behind   13 on
4 between   9 In front   14 next
5 along   10 on   15 into

26 Prepositions (2)

A 1 in   4 with   7 with
  2 with 5 with   8 in
  3 with 6 with   9 with

B 1 without spending   4 by practising
  2 by using   5 by playing
  3 without having   6 without feeling

C **WORD FOCUS** B
  1 in   4 in; with   7 By
  2 without   5 with   8 with
  3 with   6 by

D 1 in a suit
  2 with about 50 employees
  3 with a view over the city
  4 without stopping for lunch
  5 by creating advertisements for other companies
  6 with a good salary
  7 by doing research with customers

E 1 in   3 at   5 on
  2 at   4 by

F 1 At   5 by   9 by
  2 At   6 on   10 in
  3 In   7 in   11 in
  4 on   8 in

G 1 with   5 on   9 by
  2 with   6 on   10 without
  3 on   7 in
  4 on   8 on

27 Reported speech

A 1 he didn't know
  2 (that) she couldn't believe
  3 I was going to complain
  4 he would be
  5 (that) they wanted
  6 he/she was beginning
  7 (that) the train hadn't moved
  8 the same thing had happened

B 1 had started   7 was   13 was going to be
  2 was having   8 had to go   14 wouldn't be
  3 was   9 could meet   15 would give
  4 were   10 would be   16 would wait
  5 was doing   11 hadn't seen
  6 loved   12 couldn't meet

C **WORD FOCUS** out
  1 told Anne that I was
  2 told Mary that Neil wouldn't do
  3 told Wendy that Neil was going to start
  4 told Elaine that Bruce couldn't get
  5 told George that Bruce had asked
  6 told Oliver that Kate had bought
  7 told Diane that Kate's new dress didn't suit

D 1 when I could start
  2 what my ambitions were
  3 how much I was earning
  4 where I had seen
  5 why I wouldn't be able to
  6 when I was going to get back

E 1 what time the museum opened
  2 if / whether the shops would be
  3 how much a travel card cost
  4 if / whether she had left
  5 if / whether the festival had started
  6 where he / she / they could find
  7 if / whether it was going to stop
  8 if / whether I liked

F 1 (that) I couldn't sleep
  2 me to shut up
  3 him not to be
  4 him not to make
  5 me (that) he wasn't going to turn
  6 him (that) I would call
  7 (that) he didn't care
  8 me to go away
  9 them to come
 10 him not to disturb
 11 (that) he didn't want

28 Relative clauses

A 1 He works for a company which sells sports equipment.
  2 He has relatives who have been in Australia for many years.
  3 He has a wife who got a job as a teacher at a local school.
  4 They live in a nice house which is very close to the beach.
  5 They have three children who love living in Australia.

B
1 who plays
2 that's just finished
3 that won
4 that started
5 who also works
6 who helps
7 that happen
8 who does
9 that show
10 who starred

C **WORD FOCUS** **A** groceries **B** (a) takeaway
1 who lives in the next apartment will help
2 that sells basic groceries is
3 who owns the shop speaks
4 that does really good food is
5 who cleans the apartment comes
6 that tells you all about events in the city is

D
1 who she knows
2 which nobody else will get
3 which I'm sure
4 which you showed
5 which I bought
6 who I haven't seen
7 which she didn't like
8 who I always enjoy

E
1 who we met
2 when we went
3 that another guest at the hotel took
4 where we stayed
5 whose names I can't remember
6 that I bought
7 who we made friends with
8 whose bag got lost

F
1 that / which is the tallest in the world.
2 that / which Louis Armstrong played.
3 who / that people called 'The King'.
4 that / which William Webb Ellis invented.
5 where the President of the US lives.
6 who / that made the Star Wars films.
7 when the Beatles became famous.
8 who / that discovered penicillin.
9 whose capital city is Helsinki.

29 Conversational English

A
1 I'm not
2 I didn't
3 I am
4 you can't
5 I did
6 I will

B **WORD FOCUS** **B**
1 Has he?
2 Is she?
3 Does she?
4 Haven't you?
5 Isn't she?
6 Doesn't she?
7 Did he?
8 Were you?

C
1 Are you? I'm not.
2 Do you? I don't.
3 Can't you? I can.
4 Aren't you? I am.
5 Don't you? I do.

D
1 haven't you?
2 have you?
3 won't you?
4 wasn't it?
5 didn't they?
6 do you?
7 will you?
8 is he?

E
1 So am I.
2 Neither / Nor did I.
3 So is mine.
4 Neither / Nor could I.
5 So do I.
6 So have I.
7 So does yours.
8 Neither / Nor am I.

F
1 do too
2 so are
3 couldn't either
4 haven't either
5 is too
6 neither / nor can
7 does too
8 can't either
9 neither / nor is
10 so does

G
1 Don't you? I do.
2 are too
3 So do
4 neither / nor does
5 too
6 Have they?
7 Neither / Nor do
8 isn't it?
9 so does
10 does too
11 can't either

30 Clause and sentence building

A
1 I'm still working
2 I still have
3 I still don't like
4 I'm still not
5 I'm still applying
6 I still haven't found
7 you can still meet

B
1 I've only been
2 ✓
3 ✓
4 I'm only going to stay
5 ✓
6 I can only speak

C
1 ✓
2 Also,
3 ✓
4 am / 'm also learning
5 have / 've also travelled
6 can also type / can type too

D
1 also
2 still
3 only
4 only
5 still
6 only
7 Also
8 only
9 too
10 still
11 only
12 still

E
1 so that
2 because
3 because of
4 so that
5 so
6 so
7 because of
8 because

F **WORD FOCUS** **A** exhibits **B** souvenirs
1 stayed at college instead
2 Though the guided tour was short
3 instead of listening to the guide
4 except (for) the interactive exhibits
5 Apart from me
6 Although I didn't learn a lot

G
1 still
2 instead
3 so
4 only
5 Although
6 Also
7 apart
8 Instead of
9 because of
10 too
11 so that
12 except

Answer key Over to you

01 Present continuous
- I'm sitting at my desk.
- My brother is studying at college.
- I'm going to the cinema next Friday.

02 Present simple
- I catch the bus to school.
- My favourite programme starts at 8.30 tonight.
- I listen to music a lot but I'm studying English at the moment.

03 Past simple and past continuous
- I met my best friend 10 years ago.
- A year ago, I was learning to drive.
- I was sitting at home when I heard a noise.

04 Present perfect
- I've performed in a play.
- I've done some shopping today.
- I've just eaten my lunch.
- I haven't had a full-time job yet.

05 Past simple and present perfect
- I've learnt how to play the guitar. / I learnt three years ago.
- I last saw a film two weeks ago. / I haven't seen a film for two weeks. I haven't seen a film since March.

06 The future
- I'm going to get a well-paid job.
- My team is going to win its match next week.
- I don't think I'll get married for a long time.

07 Question words
- What are you working on at the moment? / Where did you grow up? / How did you become successful?
- How much does a flat cost? / How many people live there? / How hot does it get?

08 Subject and object questions
- Who lives next door? Who has bought a new car? / Who got a new job last year?
- Who is she going out with? / What did she win last year? Which team does he play for?
- Who lives at 10 Downing Street? / What did Enid Blyton write? / Which country did the dancer Rudolf Nureyev come from? / Whose face appears on a $100 note?

09 Can, could, and would
- Six months ago I couldn't play a musical instrument but I can play the guitar now. / Years ago, I could climb trees but I can't do that now.
- I can enjoy myself at weekends. / I can't travel abroad next year. / I wanted to go to the concert but I couldn't get a ticket.
- Can I try on that jacket, please? Could I return this CD? Could you help me, please? Would you put it in a bag, please?
- I can take my bike to school. / We can't/aren't allowed to use mobile phones at school.

10 May, might, could, and should
- I may get rich. / I might live in another country.
- People may not continue to damage the environment. / Life might not be so difficult for some people.
- I could do much better at school. / I could become a professional musician one day.
- My team should win its next game. / I shouldn't feel very tired when I get home tonight.

11 Must and have to
- I must/I have to go to the bank today.
- You have to move pieces around a board. / You mustn't move twice.
- I have to pay rent every month.
- I don't have to work at weekends.
- You must visit the art gallery.

12 Should
- I should be nicer to my little brother. / I shouldn't watch so much TV.
- You should join a club. / I don't think you should buy a lot of expensive equipment.
- You should get a job for part of the time. / You shouldn't waste your time doing nothing. / I suppose you could try to get a job abroad. / I'd save up some money and I'd go travelling. / I wouldn't stay at home watching TV all the time.

13 The infinitive
- I forgot to phone my friend last night. / I'm planning to see a film this weekend. / I try not to be horrible to people.
- I want to get a good job. / My parents want me to go to university.
- I should work harder. / I might not go out with my friends this week.
- Our teachers make us work hard. / Yesterday my parents wouldn't let me play on the computer.

14 The -ing form

- I like living in this city. / My team keeps losing matches. / My phone has stopped working.
- Running is a very good form of exercise. / Making friends has always been easy for me.
- I'd like to have something to drink now / I'd like to start a company when I'm older.
- My brother went to Britain to study at a college. / To solve the problem, I asked a friend for help.

15 The passive

- Last week, I was given a lot of homework at school.
- The school year is divided into three terms. / Some new classrooms have been built at my school. / We are going to be tested in English next week.
- Tickets can be bought at the box office. / Forms must be received before the end of the week.
- Our house was built by my grandfather; My grandfather built our house. / The school concert will be organized by the music teacher; The music teacher will organize the school concert.

16 Conditionals

- If I get some good qualifications, I'll get a good job. / If we don't take action on the environment, it will be a disaster.
- If I ran the country, I'd change a lot of things. / If I could afford it, I'd travel around the world.
- If everyone was nicer to each other, we'd all be a lot happier.

17 Connecting future clauses

- The country won't change unless we get a different government. / As long as I keep working hard, I'll do well at school. / I won't go to live in another country even if I get the chance. / I'm going to get a qualification in English in case it is useful to me in the future.
- When I'm older, I'm going to travel the world. / As soon as I get home tonight, I'm going to play some music. / I'm going to send some emails before I go to bed tonight. / I'm going to learn English until I'm fluent at it. / After/When I've had dinner tonight, I'm going to do my homework.

18 Articles

- I can see a picture. The picture shows some buildings.
- I bought some clothes in a clothes shop. I bought some clothes in the new clothes shop in … Street.
- I don't usually eat biscuits. / I like fruit.
- I ate the biscuits that were on the table. / I put the fruit into my bag.
- I think that drugs are a big problem today. The drugs that people take can be very dangerous.
- It was made in the USA. / I've never been to Asia. / I don't speak French. / I like rap. / I can play the piano. / I always eat breakfast. / Maths is my favourite subject. / I'm good at chess.

19 Pronouns and possessives

- My neighbours: They are very friendly. I often talk to them.
- I have a guitar. My guitar is electric. That guitar is mine.
- My grandfather built the house himself. / I enjoyed myself when I went to France.
- My friends and I text each other frequently.

20 Quantifiers

- There are no cinemas. / Most people live in apartments.
- Some of my work is very difficult. / A lot of our lessons are fun.
- All my friends like football. / Some of my friends go to night clubs.
- I had a few potatoes. / I put a little sugar in my coffee.
- I don't ready many magazines. / I don't listen to much music.
- I saw a horror film last week and a lot of it was very frightening. / I took a lot of photographs but none of them were good.

21 Pronouns and determiners

- I like fast motorbikes but I haven't got one. / My shoes are old and I need new ones. / I like his films but I haven't seen the new one. / I often wear jeans but the ones I wear are cheap. / That's one of my favourite films.
- I want to get another camera because my camera isn't good enough. / I like painting and my other hobby is acting. / I really like dancing with other people. / Some of the photographs were good but the others were rubbish.
- I had something to eat when I got home. / I said goodbye to everybody and then I went home. / No one phoned me last night. / I didn't go anywhere on Friday.
- A man said something rude to me. / I watched the news last night but I didn't watch anything else.

22 *There, it, this, that, etc.*

- There is a big canteen where I have lunch. / There are about 20 classrooms. / There have been lots of changes. / There are six of us in my department.
- It's half past four. / It's Tuesday. /It's March. / It's the twelfth of March/. It isn't far from my house to the bus stop.
- It's cold today. / There might be rain tomorrow.
- It was easy for me to find a job. / It was kind of my friend to lend me some money. / It was great to travel last year. / It was lucky that I met my girlfriend.
- This is my bedroom. This room is my bedroom. / That's my computer. That computer is mine. / These are my DVDs. These DVDS are mine. / Those are souvenirs I got in Britain. Those things are souvenirs I got in Britain.

23 Comparison of adjectives

- Elaine is shorter than Kate. / Elaine's hair is longer than Kate's. / Elaine is more generous than Kate. / London is older than New York. / The underground in London is better than the underground in New York.
- I'm not as lucky as Pete.
- The best restaurant in this city is … / … is the most famous building in this city.

24 Adverbs

- My mother shouted at me angrily. / The assistant spoke to me politely. / My friend came quickly to my house.
- I can play the guitar better than Alex. / I didn't finish my work as quickly as Alex.
- I had an extremely good day yesterday. / I did fairly well in my exams. / I had a fairly nice meal for lunch. / I saw quite a good film last week. / I was completely exhausted when I got home yesterday.
- James is much richer than George. / David is a lot funnier than Ian. / Jane works far harder than Simon. / Alison is a bit more reliable than Cassie.

25 Prepositions (1)

- I live in … Street. / I live in the south of …. / I live at 42 …
- I keep my books in my desk. / I study in Room … / Reception is on the ground floor.
- There's a bin under the desk. / There's a cupboard next to the door.
- The bus goes past the cathedral. / I drive round a big roundabout. / I walk along the main street.
- We went on holiday by plane. / I went to my friend's house on my bike. / I came home from the party in a taxi.

26 Prepositions (2)

- She was in jeans. / He's a man with short hair.
- It's a machine with a lot of buttons.
- I repaired it with glue. / I got the answer by phoning a friend.
- I crossed the road without looking to see if any cars were coming.
- I started my course at the end of January. / At first I enjoyed the course but then …/ I applied for lots of jobs and at last I got one.
- My course finishes in six months. / I'm hoping to travel a lot in the future. / In the past, it was easier to find a job.
- I paid for the books by cheque.
- I spoke to him on his mobile phone. / I looked on the internet.

27 Reported speech

- My friend Jake said that he wasn't feeling very well yesterday. / My brother told me that he would take me to my friend's house in his car. / I told the person on the phone that I couldn't understand her. / My friend said that he was going to meet his girlfriend in a café.
- He asked me what my name was. / A friend asked me what I was going to do at the weekend. / A friend asked me if I could lend her some money. / Someone asked me whether I had heard the news.
- A friend asked me to give her some advice. / The teacher told us to be quiet.

28 Relative clauses

- I've got a friend who is very good at karate. / The person who sits next to me at school is usually Mike. / I've got a computer that doesn't work properly. / The job that my father does involves a lot of hard work.
- It's good to spend time with people who you really like. / The people who I spend time with have the same opinions as me. / It's a newspaper that millions of people read. / The programmes that my parents like are often very boring for me.
- That was the place where I first met my girlfriend. / That was the moment when I decided to change my life. / She's a friend of mine whose clothes I sometimes borrow.

29 Conversational English

- Will you be open on Sunday? ~ Yes, we will. / Can I try on these trousers? ~ Yes, you can.
- I'm getting married tomorrow. ~ Are you? / I've decided to leave the country. ~ Have you?
- A lot of tourists go there, don't they? / It doesn't have a very good football team, does it?
- He likes computer games. ~ So do I./I do too. / She's been to France. ~ So have I./I have too. She's been to France and so have I/and I have too.
- He doesn't like maths. ~ Neither/Nor do I./I don't either. / She can't drive. ~ Neither can I./I can't either. He doesn't like maths and neither do I/and I don't either.

30 Clause and sentence building

- I started learning English last year and I'm still learning it. / I've only been abroad once. / I play tennis and I also play golf. / I like action films and I like horror films too.
- I shouted at my friend because I was angry with him. / I didn't go out because of the weather. / I didn't sleep well so I felt tired the next day. / I used the internet so that I could get the information I needed.
- Instead of watching TV last night, I read a book. / I didn't watch TV last night. I read a book instead.
- Apart from Jimmy, nobody in my class likes baseball. / I haven't been to any big cities except (for) Paris.
- Although I don't do much exercise, I'm quite fit. / Though I'm usually quite calm, I sometimes get very angry.

Index

A

a 70-3, 125
    or no article 72, 125
    or **the** 70, 125
a bit 96, 126
a few 78, 125
a little 78, 125
a lot 96, 126
a lot of 78
ability 34
above 98, 126
absolutely 96, 126
across 100, 126
active forms, compared with passive 60
adjectives 90-3
    after articles 70
    after something/anything 84, 126
    as... as 92
    comparative 90-3, 96, 126, 132
    comparative with **get** 90
    with **how?** 28
    irregular 90, 92
    with **it's** 86
    possessive 74, 116, 125
    superlative 92, 126, 132
adverbs 94-7, 126, 132
    comparative 94, 96, 126
    of degree 96
    irregular 94, 132
    of manner 94, 126
advice 46, 62, 66
after 68, 125
ago 20
agreement 50, 116
all 78
along 100, 126
already 16
also 118, 128
although 120, 128
an 70-3
and 116, 127
another 82, 126
answers, short 114-17, 127
any 78, 80, 126
anybody 84
anyone 84
anything 84
anywhere 84
apart from 120, 128
arrange to 50
articles 70-3, 125
    without 72, 125
as long as 66, 125

as many 92
as much 92
as soon as 68, 125
as....as 92, 94, 126
ask 27, 108, 127
at 98, 104, 126, 127
    or **in** 98
    time phrases 104
at the beginning 104
at the end of 104
at first 104
at last 104
auxiliary verbs 26, 32, 114

B

be
    + past participle for passive 58
    Past Simple 10
    Present Continuous 2
    questions 26
    there is/are 86
be going to 22, 58, 106, 124
because 120, 128
because of 120, 128
before 68, 125
behind 98, 126
beside 98, 126
between 98, 100, 126
but 120
by 100, 102, 104, 126, 127
    + **-ing** 102, 127
    + agent in passives 60, 124
    or **on** 100, 126
    time phrase 104

C

can 34-7, 123
    ability 34
    changes to could in reported speech 106
    permission 36
    questions 34, 36, 114
    requests 36
cannot 34, 36
can't 34, 36, 123
    ability 34
    impossibility 34
    permission 36
clauses
    building 118-21, 128
    see also conditional clause; relative clauses
comma 62, 64

comparatives
    adjectives 90-3, 96, 126, 132
    adverbs 94, 96
completely 96, 126
conditional clauses 66-9
conditionals 62-5, 125
    First Conditional 62, 125
    negative 62, 64, 125
    Second Conditional 64, 125
conversational English 114-17, 127
could 34-7, 38-41, 123
    ability 34
    after so that 120
    if conditionals 64, 124
    permission 36
    possibility 34, 40
    in reported speech 106
    requests 36
    or **should** 48, 123
couldn't 34, 36, 64, 123, 140
    ability 34
    impossibility 34

D

decide to 50
    determiners 70-89, 126
    and pronouns 82-5, 126
did/didn't 114
do
    Present Simple 6
    in questions 26, 30, 44, 114
does, Present Simple 6
doesn't 6
don't 6, 114
don't have to, or **mustn't** 44
down 100, 126

E

each other 76, 125
either 116, 127
else 84, 126
emphasis 16, 66, 96, 118
even if 66, 125
ever 16, 20
every 84, 126
everybody 84
everyone 84
everything 84
everywhere 84
except (for) 120, 128
extremely 96, 126

Index | 153

F

fail to 50
fairly 96, 126
far 96, 126
finish, with **-ing** 54
First Conditional 62, 125
for 20
forget to 50
formality 36, 42, 58, 120
future 22-5, 122
    be going to 22
    conditionals 62-9
    connecting sentences 66-9, 125
    Present Continuous 4
    will and **shall** 24

G

get, with a comparative adjective 90
go
    + **-ing** 54
    Present Perfect forms 20
going to see **be going to**
guess 40, 48

H

had, + past participle 106, 133
have
    + past participle 14
    Present Simple 6
    in questions 26
have to 42-5, 123
    don't/doesn't have to 44
    question form 44
he 74
    + verb form 6, 30
her 74
hers 74
herself 76
him 74, 90
himself 76
his 74
hope to 50
how? 26
    + adjective 28
how far? 28
how long? 28
how many? 28
how much? 28
how often? 28
however 128

I

I 74
I don't mind 54
I'd 48, 123
if conditionals 62-5, 66
    negative 62, 64
    Present Simple 62
    questions 62, 64
        in reported speech 108, 127
imperative 62
in 98, 100, 102, 104, 126, 127
    or **at** 98
    or **on** 98, 100, 126
    time phrases 104, 127
in case 66, 125
in front of 98, 126
in order to 128
infinitive 50-3, 86, 124
    or **-ing** form 56
    after modal verbs 52
    form and past participle 14
    to + infinitive 50, 86, 124
    to + infinitive at beginning of a sentence 56
    to + infinitive as a link 56
    to + infinitive in reported speech 108
    without **to** 52
-ing 54-7, 124, 130
    after certain verbs 54
    after **mind** 54, 56
    by + 102, 127
    forms of verb 54-7, 130
    go + 54
    or infinitive 56
    with **it's** + adjective + 86
    with **liking/not liking** 54
    nouns in 54, 58
    object after 54, 124
    Present Continuous 2
    as subject of a sentence 54, 124
    without + 102, 127
inside 98
instead (of) 120, 128
intend to 50
into 100, 126
it 74, 80, 86, 126
    + **is** or **there is** 86, 126
    + verb form 6, 30
its 74
it's 86
itself 76

J

just 16

K

keep, with **-ing** 54
know 6

L

let 52, 124
    negatives 52
like 6, 54
    + **-ing** 54

M

make 52, 124
manage to 50
many 80, 126
may 38-41, 123
    future 38
    or **might** 38, 40
    possibility 38, 62
me 74, 90
me too 116
might 38-41, 62, 123
    future 38
    or **may** 38, 40
    or **should** 48
mightn't 38
mind, with **-ing** 54, 56
mine 74, 116
modal verbs 34-49, 58, 60, 114, 124
    + infinitive without **to** 52, 124
    passive 58, 124
more, + adjective/adverb 90, 94
most 78
the most 92
much 80, 96, 126
must 42-5, 123
    for the future 42
    necessity 42
    recommendations 42
    rules 48
    or **should** 48
mustn't 44, 48, 123
    or **don't have to** 44
my 74
myself 76

N

near (to) 98, 126
necessity 42, 66
negative forms 2, 44, 50, 52, 62, 64, 80, 114, 116
neither/nor 116, 127
never 16, 20
next to 98, 126
no 80, 126

no one 84
no/yes questions 114
nobody 84
none 80
nor 116, 127
not
  + **to** infinitive 50, 124
  as... as 92, 94
  as many + plural noun 92
  as much + uncountable noun 92
  with **tell** in reported speech 108
nothing 84
nouns
  in **-ing** 54, 56, 58
  with articles 70-3, 125
  countable 72
  plural, with **which?** or **what?** 26
  plural forms 129
  singular, with **which?** or **what?** 26
  uncountable 28, 72, 78, 80, 88, 92, 125
now 8
nowhere 84
number, + **of** + pronoun 86, 126

O

object pronouns 74, 90, 106, 125
object questions 30-3, 123
of, with quantifiers 78, 80, 82, 126
off 100
offer to 50
on 98, 104, 126, 127
or **by** 100, 126, 127
or **in** 98, 100, 126
one 82, 126
  of **these/those** 88, 126
  the one 82, 126
ones 82, 126
  the ones 82, 126
only 118, 128
onto 100
opinions 40, 46, 90
opposite 98, 126
orders 42, 48, 52, 62, 108
other 82, 126
  each other 76, 125
  the other 82, 126
others, the 82, 126
our 74
ours 74
ourselves 76
out of 100, 126
outside 98
over 100

P

parts of the body 74, 102
passive sentences 58-61, 124
  with **by** + agent 60, 124
  going to 58, 124
passive tenses 58-61, 124
  compared with active 60
  modal verbs 58, 60, 124
past 100, 126
Past Continuous 10-13, 58, 122, 133
  forms 10, 133
  passive 58, 60
  or Past Simple 12
  in reported speech 106
past participle
  had + for Past Perfect 106
  have + 14
  irregular verbs 14, 131
passives with **be** 58
  regular verbs 14, 130
Past Perfect
  forms 133
  in reported speech 106
Past Simple 10-13, 18-21, 60, 122, 133
  be 10
  forms 10, 133
  if conditionals 64
  irregular verbs 10, 131
  negative 10
  passive 58, 60, 124
  or Past Continuous 12
  and Present Perfect comparison 18-21, 122
  questions 10
  regular verbs 10, 130
  in reported speech 106
permission 36, 44, 48, 52
plan to 50
politeness 36, 54, 56
possession, **whose** 26, 112
possessives 74-7, 125
  adjectives 74, 116, 125
  pronouns 74, 90, 125
possibility/impossibility 34, 38, 40, 48, 64, 66
prepositional phrases 104, 127
prepositions 98-105, 126-7
  of movement 100
  of place 98, 126
Present Continuous 2-5, 60, 122, 133
  -ing form 2, 133
  for the future 4
  passive 58, 60
  or Present Simple 8
  questions 2
  in reported speech 106

Present Perfect 14-17, 18-21, 60, 122, 133
  forms 14, 133
  for future sentences 68, 125
  negative 14, 20
  passive 58, 60, 124
  and Past Simple comparison 18, 122
  questions 14
Present Perfect Continuous, forms 133
Present Simple 6-9, 60, 122, 133
  after **if** in conditionals 62
  do/does 6
  forms 6, 129, 133
  for the future 6, 125
  for future sentences 66, 68
  have 6
  in case 66
  negative 6
  passive 58, 60, 124
  or Present Continuous 8
  questions 6
  in reported speech 106
probability 12, 40, 48, 62, 64
promises
  to + infinitive 50, 56
  will 24
pronouns 74-7, 125
  + adjective 84, 126
  + **else** 84, 126
  and determiners 82-5, 126
  object 74, 90, 106, 125
  possessive 74, 90, 125
  reflexive 76, 125
  subject 74, 125
  this/that, **these/those** 88
punctuation 62, 64

Q

quantifiers 78-81, 125
question tags 114, 127
question words 26-9, 108, 122
questions 26, 80
be 2
if conditionals 62, 64
object 30-3, 123
in reported speech 108, 127
short 114, 127
subject 30-3, 123
yes/no 114
quite 96, 126
quite a 96, 126

R

really 96, 126
reason 26, 52, 56
reckon 40

reflexive pronouns 76, 125
   with certain verbs 76
   subject + verb + 76
   subject + verb + object + 76
relative clauses 110-13, 127
   after **the** 70
remember to 50
reported speech 106-9, 127
requests 36, 50, 108
result 14, 26, 64, 120
round 100, 126

S

said 106
say 106, 127
Second Conditional 64, 125
sentences
   building 106-21, 128
   connecting future 66-9, 125
shall, and **will** 24
she 74
   + verb form 6, 30
should 38-41, 46-9, 62, 123
   compared with other modals 48, 123
   do you think I should? 46
   I think we should 46
   questions 46
shouldn't 40, 46, 123
since 20
so 116, 120, 127
so that 120, 128
some 78, 126
somebody 84
someone 84
something 84
somewhere 84
still 118, 128
stop, with **-ing** 54
subject pronouns 74, 125
subject questions 30-3, 123
superlative adjectives 92, 126, 132
suppose 40, 48

T

tell 106-9, 127
   + object + question word 108
   + object + **to** infinitive 108
   + object pronoun (**that**) 106
tenses 1-25, 122, 129, 130, 133
   changes in reported speech 106
   verb tables 133
than
   comparative adjectives/adverbs with 90, 94, 126
   possessive pronoun with 90

that 88, 110-13, 126
   relative clauses 110-13, 127
   or **this** 88
   use or not in reported speech 106
the 70-3, 125
   + relative clauses 70
   + superlative adjective 92
   or **a** 70, 125
   or no article 72, 125
their 74
theirs 74
them 74, 78
themselves 76
there 86, 126
   or **it** 86, 126
there is/there are 86
these 88, 126
   or **those** 88
they 74
think 6, 8, 40, 46
third person form of verb 30
this 88, 126
   or **that** 88
those 88, 126
   or **these** 88
though 120, 128
through 100, 126
time 26, 86, 104, 112
time clauses 66-9
to
   + infinitive 50, 56, 86, 108, 124
   preposition 100
told 106, 108
too 116, 118, 127, 128
totally 96, 126
towards 100, 126
try to 50

U

under 98, 100, 126
unless 66, 125
until 68, 125
up 100, 126
us 74

V

Verb Tables 133
verbs 1-25
   + object + **to** infinitive 50
   + **to** infinitive 50
   forms of irregular 14, 131
   forms of regular 130
   forms and structures 50-69, 129, 130, 131, 133
   with reflexive pronouns 76

very 96, 126

W

want 6, 8, 50, 56, 124
want to 50, 124
was 10
we 74
were 10
What? 26, 32, 127
   subject and object 32
when
   clauses 68, 112, 125, 127
   and Past tenses 12
When? 26
where 112, 127
Where? 26
whether 108, 127
which 110-13, 127
Which? 26, 32
while, and Past Continuous 12
who 110-13, 127
   subject and object questions 30
Who? 26, 30
Who's? 30
whose 112, 127
Whose? 26, 32
Why? 26
will
   change to **would** in reported speech 106
   conditionals 62
   and **shall** 24
with 102, 127
without 102, 127
   + **-ing** 102, 127
won't 52
would 34-7, 123
   after **so that** 120
   if conditionals 64, 124
   permission 36
   in reported speech 106
   requests 36
   or **should** 48
would like 56
wouldn't 48, 52, 123

Y

yes/no questions 114
yet 16
you 74
your 74
yours 74
yourself 76
yourselves 76